Successful Teaching

Successful Teaching

What Every Novice Teacher Needs to Know

Edited by
David Schwarzer and Jaime Grinberg

ROWMAN & LITTLEFIELD
Lanham • Boulder • New York • London

Published by Rowman & Littlefield
A wholly owned subsidary of The Rowman & Littlefield Publishing Group, Inc.
4501 Forbes Boulevard, Suite 200, Lanham, Maryland 20706
www.rowman.com

Unit A, Whitacre Mews, 26-34 Stannary Street, London SE11 4AB

British Library Cataloguing in Publication Information Available

Library of Congress Cataloging-in-Publication Data

Names: Schwarzer, David, editor. | Grinberg, Jaime, editor.
Title: Successful teaching : what every novice teacher needs to know / edited by
    David Schwarzer and Jaime Grinberg.
Description: Lanham, Maryland : Rowman & Littlefield, [2017] | Includes
    bibliographical references.
Identifiers: LCCN 2016051971 (print) | LCCN 2016054022 (ebook) |
    ISBN 9781475825282 (cloth : alk. paper) | ISBN 9781475825299
    (pbk. : alk. paper) | ISBN 9781475825305 (electronic)
Subjects: LCSH: First year teachers. | Effective teaching.
Classification: LCC LB2844.1.N4 S85 2017 (print) | LCC LB2844.1.N4 (ebook) |
    DDC 371.102—dc23
LC record available at https://lccn.loc.gov/2016051971

∞™ The paper used in this publication meets the minimum requirements of American National Standard for Information Sciences—Permanence of Paper for Printed Library Materials, ANSI/NISO Z39.48-1992.

Printed in the United States of America

Contents

Acknowledgments

DAVID SCHWARZER'S ACKNOWLEDGMENTS

Writing and editing a book is a complex and laborious endeavor. Therefore, there are many people that I would like to thank and acknowledge. First, I would like to acknowledge my colleague and friend Dr. Jaime Grinberg for all his support, guidance, and help during the process—I am glad we were able to bring this book to completion and remain good friends—*Gracias* Jaimito! Second, I would like to thank all the graduate assistants (and now published authors) that helped managing the editorial work of this book (in chronological order):

Michael Molino helped with the beginning conceptualization of the book and its proposal. Your annotated bibliographies and countless hours of discussion about the content of the book are greatly appreciated—*Merci* Monsieur Molino!

Sejal Rana helped tremendously with managing the different drafts of the chapters by each one of the contributing authors, to schedule the editorial meetings, and to provide ongoing support to all the participants. Without your help this book would not have come to completion in the way it did. Thank you, Sage!

A special mention to all my academic mentors who believed in me (even when I did not do so myself) at the beginning of my academic career in English in the United States: Ken and Yetta Goodman for their unwavering support and friendship, and Denny Taylor for writing a dedication to me in one of her books years ago which read, "Looking forward to reading your second, third book . . ." This is my fifth book, and you are in the acknowledgment section!

I would also like to acknowledge my family and friends for countless hours of listening to all the comments that were made about this book during dinner, lunch, family events, etc.—Thanks!

Finally, I would like to thank my children Noa and Ofer; Ariel and Tamar for all their love and support—I am very proud of you!!! And my wife of thirty years this July 17, 2016, Taly Schwarzer—without your help, support, and care, my career would have been very different—*Toda Raba!*

JAIME GRINBERG'S ACKNOWLEDGMENTS

After long conversations discussing the relationship between conceptual frameworks, research approaches, and practice implementation vis-à-vis novice teachers, my friend and colleague David Schwarzer proposed the idea of a manuscript that would serve as a consulting guide for novice teachers and their mentors. Thank you, David, for your thoughtfulness, organization, expertise, tenacity, humor, and hard work. I want to thank our assistants, Michael Molino and Sajal Rana, whose contributions David already exalted. In particular, I would like to thank Joe DiGiacomo, who has done invaluable work. Furthermore, he has been patient, energetic, insightful, flexible, and efficient, including during the added task of coauthoring one of the chapters.

I will be remiss if I do not thank all the contributors to this book from the bottom of my heart. Each one of them individually and collectively understood the concept and accepted our suggestions graciously. But, most importantly, their chapters taught me much not only about content, but also about how to write intelligently and in an accessible and sophisticated way. Thank you for your meaningful work and your invaluable contributions!

David and I are grateful to Sarah Jubar, at Rowman & Littlefield. She trusted us with the project, saw value in it, and guided us throughout the process with her expertise, patience, and graciousness. Thank you, Sarah!

I also want to acknowledge the support of the College of Education and Human Services at Montclair State University and in particular the magnificent group of friends and colleagues in the Department of Educational Foundations.

My children, Hannah and Aharon, Mihal and Sam, and Ben, have always helped me keep things in perspective and challenged me to maintain a humble disposition by forcing me to recognize that social and emotional experiences and relationships are more important than academic vanity. My wife, Katia Goldfarb, is not only my friend and my colleague for too many years to count, but she is my most challenging critique when it comes to academic work. She is an accomplished scholar and leader in her own right, and any tolerance she displays toward my intellectual limitations is out of our mutual enduring love.

I want to dedicate this work to my two granddaughters, Eliana and Ilanit. May this book serve their future teachers well!

Introduction

David Schwarzer and Jaime Grinberg

Teaching is a very complex skill to develop effectively and efficiently over time. Teacher preparation programs promote both theoretical and practical experiences, but many times are not able to help students balance between these two important aspects.

In terms of theoretical experiences, several discrete areas of expertise are usually taught: introductory courses on psychology, sociology, or human development; some courses are related to specific content-area knowledge and pedagogy; some are related to broad curricular issues; and some are related to concrete skills needed in teaching.

In terms of practical experiences, several opportunities inside and outside of schools and classrooms are available for novice teachers in the program: observations of students and teachers as part of field experiences; shadowing students and or teachers; tutoring students one on one or in small groups; and a final full semester of student teaching.

However, the integration of both theoretical and practical experiences is left mostly to novice teachers and their mentors during their first years of teaching. While several universities offer induction programs to help novices and their mentors with this transition, a significant number of practitioners do not enjoy such opportunity.

Research suggests that the attrition rates for newly certified teachers within the first three to five years of teaching are staggering (Ingersoll & May, 2011). This significant finding might suggest that there is need for more effective support and scaffold strategies to help novice teachers during their student-teaching semester as well as during their first five years of teaching. It is important to mention that many school districts are reacting to the alarming attrition rates by providing mentoring structures to support new teachers. These programs aim to help novice teachers to acclimate to the school district while becoming more effective and efficient. Having a balanced tool that includes theory and practice, as well as full tool kit with activities to

1

encourage self-evaluation and reflection, may greatly benefit both the novice teacher and the mentor to focus their observations and conversations about classroom practices.

The practice of teaching has been defined as filled with uncertainties (Floden & Clark, 1988). The meanings of uncertainty in terms of teaching can be multiple and go into the practical beyond the philosophical underpinnings of epistemological or pedagogical problematizations. For example, many situations unfold in unexpected ways because of questions, misconceptions, misunderstandings, external factors that could impact the day in the school, behavioral issues, personal situations of students, or other factors are not under laboratory controlled experimentations. Nevertheless, it is imperative to plan not only for certainty, but also for uncertainty by having detailed approaches and strategies for different eventualities.

Planning, of course, is a sine qua non for successful practice. More experienced teachers, through time and learning, develop a better sense of how to prepare for uncertainty and often they develop too what has been defined as "Pedagogical Content Knowledge" (Shulman, 1986), which refers to the ability that teachers have in order to connect different content with students in sophisticated and relevant ways.

Seasoned teachers plan in a way in which they have prior understanding of where some difficult or challenging topics might demand different and alternate approaches to teach them, and know enough about their students' characteristics to recognize how to adapt and modify their instruction, thus reducing levels of uncertainty. A less experienced teacher or a novice teacher needs to plan accordingly too and needs to engage in the act of self-reflection, which must be systematic and critical if the practitioner is to learn successfully from his or her own experience. Furthermore, such systematic reflection could be framed as an essential part of conceptualizing teaching as a form of research and engaging in data gathering about their own practices and their students' learning, thus performing variations of practitioner or action research with the goal of improving their own practices.

In each chapter of this book not only do we give numerous examples of practice and conceptual background on different relevant topics, but we also provide easy-to-follow and short self-reflection questions and checklists to facilitate not only planning, but also assessment of one's own practice with the expectation of minimizing uncertainties at least in terms of instruction and to recognize what elements of instruction are central to consider.

Beyond teachers' own control of their practices, there are external factors that condition life in schools and in classrooms, which also create uncertainties. Many teachers in general and novice teachers in particular face unreasonable demands since often the merits of their own teaching are evaluated on the basis of students' performance in high-stakes standardized tests. Such tests are not designed with consideration of particularities and conditions of any particular student, classroom, or school. As such, in terms of educational policy, there seems to be incompatibility and misalignment between the assessment instruments (standardized tests), the state expectations in terms of standards, the curriculum in terms of what the experts in the disciplines suggest it is important to know, and the type of pedagogies that the teacher believes are relevant to connect students with the content they are learning.

Such tensions and pressures exacerbate uncertainty when teachers have to make so many instructional decisions before, during, and after teaching. The different chapters in this book provide frameworks to better understand, plan, apply, and reflect about practice as a way to also minimize the uncertainties that emerge as a result of the policy conditions that impact life in the classroom.

This book aims to serve as a scaffolding tool for both novices and their mentors, whether they are part of university induction programs or district-based adaptation and development programs and for those who do not have such structures in place. Likewise, it serves as a guide for novice teachers who want to consult or have a companion reference for their own teaching needs.

BOOK OVERVIEW

The book that you are about to read is an edited volume that seeks to provide you, a novice teacher, with a practical guide to help you transition from teacher education student to independent, reflective, and autonomous classroom teacher. It will also serve as a scaffolding tool for mentor teachers who are assigned to support novice teachers during their first years in the field. Novice teachers can use this comprehensive resource as a way to connect the overarching conceptual themes and big ideas from their teacher education courses to their classroom practices. This book is designed to encourage you to make more intentional and pedagogically sound decisions during your beginning teaching experiences, whether it is fieldwork observations, student teaching, or the first years in the classroom.

This book covers a variety of educational issues, including: getting to know your students, families, and communities; curriculum development; and pedagogical decisions. Each of these sections contains more specific chapters that will be devoted to a particular concept such as assessment, planning instruction for diversity, integrating technology across the curriculum, and so on. The chapters are designed with the following features: vignettes, concrete applications, checklists for self-evaluation, questions/activities for self-reflection, extension materials, and a glossary of terms. These features ensure the connections between conceptual and practical aspects of teaching.

Examples from numerous content areas are presented throughout different chapters in the book as opposed to only commonplace subject areas such as math, language arts, and science.

As experienced teacher educators, the authors of the book have found over the years that students entering the fieldwork and students teaching semesters have difficulty translating theory into practice. Furthermore, the literature points to a significant gap in the transition from student to teacher that cannot be addressed solely through mentoring programs. This book serves as a bridge between pedagogical theory and the realities of the twenty-first-century classroom.

This book is an indispensable reference tool for novice teachers, enabling them to improve their instructional methodologies, understand relevant conceptual ideas from experts in each particular field, and carry out important classroom tasks such as managing students, creating a community of learners, assessing student understanding, and collecting data. It is also an invaluable tool for teacher mentors when discussing their observation insights with their mentees.

Individual readers will be able to utilize it as a resource before, during, and after instruction. Users of this book will also be able to assess their own growth by completing self-assessments, checklists, questionnaires, and activities for self-reflection that will incite them to think more critically and reflectively about their progress while reading through the guidebook.

CONTENT OF THE BOOK

This book was designed as a readable and approachable compendium of chapters. It is written in a direct and useful style to promote deep reflections and useful insights for all audiences. The language avoids jargon and is accessible to any layperson interested in education. Conceptual issues and citations are kept to the minimum required to contextualize the main concept of each chapter. The other features of the book are engaging and easy to follow.

Features and Benefits of the Book

1. Conceptual Information: Each chapter includes a few pages of conceptual information about the central topic of the chapter. This section is not meant to "teach" a new concept that the novice teachers do not know yet, but rather to remind them of its importance and parts of its complexity.

2. Vignettes: Each chapter includes a few real-life vignettes that exemplify a situation that the author of the chapter has experienced while mentoring novice teachers in the past. For example: "A novice teacher is teaching a lesson while some students in the class seem completely disengaged. The student teacher did not remember if he had surveyed students' interests in the topic at hand."

3. Concrete Applications: Each chapter provides ten concrete applications of topics to be implemented in the next lesson-planning session. These concrete applications/tips are the result of years of mentoring novice teachers in the field. For example: "Appendix 1 provides you with ten general questions used in many disciplines to survey students' interest in a topic."

4. Checklists for Self-Assessment: Aircraft pilots, surgeons, and lawyers have implemented checklists designed to focus their attention while performing their jobs. These checklists are not meant to *teach* the fundamentals of the profession, but are rather meant as a protocol that professionals in the field can consult when needed. With this in mind, each chapter of our book contains tools for self-assessment and criteria to focus the attention of the novice teacher in order to remember all the complex aspects of teaching during his/her first taxing years. Each chapter includes one checklist (ten to fifteen items) that should be used as a self-evaluation tool.

   Moreover, the final chapter of the book includes a comprehensive master checklist (all the items covered in the different chapter of the book) that can be used daily both by the novice teacher and/or by the mentor teacher to center their attention throughout the process.

5. Questions/Activities for Self-Reflection: Each chapter includes a list of questions (three to five) and/or a few activities (three to five) that actively helps novice teachers to self-reflect. For example: "Have you surveyed your students' interest in the topic you are about to teach? Use the appendix provided to survey their interests."

6. Extension Materials: Each chapter provides a few examples of multimedia extension materials that could be used as learning references—it could include video clips, articles, newspaper articles, and other resources for novice teachers on the topic of interest. For example, an edutopia.org video clip of a novice teacher explaining the importance of surveying their students' interests and their implication for lesson planning.

7. Glossary of Terms: Each chapter includes some of the central terms that are explained in detail throughout the chapter and then defined again at the end of the chapter.

List of Content Components

This book is composed of four distinct sections:

Section 1—Getting to Know Your Students, Families, and Communities

In this section, novice teachers are reminded of the importance of the context where the teaching and learning occurs. Conversations about social justice, cultural and linguistic diversity, inclusive education as well as families and communities are explored.

Section 2—Curriculum Development

In this section, novice teachers are encouraged to reflect on the different aspects of curriculum development in general and lesson and unit planning in particular. Moreover, conversations about interdisciplinary teaching and learning, the use of technology in the twenty-first century, and literacy integration across the curriculum are discussed.

Section 3—Pedagogical Decisions

In this section, the reader is prompted to look at the arsenal of tools that were provided during their teacher preparation program and decide which ones are most useful for the lesson at hand. Conversations about project-based learning, grouping strategies, dialogical teaching, and other important pedagogical decisions are discussed here.

Section 4—Putting It All Together

In this section, novice teachers are encouraged to effectively and efficiently integrate both theoretical and practical aspects of their developing trade by using action research and a master checklist to guide their beginning steps into the profession. Moreover, this section might be the most useful for administrators and mentors interested in using practical tools during their observations of new teachers in the field.

WHAT'S NEXT?

We invite you to take advantage of the insights of these experienced educators as reflected in the different chapters of this book. However, each chapter requires some "homework" on your part as a reader. You should assess the relevancy of what is presented to the realities and conditions of your own classrooms. You should also transfer from the conceptual presentations and from the examples, vignettes, and tips offered, to the grade you teach and/or to the subject matter you teach.

While not all is generalizable, the examples and suggestions in the chapters are meant to provoke your thinking and make the relevant connections to your own needs. Hence, these are not a recipe to bake a cake or steps to follow in the assembling of a bookshelf. These are structural elements of successful teaching that have to be transferred, translated, integrated, modified, and adapted as relevant to your own experience.

Finally, we have created a website that provides all live links to extension materials listed in all the chapters. Please explore this website since we will keep updating it throughout the coming years.

The link to our website is http://successfulteachingbook.weebly.com/

REFERENCES

Floden, R., & Clark, C. (1988). Preparing teachers for uncertainty. *Teachers College Record, 89*(4), 505–524.

Ingersoll, R., & May, H. (2011). *Recruitment, retention, and the minority teacher shortage*. Philadelphia, PA: University of Pennsylvania, Consortium for Policy Research in Education.

Shulman, L. (1986). Those who understand: Knowledge growth in teaching. *Educational Researcher, 15*(2), 4–14.

Section I

GETTING TO KNOW YOUR STUDENTS, FAMILIES, AND COMMUNITIES

Chapter 1

Connecting Students' Cultural Expressions to the Curriculum

Danné E. Davis

Socially constructed cultural identity markers such as sounding Black, acting White, and talking Puerto Rican (Augenbraum, 1993) have long been ascribed to students. In response, teachers adopt culturally responsive curricula and pedagogy (Gay, 2002; Irvine & Armento, 2001; Ladson-Billings, 1995; Villegas & Lucas, 2002). Today, various manifestations of femininity and masculinity are increasingly accompanying students into classrooms.

While teachers of young students expect fixed and familiar *gender expressions*, young schoolchildren in particular are revealing dynamic, unconventional, and fluid gender identities. These gender expressions are another example of a socially constructed cultural identity marker. This chapter aims to increase awareness of and responsiveness to students' nuanced and nonconforming gender expressions as cultural identity markers.

Effective teaching requires meaningful connections between students and the curriculum. Connections are formed when the content and instruction are pertinent to students' lives inside and outside of school (Gay, 2002; Irvine & Armento, 2001; Ladson-Billings, 1995; Villegas & Lucas, 2002). However, when teachers are unaware of students' actual cultural identities—for example, nonconforming gender expressions—establishing meaningful student-curriculum links is difficult. This chapter offers resources to develop teacher responsiveness to students' nuanced and nonconforming gender expressions that will ultimately connect *all* students to the curriculum.

DEFINING GENDER EXPRESSIONS

Gender expressions are socially constructed exhibitions of feminine and masculine *culture*. Lev (2004) defines "gender expression" as one of four social-sexual categories "enacted and performed by human beings" (p. 84). In most instances, mainstream culture presumes that gender expressions will align with a person's natural—natal—biology and physiology. Aultman (2014) details the evolution of the term "cisgender," which, along with cis and cisnormative, is contemporarily used to designate people whose gender expression is in synch—at least from a conventional sociocultural perspective—with their birth-assigned sex.

An example of this presumptive alignment is for "girls to be girls" and "boys to be boys"; their *performance* and behavior correspond with conventional expectancies of *being*. This presumption is especially true of elementary teachers. Many first days are filled with gender-specific pronouns—*she* and *her* to refer to apparent girls, *he* and *him* for seemingly boys. It is unlikely that an elementary teacher would think to call a feminine-looking girl a boy or vice versa. Although fitting substitutes, the use of gender-neutral pronouns such as the familiar *they* or new inventions *ze* and *ne*—signaling liberation— is unlikely (Feinberg, 2006).

Natal females—girls born female—are expected to be girlish and ladylike. They are presumed to embrace trendy fashion, exhibit gentility, and enjoy doll play. For natal males, masculine performance is considered typical. Teachers usually anticipate boys to present themselves as rugged and tough. These inclinations toward conforming gender and sexuality cultural identity markers are especially commonplace for teachers of young learners (Swartz, 2003). Moreover, teachers tend to construe that these socially constructed performances remain fixed and unchanged.

Nuanced gender expressions and gender nonconformity are rising in visibility. Butler (1990) acknowledges these performances as socially constructed as well but influenced by society rather than biology. Natal maleness and femaleness in themselves do not dictate gender expressions, according to Butler. Rather, masculinity and femininity, as they are defined and enacted throughout society, inform gender expressions. Given the range of human diversity and lived experience, there are myriad iterations of boyhood/manhood and girlhood/womanhood. Varied external sociocultural forces contribute to dynamic gender expressions.

Jourian (2015) also recognizes the social construction of gender as influenced by outside forces. However, masculinity and femininity occur as expected, unexpected, *and* amalgamation. Gender is fixed as well as fluid. In these instances, a teacher will anticipate conforming performances such as girls as girls and boys as boys—these are fixed. In addition, that same teacher will not be shocked by nonconforming presentations of girls *as* boys, boys *as* girls, *along with* other alternate expressions or uniquely blended ways of *being*—these performances are fluid.

Students with fluid gender identities usually present themselves in varying ways. Their performance will move back and forth, borrow, exchange, blur, and recreate identity. These personal performances are unique, dynamic, and growing in visibility particularly among young schoolchildren. The increasing visibility of unexpected gender expressions makes it critical to develop methods for strengthening teacher responsiveness to this cultural identity marker.

INCREASED NUANCED GENDER EXPRESSIONS

While adults may believe that alternate gender expressions are irrelevant to young people, pop culture suggests otherwise. The numerous depictions of uniquely situated youth in broadcast and print media bring to mind the adage "art imitates life." TLC's reality television series, *I am Jazz* and PBS's Frontline documentary *Growing up Trans*, are modern examples of actual nonconforming gender youth trying to live ordinarily. Alternate gender depictions also exist in children's literature. Implicit trans*cultural identities already exist in children's picture storybooks and supplemental resources, with increasing visibility of expressed narratives in commercial imprints, self-publications, and electronic texts (Davis, 2016).

This increased visibility in popular culture is likely due in part to the escalation of nuanced and nonconforming gender expressions at younger ages (Greytak, Kosciw & Diaz, 2009). As early as age seven (Grossman, D'augelli & Frank, 2011) and in elementary grades (GLSEN & Harris Interactive, 2012) schoolchildren have and continue to perform unique gender expressions. Amid the increasing presence of gender nonconformity are new calls from young people to address gender as a cultural identity marker in the early grades (Jennings, 2015).

Educators also stress an urgency for classroom teachers to move beyond conventional views of gender (Pyne, 2014). Isolated school districts and individual teachers are likely developing approaches to respond to nuanced gender expressions in their work (see Meyer, 2015). In 2011, California blazed another trail in public education. The west coast state became the first in the United States to pass legislation requiring coverage of the historical events and contributions of lesbian, gay, bisexual, and transgender (LGBT) people in the state curriculum (Lovett, 2011). Titled the Fair Education Act, the curriculum includes gender-nonconforming cultural identities and perspectives.

ACKNOWLEDGE, CONNECT, AND ENGAGE (A.C.E.)

A.C.E. is a three-component approach designed to strengthen *teacher responsiveness* to students' nuanced and nonconforming gender expressions. The components require teachers to (1) *acknowledge* students' gender expressions, (2) connect students' gender expressions to the curriculum, and (3) engage *all* students through meaningful teaching.

To provide a concrete application of the approach, A.C.E. is discussed below against two classroom vignettes. Both vignettes draw on actual classroom events composed to aid teachers in their comprehension and implementation of A.C.E. There is a trajectory of the components in that a teacher must recognize the unique identity of his or her students before any culturally relevant teaching is possible. As aforementioned, establishing student-curriculum connections benefits every learner.

Introducing Kirsten

Two years ago Kirsten earned her MAT from a progressive teacher education program. Since then she has been teaching kindergarten in an underserved community. Kirsten deems herself a culturally responsive teacher committed to her primarily Afro-Caribbean and African American students. Veteran kindergarten teachers in her district advised her to set up learning centers by familiar gender-specific designations. In the pink area, the girls play princess, beauty shop, or medical receptionist—roles the veteran teachers believe best suit the girls in Kirsten's classroom. Occasionally, the Afro-Caribbean girls imagine themselves as beauty shop owners while the African American girls mimic medical doctors. In response, Kirsten says, "Maybe some of you will manage a beauty shop, but being a Black female doctor . . .?"

Most of the time, the girls' gender performance aligns with Kirsten customary view of girls as feminine and trendy. Yet, at times the Afro-Caribbean and African American girls imagine themselves as business leaders and white-collar professionals. This image countervails traditional gender roles and hegemonic perspectives. From a cultural perspective, hegemony is the dominance over and suppression of a group of people by another (Bates, 1975). The girls' portrayals as privileged and empowered contrasts hegemonic notions about people of color relegated to low status.

Although labeling herself a culturally responsive teacher, Kirsten's actions seem culturally repressive. The center design reflects a tiered sociocultural arrangement of white male leaders and decision-makers and females of color in helping and supporting roles. To acknowledge students' gender expressions and demonstrate culturally responsive teaching, Kirsten needs favorable views of her female students that support their genuine interests. Encouraging imaginative play of nontraditional gender roles, making optimistic and not cynical statements, and developing affirmations for the girls as well as *about* them would be supportive.

Sports provide avenues to connect students' gender expressions to the curriculum. Instead of minimizing the girls' ability to become managers or physicians as adults, Kirsten should tap into their interests regarding those professions. One approach would be crafting a lesson about sports managers. To engage all students through meaningful teaching, Kirsten could plan an exploration of baseball team managers for the girls *and* boys. With its high profile in the United States, baseball has many popular managers. Also fitting are lessons about managers—from front office to equipment room—in sports such as tennis, hockey, and basketball, played by both women and men. Expanding the exploration to managers of color affords another curricular link.

Digital and craft media can help establish connections to the arts. All students could take virtual visits to explore the geography of female sports managers. To document their learning, students could create digital or paper collages. In response to the empowered and privileged image the Afro-Caribbean and African American girls have of themselves, Kirsten should help all of her students create vision boards of themselves as professionals, for example, managers, leaders, doctors, and so on. Creating opportunities for schoolchildren to use tempera colors akin to skin tones to paint self-portraits of their future selves demonstrates meaningful teaching.

As recommended by her grade-level colleagues, Kirsten has a designated center for the boys in her classroom. Painted blue, the area contains trucks, blocks, and tools. Drawn to the sparkly princess clothes and tiaras, there's always one boy insisting on playing in the pink area. Fearful of peer and parent reprisal, Kirsten forbids the boys. "When I say no, they scream at me and say they just want to play. Some say they aren't gay—don't know where that comes from—but that they want to play like the girls and feel like a princess. I tell them no, suggesting instead they build a castle. Doing what's right is often difficult."

Despite graduating a progressive teacher education program, Kirsten manages to repress the interests of students—this time the boys in her classroom. By disallowing the boys to be whatever they want, Kirsten is misinterpreting and dismissing their interests. As a self-described culturally responsive teacher, she should not fear reprisal and attend to the boys' desire to play dress-up. Kirsten needs to acknowledge the gender expressions of the small group of boys in her classroom. Their interest in feminine associative play, namely dressing up, may simply be that. For the most part, the boys indicate just wanting to play.

In response to the boys' assertions of not being gay, Kirsten missed an opportunity to tap into students' verbalized *self-determination*—the chance to name, define, and identify who they are and how they see themselves. Despite her valuing drama and play, as evident in the classroom centers, creativity and imagination are only permissible by Kirsten's design. Acknowledging nuanced gender expression permits *all* children to "perform" on their terms. Removing artificial barriers and restrictions—pink girl center and blue boy center—will likely result in newly imaged and self-determined performances.

Children's literature containing themes of gender nonconformity can connect students' gender expression to the curriculum. From the common core, to individual state curricula, and professional reading associations, teachers are expected to develop students' literacy skills via fiction and nonfiction. In recent years, many progressive educators have been moving toward critical literacy requiring learners to interact with texts to uncover and critique messages of power and inequality. Children's picture storybooks depicting young girls and boys in nontraditional roles, positions of power, and fluid and ambiguous genders exist.

Consider the story of *10,000 Dresses* (Ewert & Ray, 2008). The main character is a natal male named Bailey. Despite Bailey's recurring dreams about dresses, he is prohibited from wearing them. In fact, Bailey's social restriction is similar to the ways in which the children are limited in Kirsten's class. Eventually, Bailey meets Laurel, and together they collaborate to make a dress for Bailey to wear. Text-to-self, text-to-world (others), and text-to-text connections are common comprehension strategies. Establishing these links enables self-determination, empathy, and awareness.

The storyline and illustrations of *10,000 Dresses* invite rich arts and crafts lessons. Students could study popular clothing designers and they may be surprised to realize the male dominance of commercial dressmakers, including the late African American Willi Smith and Jason Wu, who were credited with designing for U.S. first lady Michelle Obama. Another idea allows students to draw, paint, and sew dresses. Students could learn to sew well enough— or prepare pieces for someone else to assemble—as a service project. Kids Helping Kids programs provide meaningful opportunities to practice empathy and help other people. Many schools, communities, and places of worship sponsor these kinds of activities that foster civic engagement and awareness.

The GLBT Roundtable of the American Library Association, the Gay, Lesbian, and Straight Education Network (GLSEN), and Teaching Tolerance reflect a sundry list of online resources having books, summaries, and supplemental curricular resources. Children's picture storybooks offer powerful critical literacy messages for children *and* adults. It would benefit Kirsten's teaching to know that since 2000, children's books featuring boys and dresses, dressmaking, and other female associative expectancies have been on the rise (Davis, 2016). Placing this genre of alternate narratives in the learning centers would better serve the students.

Like all kindergarten teachers, Kirsten is expected to develop her students' literacy skills. To that end, children's literature with messages of nuanced gender expression is useful. The children may read and analyze the text alone, with partners, or as a read aloud. Having the books in the centers affords students the freedom and flexibility to interact with the texts. This arrangement, as an approach to engage all schoolchildren through meaningful pedagogy, naturally dovetails with curricular connections.

The aforementioned recommendations are pertinent to teachers who need to develop their responsiveness to natal male students' nuanced gender expressions. In addition to Kirsten's case, other general tips exist (see tips that follow).

Tips on Gender-Specific Colors

Avoid the notion of gender-specific colors. Blue for boys and pink for girls are artificial identity markers that spiked in popularity as a marketing ploy for department stores. Instead:

- Plan a lesson or unit on the history of this color phenomenon. Consider the guiding question: "Who said pink is for girls and blue is for boys?"
  - Interview people to determine what they know.
  - Visit clothing stores to see how colors are used and presented for marketing purposes.
  - Identify gender-specific color use with baby items.
  - Invite vendors and designers to the classroom.
- Use pink for boys and blue for girls.
- Avoid using the colors, at least as gender identity markers.

Learn to mix pink and blue paints and then use the new color in and around the classroom.

Tips on Gender-Neutral Drama

Establish gender-neutral drama and play spaces.

- In the spirit of democracy—a social studies concept—let students decide where to play.
- In the spirit of self-determination let students decide how they'd like to perform and present themselves.
- Choose drama and play center themes *with* the students—they may identify topics beyond a teacher's radar.

Let students select which items to include in the drama and play spaces.

Tips on Diverse Guest Speakers

Invite diverse guest speakers from the community to your class.

- Host people, of varying cultural identities, who perform jobs familiar to young students.
  - Pediatric health providers, transportation workers, shopkeepers, construction workers, professional athletes, celebrities

Help students plan "good questions" to ask their community friends.

Introducing Mr. Brown

Mr. Brown and his 24 fourth graders are preparing their classroom for the fifth grade. The school practices "looping," so they'll be together next year. To capture the moment, Mr. Brown and the students took a selfie and then posted the picture to the class website. On the first day of school the following year, Mr. Brown counted 24 faces, but seemingly there was an additional girl. "C'mon," he said. "Let's visit our class webpage to see how we've changed." When the webpage loaded, Mr. Brown's noticed someone was missing. "Where's Michael?" he asked. "Right here Mr. Brown," said a firm voice. "But I go by Mikela now 'cause I'm a girl."

Rather than ask for Michael's whereabouts, Mr. Brown should have created an opportunity for students to (re)introduce themselves. This could have happened during the morning meeting or as the first formal lesson for the day. Allowing students to self-identify enables them to name, define, and identify their cultural identity markers. This exercise of self-determination would position Mr. Brown to acknowledge students' gender expressions by meeting Mikela and sidestep asking for Michael. Young people enjoy talking about themselves and discussing their families, which is a great way to build teacher responsiveness.

As stated earlier in the chapter, increasing numbers of schoolchildren are exhibiting nuanced gender expressions. Some youth, similar to the students in Kirsten's class, simply want to perform in unexpected ways. Their behavior is a superficial presentation of how they see and understand themselves at one moment in time.

Then there are other students such as Mikela whose cultural identity goes beyond superficial presentation to representing their *being*. Mikela is not simply wearing a costume or playing a role like the boys in Kirsten's class. The boys expressed wanting to play *like* the girls not *as* girls. By contrast, Mikela has a new cultural identity. *She* understands herself in new ways and is now living—or *being*—that new person. This is an important awareness for Mr. Brown, especially to make the classroom conducive to learning.

Other examples of possible morning meeting questions include the familiar, "What did you do during the summer?" However, inviting students to talk about "how they've changed since last year" taps into their last day of fourth grade from last year, demonstrating continuity and connecting students' gender expressions to the curriculum.

The topic of transitions is another approach to establishing student-curriculum connection in this instance. Transitions are changes and shifts. They occur in nature and they are helped by human beings. Clearly, Michael has transitioned to Mikela. A lesson on change and transitions is pertinent to science concepts, particularly biology and geography for young learners.

Educators also have legal obligations for gender inclusivity. Title IX disallows schools to practice sexdiscrimination (see "Tips on Gender Laws"). If a natal female wants to play baseball, a school cannot simply deny her because of her gender. Moreover, regardless of how a student identifies and whether those performances and expressions change annually, monthly, or daily, there is growing obligation for schools to accommodate students according to their self-determination (Weiss, 2014). Self-determination is also an approach to engage all schoolchildren through meaningful teaching (see "Tips on Gender Identity").

Tips on Gender Laws

• Know the law. Title IX is a federal law that prohibits sex discrimination in education. Sure it's known for granting students equal access to academics and extracurricular activities on school campuses. Yet, Title IX also prohibits gender-based discrimination against female, male, and trans* fluid students.
• Learn what the federal government says about Title IX and sex discrimination.
• Permit students access to bathrooms and locker rooms that match their self-determined gender identity. Search the Internet to learn about the case of Coy Mathis.

Advocate for gender-neutral or uni-bathrooms in your school. Within the last five years, elementary schools from New England to California have eliminated gender-specific bathrooms.

Tips on Gender Identity

• Use the correct names, nouns and pronouns.
• Allow students to name themselves and refer to them by that name.
• Address students by the pronoun that corresponds to their stated gender identity.

- Be mindful that students may switch among genders or indicate an unfamiliar identity. For a day, week, or entire school year a student may identify as female and then at other times, may identify as male or vice versa or another gender. Accommodate the shifts.

Let students "out" themselves. Educators should maintain the confidentiality of students' gender or transidentity.

CONCLUSION

The purpose of this chapter is to advance teacher responsiveness to students' gender expressions. Well into the twenty-first century, it is critical for teachers to recognize the range of socially constructed differences among students, especially young schoolchildren. For decades, teachers attended to the racial, ethnic, and linguistic cultural identities of their students. Today, teachers must also attend to the gender cultural identities of their students.

While adults might expect gender nonconformity and gender variance among middle- and high-school students, current trends reveal that preschoolers and lower- and upper- elementary schoolchildren perform nuanced and nongender-conforming gender expressions. Whether changes in identity are superficial or biological, innate or external, teachers must be responsive to the actual cultural lives of their students. This responsiveness is especially critical for students' academic and social development.

Tips on Cultural Similarities

Gender is one example of countless cultural identities. To understand similarities among differences, try

- rereading this chapter replacing gender with race, ability, ethnicity, or socioeconomic status. Do the same for the tips.
- using art or digital media to create a picture of a garden. Design one where all images are the same; the other where no images are alike. Compare. How do the pictures make you feel? Now image how school, your neighborhood, or family would look and make you feel if everyone were the same.

A responsive teacher is a professional who knows his or her students well and uses this knowledge to make learning relevant and school safe. Acknowledging students' gender expressions, connecting these gender expressions to the curriculum, and engaging *all* students through meaningful instruction are offered as a three-component approach to begin to strengthen teacher responsiveness to students' nuanced and gender-nonconforming cultural identities (Table 1.1).

Table 1.1 Self-Assessment

A.C.E. Component	Yes	No	Opportunity to Advance
Acknowledge Students' Gender Expressions			
1. Ask students for their preferred pronouns. 2. Where appropriate, use gender-neutral pronouns such as *they, ze,* and *ne.* 3. Use students' correct first and last name pronunciations 4. Accept students' self-determined expression and performance			
Connect Students' Gender Expressions to the Curriculum			
1. Encourage imaginative play and performance of nontraditional gender roles. 2. Integrate children's literature representing the range of gender nonconformity and trans* cultural identities. 3. Link students' gender interests and expressions to mandatory subject area content. 4. Align students' gender interests and expressions with explicit curriculum standards—see Common Core, IRA/NCTE.			
Engage ALL Students through Meaningful Teaching			
1. Integrate twenty-first-century technology into teaching and the classroom—for example, electronic devices, digital tools, online sources. 2. Provide students with multicultural craft products. 3. Create opportunities for students to express and perform as they see their cultural identities. 4. Teach cultural identity affirmations to students and yourself. 5. Design lessons and plan meaningful instruction on the basis of current student interests and perspectives. 6. Explore opportunities for community service and outreach. 7. Respect students' civil rights.			

Table 1.1 Self-Reflection (*Continued*)

	Yes	No	*How did I A.C.E. Today?*
Acknowledge Students' Gender Expressions			
1. Whose gender expression seemed different today and how? 2. When were students referred to by name, pronoun, or cultural identity? Which ones? Why? 3. How were students' gender expressions and/or cultural identities acknowledged? 4. How are colleagues acknowledging students' gender expressions? 5. What changes are necessary to better acknowledge students' gender expressions in the future?			
Connect Students' Gender Expressions to the Curriculum			
1. Which subject areas are students required to learn? 2. How do students' gender expressions align with required subject areas? 3. What connections are possible between students' gender expressions and subject matter content? 4. How are colleagues connecting to students' gender expressions? 5. What changes are necessary to better connect students' cultural identities to standards?			
Engage ALL Students through Meaningful Teaching			
1. How were cultural identities regarded or disregarded throughout the day? 2. How did students demonstrate being engaged or disengaged during lessons? 3. Who or what can help to better involve and respect all students? 4. What changes are necessary to better engage students in the future?			

APPENDIX 1: EXTENSION MATERIALS

Readings

1. GLSEN & Harris Interactive. (2012). Playgrounds and prejudice: Elementary school climate in the United States. A survey of students and teachers. New York: GLSEN.
2. San Francisco elementary school switches to gender-neutral bathrooms for little kids. http://dailycaller.com/2015/09/08/san-francisco-elementary-school-switches-to-gender-neutral-bathrooms-for-little-kids/#ixzz3qP4F18eh.
3. San Francisco school adopting gender-neutral bathrooms. http://www.sfgate.com/bayarea/article/Bathrooms-at-Miraloma-Elementary-in-S-F-go-6481544.php; http://dailycaller.com/2015/09/08/san-francisco-elementary-school-switches-to-gender-neutral-bathrooms-for-little-kids/.
4. Tips for teachers—ally yourself with LGBT students. http://www.tolerance.org/toolkit/tips-teachers-ally-yourself-lgbt-students.

Gender-Neutral Pronouns

http://www.citylab.com/navigator/2015/09/ze-or-they-a-guide-to-using-gender-neutral-pronouns/407167/.

Audio/Video

1. Judith Butler: Your behavior creates your gender. https://www.youtube.com/watch?v=Bo7o2LYATDc.
2. A child moves from she to he with confidence. http://www.wnyc.org/story/child-goes-she-he-confidently/.

Websites

1. Gay, Lesbian, and Straight Education Network (GLSEN). http://www.glsen.org/.
2. Title IX and sex discrimination. http://www2.ed.gov/about/offices/list/ocr/docs/tix_dis.html.

Multicultural Craft Media

F-H Community Service Sewing. http://extension.usu.edu/files/publications/factsheet/pub__4334920.pdf.

Kids Love Stitching Community Service Projects Too! http://fascinationin-
fabrics.com/bobbis-sewing-blog/?p=166.
Pacon. http://pacon.com/?s=multicultural&orderby=relevance (construction
paper and "hair").
Crayola. http://www.crayola.com/ (crayons, markers, finger paints).
Colors of My Friends (tempera paints).

For Students

Readings

1. Bergman, S., & Malik, S. (2012). *The adventures of tulip, birthday wish fairy*. Toronto, ON: Flamingo Rampant.
2. Broadhead, T. (2014). Meet Polkadot. http://www.amazon.com/Meet-Polkadot-The-Series-Book-ebook/dp/B00LLXY9T8.

Resources

The Genderbread person 2.0. http://itspronouncedmetrosexual.com/
wp-content/uploads/2012/03/Genderbread-2.1.jpg.

GLOSSARY OF TERMS

Cisgender—someone whose gender "matches" their sex assigned at birth; the opposite of transgender.
Culture—a set of defined roles, values, beliefs, and attitudes that characterize a group of people or organization.
Gender—the distinct, dynamic, combination, or absent demonstration of masculinity and femininity.
Gender expression—the manner in which a person demonstrates distinct, dynamic, combination, or absent masculinity and femininity; the behavior may or may not align with a person's birth-assigned sex.
Empowerment—self-initiated growth achieved through a combination of decision-making power and increased self-esteem.
Fluidity—a sensibility of self as more than one gender at the same time or different times; gender is nonbinary, neither male nor female, but instead is a spectrum of identity.
Performance—a person's outward presentation of self; behaviors of identity influenced by one's internal sense of self, external factors, and/or a combination.
Self-determination—the opportunity to freely decide one's personhood, identity, and fate without an external influence.

Teacher responsiveness—an educator's awareness of the comprehensive past and present-day realities of *all* students and the ability to justly incorporate those facts into the curriculum.

Transgender—has become an umbrella term for someone whose gender identity differs from their birth sex; trans* is sometimes used because of the range of trans identities.

REFERENCES

Augenbraum, H. (1993). *Growing up Latino: Memoirs and stories.* New York: Houghton Mifflin Harcourt.

Aultman, B. (2014). Cisgender. *Transgender Studies Quarterly, 1*(1–2), 61–62.

Bates, T. R. (1975). Gramsci and the theory of hegemony. *Journal of the History of Ideas, 36*(2), 351–366. http://doi.org/10.2307/2708933.

Butler, J. (1990). *Gender trouble: Feminism and the subversion of identity.* New York: Routledge.

Davis, D. (2016). Real Lives, Relevant Texts: A Survey of B2G Children's Counter-narratives. *Multicultural Teaching and Learning, 10*(1), 10–20.

Ewert, M., & Ray, R. (2008). 10,000 Dresses. New York: Seven Stories Press.

Feinberg, L. (2006). Transgender liberation: A movement whose time has come. In S. Stryker and S. Whittle (Eds.), *Transgender Studies Reader.* New York: Routledge.

Gay, G. (2002). Preparing for culturally responsive teaching. *Journal of Teacher Education, 53*(2), 106–116.

GLSEN & Harris Interactive. (2012). Playgrounds and prejudice: Elementary school climate in the United States. A survey of students and teachers. New York: Gay, Lesbian, & Straight Education Network.

Greytak, E., Kosciw, J., & Diaz, E. (2009). Harsh realities: The experiences of transgender youth in our nation's schools. New York: GLSEN.

Grossman, A., D'augelli, A., & Frank, J. (2011). Aspects of psychological resilience among transgender youth. *Journal of LGBT Youth, 8*(2), 103–115.

Irvine, J. J., & Armento, B. J. (2001). *Culturally responsive teaching: Lesson planning for elementary and middle grades.* Boston: McGraw-Hill.

Jennings, K. (2015). Leelah Alcorn and the continued struggle for equity for LGBT students. *The Educational Forum, 79*(4), 343–346.

Jourian, T. J. (2015). Queering constructs: Proposing a dynamic gender and sexuality model. *The Educational Forum, 79*(4), 459–474.

Ladson-Billings, G. (1995). Toward a theory of culturally relevant pedagogy. *American Educational Research Journal, 32*(3), 465–491.

Lev, A. I. (2004). *Transgender emergence.* Binghamton, NY: Haworth Press.

Lovett, I. (2011, July 15). California to require gay history in schools. *The New York Times (NY)*, p. 16.

Meyer, E. (2015). The personal is political: LGBTQ education research and policy since 1993. http://www.tandfonline.com/doi/full/10.1080/00131725.2015.1069514 -abstract. *The Educational Forum, 79*(4), 347–352.

Pyne, J. (2014). Gender independent kids: A paradigm shift in approaches to gender non-conforming children. *The Canadian Journal of Human Sexuality, 23*(1), 1–8.

Swartz, P. (2003). Bridging multicultural education: Bringing sexual orientation into the children's and young adult literature classrooms. *Radical Teacher,* (66), 11–16. Retrieved from Academic Search Complete database.

Villegas, A. M., & Lucas, T. (2002). Preparing culturally responsive teachers: Rethinking the curriculum. *Journal of Teacher Education, 53*(1), 20–32.

Weiss, J. (2014). Protecting transgender students: Application of Title IX to gender identity or expression and the constitutional right to gender autonomy. *Wisconsin Journal of Law, Gender & Society, 28*(3), 331–346.

Chapter 2

It Takes a Village

Families, Contexts, and Diversity

Katia Paz Goldfarb, Jaime Grinberg, and Sejal Rana

As the saying goes, "It takes a village to raise a child." The families and communities where our children grow have been and will continue to be there long before and after children step in our classrooms. This chapter will focus on the critical need to understand, know, and care about our children's families and communities as we teach them in our classrooms and in our schools. We will look at these relationships as they shape how we think about our own instructional needs to be effective and relevant within diverse environments. This is critical given the demographics throughout the United States.

According to the Center for Immigration Studies, 22 percent of public school-age children live in an immigrant household. Also, 21 percent of school-age students live in poverty, and 49 percent of the student population are members of ethnic and racial groups other than White (Institute of Education Sciences, 2015).

More than fifty years ago, Joseph Schwab (1969), one of the giants of curriculum theory, revision, and development, established that for a curriculum to be successfully developed and implemented, besides the necessary expertise in curricular organization, it should incorporate four other dimensions: the learners, the teachers, the subject matters to be taught, and the milieu (contexts). Considering the need of novice teachers to enhance their practice and curricular skills, we want to address Schwab's context dimension by also understanding how it is shaped by systems.

In this chapter, we will discuss the system approach as a scaffolding tool for the understanding of contexts for families and schools that can serve practitioners when planning and assessing curriculum and teaching. We will pay attention also to the context of diverse communities and immigrant families vis-à-vis what teachers need to consider when teaching within such contexts. In addition, we will emphasize practices that embody working WITH families and communities and not ON families and communities.

SYSTEMS THEORY

Before we begin speaking about understanding the contexts in which our students reside, we must understand the systems that exist which influence many aspects of their lives. Bronfenbrenner's *classic ecological systems theory* (1979) provides a conceptual framework for understanding the need to pay attention to how contextual issues play in human development in general and in the development of children in particular. This theory can better explain the construct of milieu (contexts) advanced in Schwab's curriculum design and implementation proposal.

"Ecological" is a descriptor for how things are interconnected and for understanding local communities and working with families in a reciprocal, long-term, and dynamic relationship between the individual and her/his different environments. These environments are explained by subsystems called *microsystem, mesosytem, exosystem,* and *macrosystem* (see Figure 2.1). These help us understand how influential factors function in relation to each other and to individuals, groups of students, teachers, communities, families, and even the larger educational policy issues which educators need to consider when designing curriculum and instruction.

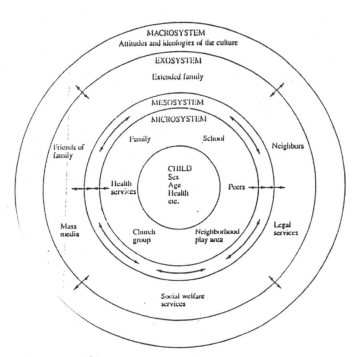

Figure 2.1   Systems graph.

The microsystem is defined as all contexts that come in immediate interaction with the individual, such as home and school, or in terms of our interest explains the context of classrooms. The mesosystem identifies the reciprocal influences between all immediate settings or microsystems, such as family-school connection. The exosystem is comprised of all social structures that impact development without immediate contact, such as parents' workplace and community. The macrosystem serves as the cultural environment that influences the individual's beliefs, values, norms, traditions, and laws—the condition of the life of communities by the social, cultural, economic, and even political circumstances under which such experiences and interactions take place. The physical space as well as the conditions and circumstances that influence these relationships are a context. Table 2.1 explains the definitions of the different systems, with examples and issues that affect students.

Contexts are a large part of the different systems, and we refer to context in multiple ways such as the context of a community, the context of a classroom, the context of present educational policy, and the context of the family. In what follows, we further explain the importance of contexts.

Table 2.1   Systems and Questions about Issues that Affect Students

System	Definition	Example	Issues Affecting Students
Microsystem	Settings in which the students come into face-to-face contact with influential people/ organizations	Family, school, peer group	Are they regarded positively? Are they accepted? Are they given an active role in reciprocal relationships?
Mesosystem	Settings in which relationships between microsystems occur	Home-school, school-neighborhood	Do settings respect each other? Do settings share values?
Exosystem	Settings in which students do not participate but significant decisions are made affecting them	Parents/guardians' place of employment, school board, local government, parent's peer group	Are decisions made with the interests of students/families in mind? Are families supported?
Macrosystem	Blueprints for defining and organizing the institutional life of the society	Ideology, social policy, values	Are some groups valued at the expense of others? Is there an individualistic or a collectivistic orientation?

CONTEXTS

Contexts are environments, informal or formal, that shape and relate to organizations, institutions, groups, and/or individuals. For instance, we can understand that neighborhoods are part of a city context, schools are part of a neighborhood context, teachers are part of the school context, families are influenced by a number of contexts, and students are influenced by these contexts beyond schools. Students, teachers, families, and/or community members could also shape or influence their contexts. While context influences knowledge, behaviors, discourse, and interactions in and out of schools, participants also influence contexts—contexts are dynamic and constructed, not deterministic!

Consequently, by understanding systems and contexts, teachers and relevant educational partners such as families, experts, and students do have the power to design, modify, and/or implement meaningful, engaging, relevant, and challenging curriculum. Furthermore, such understanding can provide enough insights to choose teaching approaches that are connected, respectful, and mindful of who the students are and that recognize students also as relevant *funds of knowledge*. In the following section we discuss and provide examples of how to better understand the local community as a context in the life of the school, the teacher, the family, and the student.

LOCAL COMMUNITY CONTEXT

In the following vignette we will learn about a teacher who realized he would have to understand his students' lives before planning lessons so that he would be culturally responsive to ensure an environment conducive to learning. Byron, a middle-school language arts teacher who was new to the school, shared the following reflections about what he did before the school year started in addition to the regular planning sessions with colleagues and supervisors in his building:

> *I began by sitting with my laptop computer and just searching around for information about the neighborhood. I found the supermarkets and restaurants. I was surprised with how many ethnic eateries I found. There are some parks but not many other types of spaces to gather. I drove around and notice that buses are hard to find, and I pondered how do students get to the movies or main street? That afternoon I went to the school and then I went out to a street corner, closed my eyes, and just wanted to listen and smell, then walked the streets of the neighborhood, bought some goods in one of the local ethnic grocery stores and sat in the park to test them. I hope I like them, I have no idea what they are, I only asked for suggestions. I basically "hanged out" around the public places with*

*the purpose of smelling, listening, and feeling the area as one way of under-
standing the community that I cannot find in the web or in magazines. Experiencing the community even if the first time was as a "tourist" gave me insights
and a way to start learning about the contexts where my future students live.*

Byron's exploration and experience is an important disposition and a way
to start thinking about how to smooth the incongruences or discontinuities
often experienced by the two worlds of the student's life, as stated above,
that of home and that of school. In this case, the microsystem of the student,
comprised by family and community places, becomes part of the knowledge
required to teach.

Nieto (2000) provides numerous examples of what she calls "cultural discontinuities" referring to the incongruence between home or local cultures
and that of the school. She provides the example about the difference in the
concept of being smart or intelligent. Although in the dominant American
culture intelligence is an innate quality (if a person was born in American
culture, then dominant societies assume you are smart), for most Latinos/as
intelligence is a learning process, often a result of investing time and energy,
which demands networks of support as those provided by family, friends, and
communities (in Latin American countries, you may score high on exams
but true knowledge is understood as being able to apply what you know).
Consequently, building on local knowledge and expertise has been identified
as an important strategy as Byron recognized and got started in his initial
exploration.

Byron's exercise initiates a process to access the knowledge required to
understand the community where children and families live, where school
resides, and where he will teach. The purpose of this process is to become
familiar with the social resources in the community and, in turn, see the community as a resource. Byron also understood that students whose background
is not culturally in congruence with that of the school's mainstream practices
have the daunting task of learning two languages—that of the academic
content like any other student of any background has to learn, and that of the
school culture, which differs with the one from home—which is not the case
for students who are part of the dominant mainstream culture since school
culture is congruent with that of the home.

Therefore, it is important to further study the mesosystem (influences that
come from the relationships between immediate contexts/settings) in which
students develop. This requires understanding the community with the intention of identifying the reciprocal influences between available organizations,
institutions, and agencies that serve the families and children and school.

Furthermore, mapping the community resources such as museums or cultural centers, as well as identifying individuals who can serve as resources

and bridges to gain access and develop relationships of respect and trust, is beneficial. In turn this would be working with locals, not on locals, and forging authentic partnerships.

The following tips provide information on how educators can start immersing themselves into the local community.

Tips on Teachers in the Local Communities

Where can I start and what can I do outside the school but in the community if I want to immerse myself in the local context?

In order to answer these questions, let's learn from history. In what follows, a group of student-teachers in New York City in 1937 describe why and how they got involved in community projects (Grinberg & Goldfarb, 2015). A key aspect of such engagement is not to do it alone, but together with colleagues and community members, often including families and students.

> We believe that a teacher's job is not only in the classroom. That while a teacher's primary responsibility is to help children grow and develop to the best of their potentialities, she has a responsibility also for the kind of world these children are growing up in. She cannot ignore the influences outside the classroom that are shaping children's lives. . . . This year we are continuing our effort for a low-income housing project. We are working with Greenwich House on their health program. We are cooperating with a public school in their after school recreation activities and we are running a Saturday Play group for neighborhood children. (p. 50)

Connecting this to present times invites educators to reflect about the ways in which teachers and students participate in and out of school and how this participation has an impact upon educational achievement. Thus, the kind of education that a student experiences is shaped by practices that favor certain ways of being and knowing.

As teachers, we are often caught up in focusing on the individual needs of students and developing curriculum and pedagogical experiences that enhance students' understanding of the world. However, how we teach and what we teach is not culturally neutral when it ignores the local ways of knowing, the local meanings, and the local needs as defined by the locals. Such act of dismissing the local contributions diminishes the contribution and connection with the mesosystem and confirms the divorce between the school and the curriculum on the one hand and the students' context on the other. Next, we briefly discuss the construct of families.

Families

Understanding families requires a comprehensive view of it as a unit of intimate, transacting, and interdependent persons that recognizes diverse structures, functions, and relationships. *Family* is defined in its broader sense as including shared biological, legal, cultural, and emotional ties with a significant commitment to each other over time. Diversity is regarded as a critical component in recognizing the complexity of families (Brown, Stewart & Goldfarb, 2006).

Family diversity refers to the variety of ways that families are structured and function to meet the needs of those defined as family members (Stewart & Goldfarb, 2007). Diversity in families should encompass different family compositions such as multigenerational families, single-parent families, blended families, LGBT-parent families, and multiracial and multiethnic families, transnational families, and immigrant families. Families may include biological children, adoptive children, and foster children.

In the case of *transnational families*, members live some or most of the time separated from each other, yet hold together and create something that can be seen as a feeling of collective welfare and unity, namely, "familyhood," even across national borders (Bryceson & Vuorela, 2002). Furthermore, transnational families tend to be more permeable to the influences of the social environment (Bacigalupe & Lambe, 2011). These families transcend the traditional systems discussed above in ecological theory because the geographical boundaries are not constraining, meaning that distant geographical spaces that bound systems also could potentially influence a local context.

For example, the macrosystem is not culturally limited only to a geographical space. Families move in and out of cultural contexts and ways of knowing according to particular situations. The exosystem is not geographical as they sustain ties with friends and institutional/legal relations in other places, physically or virtually. Refer to Figure 2.1 in this chapter to have a visual to follow along with what was just stated.

The following tips illustrate how transnational families sometimes travel during the school year for extended periods of times, which interrupts the student's education. The tips provide a suggestion on how to turn this challenge into an opportunity of learning.

Tips on Constructing an Opportunity Out of a Challenge

When in a transnational family a student is missing school for an extended period of time due to travel to visit relatives, often it is seen as a challenging academic situation. This situation can be an academic opportunity. It can be redefined capturing the possible strengths that the experience can provide for the student's learning, value of family within the school context, and firsthand knowledge to be shared in the classroom. Students can write a daily journal, take pictures, read a local newspaper, write a report, and interview family members about their lives. These documentations, for example, can serve as resources for writing, presentation, social studies, music, art, and geography among others.

Understanding of local community and working WITH families and not ON families relate to the realities of all types of families regardless of their composition. The examples given in this chapter should serve as models to create informed and relevant practices to value and strengthen the interconnectedness of schools and families in their contexts. In the following section we will discuss ways by which educators can work *with* families and not *on* families.

As novice teachers, you need to think about planning lessons. The following checklist is provided as a guide to consider, which will help scaffold and focus on incorporating these concepts in your lessons.

CHECKLIST FOR WORKING *WITH* FAMILIES

1. Are you communicating with your students' families?
   Yes _____ No _____
   Through what means? _____

2. Have you visited the neighborhood in which you teach?
   Yes _____ No _____
   What did you see, hear, or do? _____

3. Are your lessons planned so that they are culturally responsive to the students in your class?
   Yes _____ No _____
   Explain _____

4. Are there resources within the community that the families have access to?
   Yes _____ No _____
   Explain _____

5. Are there resources students have access to within the community and school?
   Yes _____ No _____
   Explain _____

6. Does your classroom represent the various cultures that exist in your student population?
   Yes _____ No _____
   Explain _____

7. Is there a school-led or parent-led program within your school that allows for parent involvement?
   Yes _____ No _____
   Explain _____

8. Are you available to your students through other means of communication?
   Yes _____ No _____
   Explain _____

Working with *Families not* on *Families*

Lynn has worked all her life advocating for the rights of marginalized children and families. In such capacity, she got involved with a promising project called "Grupo de Padres" (Parent's Group) in a school building that served a significant number of immigrants, many of whom did not speak English fluently or at all.

> *Every Friday at noon Lynn will sit in the trailer designated for "Grupo de Padres" and wait for someone to show up. After a couple of weeks of having two or three mothers come, she asked them which issues they thought were the most important, and they stated, "If you bring a lawyer to talk about immigration you will see many more of us here."*
>
> *She invited a lawyer specialist in immigration and fluent in Spanish. Indeed, fifty mothers and community members showed up. At that meeting, she asked them what other issues were affecting them. She developed a series on nutrition, practiced how to talk with teachers, with volunteers who were actually teachers from the school, worked on leadership and representation, and also created an evening and weekend English class for adults.*
>
> *At the end of that school year, district officials came to ask the group to pose in a picture to serve as advertisement of how responsive they were to immigrant families. The representatives of the group asked for an increased budget for the following year and recognition of Lynn and teachers who were crucial in their empowerment, before posing.*

Beyond understanding the families and communities where children develop, it is critical to learn how to work *with* them and not *on* them. Often families and communities are used as token or exotic illustrations to give a superficial picture of the context in which children live, giving the perception of *us* versus *them*, expert versus ignorant. An authentic work *with* the community requires time, energy, and most importantly, respect. For example, "Grupo de Padres" was formed following the practices of respect and mutual knowledge exchange. "Grupo de Padres" is part of the school with a predominantly Latino population. The group helps mostly mothers to understand the school life of their children, including rules, norms, and expectations, as well as services they can access beyond academics (Goldfarb, 1998).

As the group continued to evolve, the schoolteachers, principal, counselors, social workers, and other professionals learned to use this new resource to inform decisions. Such practice creates a safe, trusting, and respectful physical space that nurtures an environment where the mothers' voices count, in other words, a "school sanctuary."

In fostering a more comprehensive definition of family involvement, teachers need to look at the mesosytem, in this case home-school relationship, as a partnership where each institution is equally valued to serve as a resource in children's learning. In order to solicit genuine involvement from parents, the school must provide both conventional and nonconventional activities such as "Grupo de Padres."

Lynn's description, as well as the research performed on that experience (Goldfarb, 1998), point to what Delgado-Gaitan (1991) argues about activities such as open houses, parent-teacher conferences, and bilingual classrooms that "[validate] the families' social and cultural experience, which allowed [the parents to be a] part in their children's schooling, and thus [achieve] a better balance of power and cooperation between home and school" (p. 43).

The following tips offer suggestions on how to improve communication with parents regarding their student's academic environment, which can help increase parental involvement.

Tips on Communicating with Parents

There are various ways by which educators can connect with parents to keep them consistently involved in their students' education.

The following sources are apps that can be downloaded and utilized within the classroom:

1. Class Dojo: an app that marks students' progress during the day on factors like behavior and participation as well as students' social responsibilities within the class.
2. Class Messenger: an app that allows teachers to directly communicate with parents regarding any matter like plans for the day or upcoming events, or even if volunteer help is needed for any functions.

Other ways to communicate with your students' families are by creating your own website, a newsletter, sending emails to parents weekly or monthly, or even a blog in which they can also provide feedback!

The following is an example of how a teacher communicates with her students' parents:

A student-teacher created a weekly newsletter in which she began by introducing herself to the families and listing different times for parents to meet with her. The newsletter also served as a vehicle to share information on what was going on in the classroom and to disseminate some of the children's work. This newsletter, for the families, served as a window into the classroom. Parents and guardians could use the school language to ask children about their days and promote a closer connection between home and school. Another teacher worked with the elders of the community in developing stories about the local neighborhood and incorporating some of these in the curriculum.

Context: Communities and Families

Teachers often do not live in the neighborhoods where their students reside. In teaching the whole child, we need to understand the physical and social aspects of where and with whom our students live. Some of our students live in big apartment buildings, some of them live in single-family houses, some of them share their room with others, some of them sleep in a comfortable bed and some on the floor, some of them take care of younger siblings, some of them are the official translators in the family. We need to keep these aspects of our students' lives present.

Frequently schools are institutions that are geographically in the community, but culturally and socially disconnected from them. Even more, they tend to be divorced from the local community, and they deliver the same package of activities on the basis of standards and assessment tools with little relevance to the needs of the students (Grinberg et al., 2005).

In other words, there are models for schooling, architecturally speaking (gym, library, cafeteria), and all these buildings are located in different areas of the property the school is located on. The buildings all look the same and share a consistent representation of what the school portrays as its image; however it doesn't recognize or represent the life of its students and that of the surrounding neighborhood. The school does the same thing every other school does except validating or celebrating the different cultures in the community and within the school itself.

Such divorced conditions risk exacerbating a break with the values, behaviors, beliefs, and ways of knowing local communities such as that populated by large numbers and percentages of Latina/o students, hence, potentially also creating a cultural rupture between the school as a public institution and the local community where the building is located. Or as McCaleb (1994) has suggested, "Children live their lives in two worlds: that of the home and community and that of the school. When these two worlds fail to know, respect, and celebrate each other, children are placed in a difficult position" (p. vii).

Alternately, teachers can construct opportunities to connect the contexts of schools and that of the families and local communities by incorporating their local funds of knowledge into their curriculum and teaching as in the following vignette:

> Lisa is a novice teacher who has just been hired as a tenth grade physical education teacher. Her curriculum covers the most popular sports such as volleyball, basketball, flag football, and badminton. Yet, the teacher also celebrates and legitimizes the specific culture that is predominant within her physical education class.
>
> Lisa works in a district that has a large Indian population. She teaches common American sports which include volleyball, basketball, badminton, and

flag football, but she is also required to teach at least one nontraditional sport. Since a majority of the local population is of Indian descent, she decides to teach cricket as the nontraditional sport, which is widely popular in India and among Indian immigrants in America. Lisa thinks that exposing students to a sport that is not popular in America allows her students who are culturally or ethnically Indian to feel represented and legitimized. The school support for this also shows that the institution appreciates the diversity that the students have to offer and validates their culture. In addition, this curricular approach expands students' sport education knowledge. Furthermore, this provides students with another possible lifelong activity they can engage in.

By choosing cricket, Lisa is not suggesting that since the majority of the students in the district are of Asian descent (Indian) they only know how to play cricket but instead she is tailoring a unit of instruction and curricular outcomes that are culturally responsive (Villegas & Lucas, 2002) to the student population in her classroom—she is doing what Schwab argued regarding successful curriculum implementation by considering and incorporating the context (milieu) into her physical education classes. She validates the student's culture through her specific discipline. Lisa decided to build upon her understanding of the macrosystem as manifested in this case through sport cultural context and then by teaching material that is relevant to the student. She helps students feel connected and appreciated as well as acknowledged, which ultimately reflects the building of a bridge with the community context and within the school.

Another example is that of Emilia, a novice social studies teacher in an urban school with a significant number of immigrant students. She developed a unit with her ninth graders in which they collected oral histories of their families and traced their roots. This was a validating experience since for most of these children the stories of their families and of their ethnic groups are still mostly silent in textbooks and curriculum materials.

This also seems to be moving the children beyond the geographical boundaries of their present communities to "exploring" places such as Vietnam, Mexico, India, Michigan, and New Jersey. Hence, Emilia and Lisa, as well as other teachers who engage in a dynamic of learning from and with the community, "had either learned the students' language or were knowledgeable about or comfortable with their culture" (Nieto, 2000, p. 298).

The following tips provide suggestions about questions that could be asked in oral history projects and about how to develop a project involving oral histories.

Tips on Examples of Questions for Oral History Projects (modify these to be relevant according to the nature of the project)

  1. How do you prefer to be called? Did you or do you have a nickname? How did you get it?

2. When were you born?
3. Where were you born?
4. What is the origin of your family name?
5. Who were the first family members to settle in this country?
6. What brought them here?
7. Do you know any stories about your ancestors?
8. Who is a member of your family?
9. Where do they live?
10. How often do you see them? Do you call/skype/text?
11. Where did you go to school?
12. What music do you like?
13. What food do you like?
14. What sports do you like?
15. Which TV, radio programs, movies, plays, or other forms of art do you like?

Tips on How to Do an Oral History Project with Your Students

1. Find common patterns among the students within your classroom by using a lesson or unit you will teach.

   For example, if a health teacher is covering a unit on nutrition and healthy foods and recipes are part of the unit, the teacher can have students create a portfolio on families' favorite healthy food that they cook at home.

2. Once you planned and are ready to implement the lesson and/or unit, provide students with concrete guidelines to communicate with their families about the topic you want them to. Have the class to organize in groups and collaborate on what kinds of questions can be asked.

   For example, students can interview different members of their own families about what the recipes consist of, when they cook these (everyday, celebrations, etc.), and what are the ingredients necessary to create the meal.

3. After the information is gathered, have students identify the background of the recipes and locate them on a world map as well as on a map of the United States that are part of a bulletin in your room. These will represent the diverse cultures that exist within your classroom and the community as well as how different regions of the United States have different traditions.

   For example, students can pin a picture of the dishes to the maps on the bulletin board. The students then will do an oral presentation highlighting the information in their report.

4. Create a classroom project with the information obtained. The classroom project can be a book, a website/blog, roll-a-decks, or a mural within a showcase that can be placed in the hallways of the school.

For example, as the culminating activity for this project, students can create a website/blog that includes all the dishes that they are presenting, with links to nutritional information, regional information, food production, pictures, and/or a videos capturing cultural traditions in which these dishes are served. Working in groups, this project would let students explore deeper into their cultural roots, make decisions about what to include and what not to include in the website, and how to organize it; this will also validate and legitimize their own cultural backgrounds and traditions.

Below is a self-reflection that is created to reassess and evaluate your contributions to the classroom and understanding of the various contexts that exist.

1. What do I know about the school contexts?
2. How have I communicated with my students' families?
3. How do I know that I am culturally responsive?
4. Am I seeing my challenges as opportunities?
5. How am I including my students' funds of knowledge into the curriculum?
6. How have I contacted my students' parents for a variety of positive, negative, or neutral situations?
7. What do I know about my students' daily life?
8. What do I know about my student's family life?

CONCLUSION

Being able to understand and care about the students' families and communities allows educators to accommodate and modify their lessons so that the disconnect between school, family, and community is minimized at first and eventually removed. While it is essential to be knowledgeable in the discipline you teach, it is imperative to consider the cultures that exist within the classroom. Being culturally responsive allows a rapport to be built between students, families, the community, and the teachers. When academic life is infused with familial life experiences, students feel understood and appreciated which, in turn, helps academic performance.

Ways to accomplish being culturally responsive is by first visiting the environment your students and their families live in as a "tourist," making yourself "stranger" to what otherwise might be known in order to grasp more objectively what the community is like. Inviting parents to functions that involve student-parent and teacher involvement, such as teacher conferences and back-to-school nights, helps build rapport between one another. It also allows parents to be more involved in their children's education. Acknowledging students' culture and the community through the discipline that is being taught is another way of accomplishing cultural responsiveness.

When educators are able to connect the material back to the students' experiences, students are better equipped to relate and understand the material that is being taught. We have provided additional resources at the end of this chapter that will help further your understanding or provide additional ideas on how to accomplish cultural responsiveness.

Creating open pathways for communication with families is vital. It is important that educators find means to provide access for parents to their children's educational realm so that they are able to understand the norms of the classroom, whether that means through a newsletter every week or class messenger. Creating an environment where parents feel comfortable and are able to engage with education professionals allows for the community and the school to build a transacting bond.

Lastly, as an educator, reflect on the microsystems, mesosystems, exosystems, and macrosystems in which the students and their families live. They influence the behaviors, attitudes, and performances of the various social contexts within your district. It is imperative to build bridges between families, communities, and schools because "it takes a village" to educate and raise our children.

APPENDIX

DEMOGRAPHIC INFORMATION: U.S. K–12 PUBLIC SCHOOL (INSTITUTE OF EDUCATION SCIENCES, 2015)

Consider the following information and the quotations below when thinking about the contextual and system conditions of students, families, schools, and communities. In turn, this information is relevant for curricula development, adaptation, and implementation:

- In 2013, about 13 percent of White students were living in poverty, when compared with 39 percent of Black students and 32 percent of Hispanic students.
- During the 2012–2013 school year, the number of students designated as English language learners (ELLs) represented more than 9 percent of the total student population in the United States.
- During the 2012–2013 school year, about 13 percent of students received special education services.

From fall 2002 through fall 2012, the number of White students enrolled in public elementary and secondary schools decreased from 28.6 million to 25.4 million, and their share of public school enrollment decreased from 59 to 51 percent. In contrast, the number of Hispanic students enrolled during this period increased from 8.6 million to 12.1 million, and their share of public school enrollment increased from 18 to 24 percent. The number of Black students enrolled decreased during this period from 8.3 million to 7.8 million, and their share of public school enrollment decreased from 17 to 16 percent. Since 2002, the percentage of Hispanic students enrolled in public schools has exceeded the percentage of Black students. (p. 80)

Changes in the racial/ethnic distribution of public school enrollment differed by region. From fall 2002 through fall 2012, the number of White students enrolled and their share of public school enrollment decreased in all regions, with their shares decreasing by 7 percentage points in the Midwest and 8 percentage points each in the Northeast, South, and West. The number of Hispanic students enrolled and their share of public school enrollment increased in all four regions, with their shares increasing by 5 percentage points in the Midwest and Northeast and 7 percentage points in the West and South. From 2002 through 2012, the number of Black students fluctuated in the South but decreased overall in the West, Northeast, and Midwest. (p. 81)

CULTURAL KNOWLEDGE

Cultural knowledge is the process in which educators seek and obtain a deep foundation concerning various worldviews of different cultures.

- Become familiar with values, beliefs, practices, lifestyles, and problem-solving strategies of culturally/ethnically diverse groups.
- Attend classes, presentations, and events about environmental, psychological, spiritual, religious, social, economic, and structural factors that condition different ethnic groups among other topics.
- Learn about diversity within diversity (i.e., religion, gender, social class, sexuality).
- Obtain direct cultural knowledge: explore and enter places that are ethnically and culturally diverse; talk with people; look for how same cultural constructs might have divergent meanings.
- Read!
- Do not construct cultural categories and ethnic groups in generalizing terms and as deterministic and permanent.
- Avoid stereotyping: do not construct the "other" as if people were exotic or inferior or primitive.
- Interrogate yourself, your biases, your values, and your open-mindedness.

WEB LINKS

1. Tips to get to know parents as well as involved:
   http://www.educationworld.com/a_special/parent_involvement.shtml.
   http://www.edutopia.org/groups/classroom-management/783266.
2. Ways to get to know your students:
   http://www.scholastic.com/teachers/article/top-5-ways-get-know-your-students.
   http://www.scholastic.com/teachers/lesson-plan/multicultural-celebrations.
3. Classroom as a context:
   https://www.responsiveclassroom.org/what-hangs-on-our-classroom-walls/ (provides insight into changing the walls in your classroom).

FURTHER READING

Allen, J. (2008). Family partnerships that count. *Educational Leadership*, *66*(1), 22–27.

Anderson, R. E. (2015). Focusing on family: Parent-child relationships and school readiness among economically impoverished black children. *Journal of Negro Education*, *84*(3), 442–456.

Bronfenbrenner, U. (1979). *The ecology of human development.* Cambridge, MA: Harvard University Press.

Michael, S., Dittus, P., & Epstein, J. (2007). Family and community involvement in schools: Results from the School Health Policies and Programs Study 2006. *Journal of School Health*, *77*(8), 567–587.

Stoddard, K., Braun, B., & Koorland, M. (2011). Beyond the schoolhouse: Understanding families though preservices experiences in the community. *Preventing School Failure*, *55*(3), 158–163.

GLOSSARY OF TERMS

Classic ecological systems theory—dynamic relationship between the developing human being and her/his different tiers of surrounding environments.

Contexts—these are environments, informal or formal, that shape and relate to organizations, institutions, groups, and/or individuals. For instance, neighborhoods are part of a city context, schools are part of a neighborhood context, teachers are part of the school context, families are influenced by a number of contexts, and students are influenced by these contexts beyond schools. Students, teachers, families, and/or community members could also shape or influence their contexts.

Family—as including shared biological, legal, cultural, and emotional ties with a significant commitment to each other over time.

Family diversity—variety of ways that families are structured and function to meet the needs of those defined as family members.

Funds of knowledge—it refers to the knowledge that students have and bring with them to school, which is based on the cultural environments of their own families and communities (Moll et al., 2001). These include ways of communicating, language, and skills needed to sustain their own social, cultural, and economic environments, as well different manifestations of culture in terms of music, folklore, food, art, literature and literacy, land conflict resolution among other forms of becoming and being a part of their own sociocultural context (Grinberg, Goldfarb & Saavedra, 2005). Many times students find that schools do not recognize or do not value what they bring with themselves as important sources of knowledge (Grinberg, Goldfarb & Saavedra, 2005). We argue that recognizing and valuing these funds of knowledge are extremely important to build the environment that sustains a dialogical learning community.

Microsystem—contexts that have immediate interaction on students (i.e., home and school).

Mesosystem—relations between microsystems, such as home and schools, which influence one another.

Exosystem—social structures that impact development without immediate contact (i.e., parent's workplace or community).

Macrosystem—cultural environment that influences the individual's beliefs, values, norms, traditions (i.e., federal/state government, geographical location, religion, economic status).

Transnational families—when families are separated most of the time from their native lands but still hold together and create a unity, whether through visiting across national borders or calling back home to maintain contact or remain connected.

REFERENCES

Bacigalupe, G., & Lambe, S. (2011). Virtualizing intimacy: Information communication technologies and transnational families in therapy. *Family Process, 50*(1), 12–26.

Bronfenbrenner, U. (1979). *The ecology of human development*. Cambridge, MA: Harvard University Press.

Brown, T., Stewart, P., & Goldfarb, K. P. (2006). Can we please drop "Chapter 3"? The need to intertwine diversity throughout course curriculum. *The Journal of Teaching Marriage and Family: Innovations in Family Science Education*, 6, 1–27.

Bryceson, D., & Vuorela, U. (2002). *The transnational family: New European frontiers and global networks*. Oxford: Oxford University Press.

Delgado-Gaitan, C. (1991). Involving parents in the schools: A process of empowerment. *American Journal of Education, 100*(1), 20–46.

Goldfarb, K. P. (1998). Creating sanctuaries for Latino immigrant families: A case for the schools. *The Journal for a Just and Caring Education, 4*(4), 454–466.

Grinberg, J., Goldfarb, K., & Saavedra, E. (2005). *Con coraje y con pasion*: The schooling of Latinas/os and their teachers' education. In P. Pedraza & M. Rivera (Eds.), *Latino education: An agenda for community action research* (pp. 227–254). Mahwah, NJ: Lawrence Erlbaum Associates.

Grinberg, J., and Goldfarb, K. (2015). Learning to Teach for Social Justice: Context and Progressivism at Bank Street in the 1930's. *Journal of Education and Human Development*, June, *4*(2), 50–59.

Institute of Education Sciences (2015). *The condition of education, 2015*. Washington DC: National Center for education Statistics.

McCaleb, S. (1994). *Building communities of learners: A collaboration among teachers, students, and community*. New York: St. Martin's Press.

Moll, L., Amanti, C., Neff, D., & Gonzalez, N. (1992). Funds of knowledge for teaching: Using a qualitative approach to connect homes and classrooms. *Theory Into Practice, 31*(2), 132–141.

Nieto, S. (2000). *Affirming diversity: The sociopolitical context of multicultural education*. New York: Teachers College Press.

Schwab, J. (1969). The practical: A language for curriculum. *The School Review, 78*(1), 1–23.

Stewart, P., & Goldfarb, K. P. (2007). Historical trends in the study of diverse families. In B. Sherif Trask & R. Hamon (Eds.), *Cultural diversity and families: Expanding perspectives* (pp. 3–19). Thousand Oaks: Sage Publishers.

Villegas, A., & Lucas, T. (2002). *Educating culturally responsive teachers: A coherent approach*. Albany, NY: SUNY Press.

Chapter 3

Shifting the Locus of Control

Five Strategies for Creating a Twenty-First-Century Student-Centered Classroom

Maheen Ahmad and Mayida Zaal

As a preservice or in-service teacher, you've likely heard the term "student-centered" classroom. In this chapter, we explain how student-centered classrooms can be summed up in one phrase: a shift in the *locus of control*. Our framework lays down the foundational differences between a *teacher-centered* and a *student-centered classroom*. We then take a trip to a classroom and show how these values of teacher and student-centeredness play out on the ground. Essentially, we argue that it is our perception of our students that drives student-centered teaching.

In this chapter, we draw upon our experiences in the classroom (both as teachers and as learners) to share five strategies that we found most helpful when kindling student-centered classrooms that prepare students for the twenty-first century.

Now, more than ever, we need student-centered classrooms to make education meaningful for all of our students. The use of student-centered strategies is supported by multiple theories that speak to engaging young people in transformative learning practices such as "funds of knowledge" (Mercado & Moll, 1997), culturally responsive teaching (Ladson-Billings, 1995), youth participatory action research (Cammarota & Fine, 2008), and civic education (Schulz & Sibberns, 2004). Student-centered classrooms provide all of our students with the resources and space they need to truly succeed in today's rapidly changing world (SCOPE, 2014; McKenna, 2014).

TEACHER-CENTERED VERSUS STUDENT-CENTERED CLASSROOMS

Traditionally, the dynamics of the teacher-centered classroom have been such that the teacher is positioned as the "expert," the sage on the stage (King,

1993), the person in power who makes all decisions about curriculum and classroom structure and manages student behavior.

On the opposite spectrum, the dynamics of the student-centered classroom is such that the teacher is positioned as the "facilitator," the "guide on the side," the person who works with students to make decisions about classroom structure and its activities (King, 1993). A student-centered classroom is a transformative model of education that places students at the center and is better aligned with teaching philosophies that promote having students take *ownership* of their learning (Morrow, 2001; Tracey & Morrow, 2012).

A student-centered approach encourages students to make choices, direct their learning, think critically, and collaborate with others (Pedersen & Liu, 2003). As teachers in twenty-first-century student-centered classrooms, we need to provide opportunities for students to collaborate and work independently of adults. Students need to analyze and evaluate data and to explore different ways of looking at the same problem (p. 21, n.d; Wallis & Steptoe, 2006). Throughout it all, students need to be able to communicate their understanding with others and be aware of what else they need to do to improve their understanding. A student-centered classroom does all of this and more (Barell, 2003). We argue that these skills foster the leadership skills, motivation, and self-initiative that students need to effectively engage in a dynamic twenty-first-century world.

A true shift in the power dynamics necessitates that students are the ones driving the teaching. It is their performance and understanding that determines the nature of the lessons. Bear in mind that this focus on students as the driving force of the classroom does not mean that teachers appease every student demand or wish. We believe that in a student-centered classroom teachers are asked to *surrender control* but not responsibility. Teachers are the "guide on the side" and are still supervising student performance, understanding, and behavior. In a student-centered classroom, teachers simply provide students with a controlled environment in which to practice their skills.

Use the tips below to reflect on your own classroom experiences. How many of them were teacher or student centered?

Tips on Classroom Experiences

Think back to your classroom experiences. Which ones would you characterize as teacher centered? Which ones would you call student centered? Why? Jot down two to three traits of each type of class.

Teacher Centered	Student Centered
1. _____	1. _____
2. _____	2. _____
3. _____	3. _____

Inside a Classroom

Let's take a look at a few examples to see how a student-centered classroom looks like in practice. In a teacher-centered version of a lesson, the teacher would simply lecture the class about a topic and then quiz students afterward, with little to no thought about how to ensure students actually understood the material or how to engage in any contingency plans if students do not understand the material at all. The entire lesson from start to finish is very controlled and follows a series of steps. In such a teacher-centered classroom, the focus is on the teacher; he or she is essentially checking off all the things he or she had to do in the lesson and is thus satisfied having "taught" the students whether or not students understand the material.

Now, picture a classroom in which the teacher explains a topic and then has students work in groups to express their understanding of the said topic. To a casual observer, the students may look like they are loudly chatting, laughing, or even randomly walking around the classroom. But these are all intended behaviors—the teacher's ultimate goal is for students to work together to achieve a certain goal with their group.

In a well-designed classroom, students are prompted with the right questions that generate thought-provoking conversation. Or they may be competing in pairs to analyze as many texts or images hung up around the classroom as they possibly can in a given amount of time. The teacher has surrendered control by allowing students to talk or move freely. However, because students are asked to complete a very specific task, it holds students responsible for the content and curtails off-task behaviors.

To make a classroom truly student centered, the teacher would have to monitor student understanding of the content and adjust his or her teaching practicing throughout the whole lesson, not just toward the end. The students become the focus of the classroom, and it is their level of understanding that guides how the teacher teaches.

Are Our Students Empowered?

How we view our students is of paramount importance. For a long time, students were considered simply knowledge recipients (Freire, 1970). Today, we know our students are so much more than that. They are *knowledge holders* and *knowledge creators*. To believe this is to empower our students. They are capable of critical thought and autonomy, and we need to kindle these skills in our classrooms.

Now more than ever, young people have to sift through and make sense of massive amounts of content in our fast-changing information and media-saturated environments. Our students already are knowledge holders

(Jaleel & Verghis, 2015) and come to use with all sorts of experiences and information. In addition, the worldwide web has made it so that we are no longer just passive consumers of this content, but we now have the ability to be creators of content. Whether it's on social media websites, blogs, or collaborative learning platforms, young people are posting, retweeting, responding to, and creating new content. This positions young people as "knowledge creators" (Domine, 2009).

Five Strategies in a Student-Centered Classroom

Below are five strategies that are essential features of a student-centered classroom.

1. Plan Backward: Planning backward is a key strategy for teachers because it forces them to focus on what matters most (Wiggins, 1993). What do you want students to do by the end of the unit that they cannot do right now? What knowledge or skills do they need to learn to complete the final assignment? When planning your units for teaching, be very clear and pragmatic on what you expect from students.

Now, take a look at the example below of a teacher who framed her entire unit around the final project:

> *Miss A is a sixth grade language arts teacher who decided to teach persuasive appeals to her students in preparation for argumentative writing. In order to ensure that students truly understood the concepts, she wanted them to be able to create a radio commercial by the end of the unit, in which they had to effectively use the persuasive techniques they had learned. Students were informed of the project first and then were taught the various persuasive techniques that they could use. Throughout the different lessons on how to be persuasive, students were engaged, asking questions that connected the lessons to their final project. Anytime a student became unfocused, Miss A would simply remind him or her of their project and that got them on track. When the time came to draft their radio commercial scripts, students worked in groups, and most of them completed the scripts in one day.*

From day one, students knew exactly what was expected of them. Subsequently, they had a greater stake in mastering their lessons (persuasive techniques, knowing the audience, etc.) and were able to directly apply their skills and lessons to their project.

Whether you teach language arts, math, science, physical education, or any other subject area, be sure to critically analyze your own assignments. As the teacher, you know what you have been teaching, and you know your students' potentials. Use that knowledge to ensure that your assignments are valid assessments.

The beauty of backward planning is that it cultivates problem-solving skills in students and allows for greater differentiation. Since everyone knows the end goal, those who wish to go above and beyond easily can, while those who may be seriously struggling have plenty of time to get extra help or additional scaffolding. This is especially helpful for heterogeneous classrooms that include students of wide-ranging abilities. Additionally, such a setup provides students of all backgrounds with the tools and resources they need to succeed, thereby evening out the playing field (SCOPE, 2014; McKenna, 2014).

Tips on Evaluating the Authenticity of Assessments

When creating assignments (especially cumulative ones), make sure they assess exactly what you want them to assess. Use the tips below to help you evaluate the quality of your assignments.

1. Determine the purpose of the assessment. What will you use the data from this assessment for?
2. Ensure that your assessments address the skills you taught.
3. If you spend 80 percent of your time teaching certain skills, 80 percent of your assessment should also reflect that.
4. Your assessments should connect to your unit and help students achieve the overall unit goal.
5. Consider alternate ways to assess the same skills. Determine the best assessment style and use that.

2. Get Students to Drive Their Learning: Now, it is time to think about your actual lessons and activities. What will students actually be doing? Student-centered classrooms can involve a lot of physical movement and hustle bustle. How can you ensure that your classroom activities are meaningful and driving student learning as opposed to just chaos?

For nearly every activity you plan, remember your students. What do your students need to be able to do for the final assignment? How can they do that on a smaller scale? The key word here is "do." Every lesson you teach should involve students demonstrating their understanding in some way. Will they be copying notes? Will they be discussing in pairs? Will they be listening to a teacher lecture? Will they be only completing worksheets?

A fairly simple way to check the nature of your classroom dynamics is to check who is doing most of the talking in the classroom. Is it the teacher or the students? Use the tips below for a quick experiment that can help you critique your own teaching practices and determine who is driving the classroom.

Tips on Student-Centered Classrooms

Are you a sage on stage? A guide on the side? Not sure? Let the numbers speak for themselves. Try recording your lesson and count up how many minutes you spend talking to the class versus how many minutes students are given to talk and/or work. Naturally, this is not the most accurate way of determining how student centered your classroom really is, but it will give you a good idea of which end of the spectrum you are closer to. Note that a classroom in which students are speaking for a majority of the time does not necessitate that the teacher is a guide on the side, but it could.

A nice mix of activities should be selected to ensure that students are both mentally and physically on their toes. Now, of course, we are not arguing that every single classroom needs to transform itself into a field day of activities and excitement in order to be a student-centered classroom. To swing in the directions of extreme energy and extreme passivity is dangerous. But your classroom activities should demand students to do something beyond just sitting and listening.

Tips on Energy Level of Your Favorite Lesson

Think back to your life as student. What was your favorite lesson that you still remember to this day? Name a few things that you did as a student on that day. In the second column, choose if you would characterize each activity as a passive one or an active one?

Activity	Passive vs. Active
1. _____	1. _____
2. _____	2. _____
3. _____	3. _____

3. Check for Understanding; Provide Space to Teach and Reteach: Students need to have instances where they can practice the skills and knowledge they will be tested on. This way, they can get feedback on their understanding. If students struggle during these critical moments, you the teacher can step in to *reteach* as necessary. Essentially, you are building in checks for understanding to make sure that students are actually internalizing what you are teaching. Throughout a unit, students should be asked to also evaluate their understanding multiple times, so they can track their progress and growth.

Taking into account student understanding and performance is an essential part of a student-centered classroom. Instead of simply going through the motions of teaching and imparting knowledge to students, teachers need to assess their students. The activities within a student-centered classroom should be designed to reinforce content knowledge. However, how does it benefit you as the teacher to know when students are understanding and not understanding the material? Does this mean you should stop the lesson for all the students just because of a few? No.

So, what do you do with the information gathered from these checks for understanding? One of the most crucial aspects of checking for understanding is analysis. Any data that is collected through a check-in should be closely studied and used to modify the teaching rhythm as needed. In short, these checks for understanding must be true formative assessments. For instance, twenty incorrect exit tickets should prompt the teacher to go back and reteach the lesson in a different way. Or, if only a handful of students struggled with the material, then these are the students the teacher needs to conference with and review the content.

Tips on Checking for Understanding

How can you check for understanding? The purpose of a check for understanding is to determine to what extent students are understanding your material. A simple yes-no-somewhat response can gauge the classroom sufficiently to see if you need to alter your teaching.

1. *Thumbs up/thumbs down*: universal language of contentment or discontentment. Use to ask students how well they understood the lesson.
2. Provide students with color-coded sticky notes that correspond to a signal for help. Students can flag their desk if they need help.
3. Have students restate the concept in their own words to a partner or a group while you monitor.
4. Have a scale or rubric that specifies what students need to know about the concept so that they can easily point to it.
5. ELI5: May work best for older grades. Have students re-explain the concept as if teaching it to a five-year-old (Reddit, n.d.).
6. Exit Tickets: A brief activity or questionnaire students must complete at the end of the class that shows what they understood of the lesson. A common pitfall you might face is that when prompted to assess themselves, students may overexaggerate their capabilities, either intentionally or unintentionally. To mitigate this, ask students to justify their evaluation with evidence. Having a rubric or scale is a great way to make your expectations clear, and students can easily use parts of the rubric to include in their justification. Be sure to verify that student evidence supports their claims. Establishing this ongoing practice of verification will help students develop a habit of honest self-reflection (Roberts, 2015).

In one Social Studies class that I know, students must always hand in their rubrics with their projects. It's a simple habit, but it forces students to constantly be aware of what is expected of them. Subsequently, so many of the students simply evaluate themselves before submitting their work and end up ensuring they will get the best grade.

Whether social studies, physical education, or anything else, students should always be provided a rubric for each of their projects and major writing assignments, so they know exactly what is expected of them and can easily evaluate themselves.

Student-centered learning is intended to help students develop their autonomy. Encouraging students to evaluate their own understanding pushes students to take a more active role in their learning. If your goals for your students are clear, your lessons and teaching will be clear as well. Subsequently, students will be able to easily pinpoint their progress and be more driven about achieving their goals.

4. Allocate Time for a Variety of Peer Assessments: Often, peer assessment activities allow for natural teaching to occur between students. They can collaborate by providing each other solutions to their weaknesses. From a teacher's point of view, sometimes students can help each other in ways that we never can. Can group work be unpredictable? Yes, and this is one of the areas where teachers must surrender some control of the classroom. It will not happen exactly the way you want it, but that is ok. Teachers can still hold on to their sense of responsibility by generally evaluating group work effectiveness or even asking students themselves to assess their group and individual performance.

Peer assessment allows students to practice evaluating how well another person understood the concept. It can take many forms. To us, peer assessment is when at least two or more students work together to demonstrate some level of understanding either by indulging in discussion, a group activity, or by completing an assignment.

In order for students to truly take ownership of their learning, they need to know what successful learning looks and doesn't look like. For instance, if they are expected to master a math concept such as multiplying fractions, students should be able to look at another student's work and determine if the process to multiply fractions was correctly followed or not. Eventually, with enough practice, students will begin to develop a critical eye.

Tips on Teaching Students to Evaluate Work Samples

Depending on what grade you teach, getting students to successfully evaluate content can be a tricky activity. For younger grades, we'd suggest you give them three clear-cut work samples that they can differentiate into high, medium, or low. For higher grades, the more challenging work samples, the better. Then, simply ask students to sort the provided samples into categories of high, medium, or low.

Having lots of work samples will work to your advantage. Start collecting samples now in a clear place that you can always access and clearly label why you saved those specific pieces. If you have absolutely no samples at all to work with, don't fret. There are many samples of work online that you can easily search for. And of course, ask colleagues! Be sure to always delete the names of students before sharing.

The Think-Pair-Share technique is one popular strategy that many teachers use to allow for peer assessment. This involves asking students to simply turn and talk with the person next to them. It can be used to preview, practice, or even review content knowledge. Take a look at how one teacher took the Pair Share concept to a whole new level.

Ms. J is an experienced math teacher who excels at differentiating instruction for her students. In one class that I observed, she paired students up and provided them with a series of activities to do, all of which became increasingly more challenging. When I walked in, students were given puzzle pieces with complex math problems that they had to solve by working together. Then, they had to match the puzzle pieces with the appropriate answers in order to complete the assignment. Each puzzle piece had four math problems that had to be rotated to match the correct location. In short, it was a challenging assignment, one they could not complete without their partner's help.

In one particular group, because one student made a mistake, his partner showed him how to properly solve the problem. Ms. J walked around frequently to monitor student work and occasionally conferenced with the groups that needed the most help. Once students completed the puzzle, the teacher checked their work and had them move onto another challenging activity that they had to collaborate to complete. In this way, most of the period was spent reviewing mathematical concepts in a way that empowered students.

Even though this was group work, students had to rely on each other to complete the assignment and to ensure that each other's computations were correct. Students informally reviewed and retaught each other their math concepts and were held accountable by each other and the teacher. In addition, because the activities became more and more challenging, completing them all became a contest for the students, thereby increasing their engagement levels. It is important to note that despite the challenging nature, the tasks were still doable within the allotted time. If students are expected to do tasks beyond their ability, they will become frustrated (Vygotsky, 1978).

Sometimes, students do not know how to give effective feedback to each other. Because this is such a vital part of the student-centered classroom, we believe it's important to model to students how to effectively critique.

Tips on the Glow and Grow Format

Oftentimes, students struggle to assess one another because they don't know how to do so. A good teacher once suggested this method to me, and I've used it ever since. Using the Glow and Grow format, you can teach students to point out something positive that the other person did (how they glowed) and mention something they could have done to improve their work (how they can grow). It's a simple technique they can use again and again.

5. *Encourage Student Choice*: Finally, a student-centered classroom encourages and incorporates *student choice*. When it comes to the unit, take your students' preferences and interests into account. This is another area where you will have to relinquish some control.

In terms of classroom activities, a surefire way to incorporate student choice is to simply ask students. Is this an activity they would like to do again? Why or why not? Sometimes, having an honest discussion about the classroom activities can be enlightening for both the teacher and the student. For instance, when I was switching over to Google Classroom, I frequently asked students to what extent our classroom activities should be online or via paper. On the basis of their responses, I would adjust my practices and consequently faced less of a backlash from students when we tried (or didn't try) new technology.

Another way to infuse student choice is to provide students with a variety of activities to complete as opposed to asking all of them to respond to just one prompt. This can be applicable to nearly any subject area.

After a school district I know offered a workshop on differentiation, many of the teachers took what they learned and applied it in their classrooms. One particular activity became very popular, and nearly every subject area had asked its students to complete it. This activity was called the Tic Tac Toe Activity, a cumulative assignment in which students are given a selection of nine mini assignments to complete. Students were able to choose to complete any three as long as they made a row up, down, or across. When designing the Tic Tac Toe board, teachers ensured that each row had a similar level of difficulty, and the variety of thoughtful assignments allowed students to be as creative, musical, or artistic as they wished. (Fote, 2015)

The Tic Tac Toe Activity was a great hit in this school district, and despite its frequency, students enjoyed completing them because it provided them plenty of freedom. Grading activities like this can be challenging, but you can prevent a headache by creating simple rubrics for each activity. Or, you can stagger the due dates, so that only a few classes submit their work at a time.

Of course, to enable teachers to incorporate student choice, as a teacher you have to know your students. Spend time understanding their likes and dislikes and find ways to incorporate them into the lesson when possible. This will be different from age group to age group and even from year to year.

Tips on Multiple Options for Assignments

Truth be told, creating multiple options for a single assignment can be a challenge since it multiplies your workload. However, this is work that you can front-load and hopefully reuse from year to year with minor adjustments.

Tic Tac Toe Activity: Great for practicing or reviewing content!
What is it?
Arrange a three by three grid and fill each box with an assignment or problem that relates to your topic. The trick is to make sure each row is of the same complexity and requires similar effort. Students then must complete one activity per row, much like a Tic Tac Toe board.

Menu of Activities: Great for practicing or reviewing content!
What is it?
Similar to a Tic Tac Toe board, a menu of activities just allows for more flexibility. Students can choose however many assignments or only one, depending on teacher instruction. This can be great as a summative review, and each activity can review a different skill.

Another way to incorporate student choice is to tap into their funds of knowledge. Sometimes, students come to our classes as passionate experts in a field. If we don't acknowledge this or provide space in our lessons for students to share their prior knowledge, we will never know. Of course, the biggest caveat to this principle is that it has to be done within limit. We all know the dangers of students sharing too much information, and this is a rabbit hole that no teacher (or classroom) wants to be in.

Tips on Providing Space for Student Experts

It can be a challenge to balance finding time for students to share their expertise while still maintaining a steady flow of the class. Alas, there are many ways to keep comments on topic! You can preview the topic or concept by using a word cloud that includes words from your unit. Allow students to define or identify as many words of the word cloud they already know, and you will quickly get an idea of which students genuinely know the concept. At the time of this book's publication date, two of our personal favorite websites that let you customize creating your own word cloud are Tagxedo.com and Wordle.net.

Giving students the choice to choose which assignments to complete can be liberating for students. At the same time, sometimes the entire assignment needs to be completed by students. Use the tips mentioned below for classroom activities that are collaborative and performance-based and that incorporate student choice.

Tips on Great Peer Teaching Activities

Pair Share: Great for previewing, practicing, or reviewing content!
  What is it?
  Students talk to the person next to them to discuss as a pair before sharing and discussing as a class. This is a great informal way to spark conversation and help students drive the classroom.

Jigsaw: Great for practicing or reviewing content!
  What is it?
  Students are divided into five groups of five each (or four of four each). Then, they are each given a specific type of question, prompt, or image to respond to. After they complete their task at that group, one messenger from each group travels to the next group to explain their strategy while collecting information on each group's notes as well. It's a great strategy if it's planned carefully in advance and if you have enough distinct problems. The work at the end should be collected. Clear communication is a necessity, and clarification questions between students naturally abound in this strategy.

4 Corner: Great for previewing, practicing, or reviewing content.
  What is it?
  The teacher asks a question and students travel to one of the four corners of the room, depending on their answer. The four corners (more or less, depending on the question) can be labeled Strongly Agree, Agree, Disagree, and Strongly Disagree. Once in that corner, students discuss with their group and formulate a response on the basis of their discussion. Informal student teaching naturally occurs.

Gallery Walk: Great for previewing, practicing, or reviewing content.
What is it?
All around the classroom, the teacher posts up different examples of texts, images, or problems for students to analyze. Students in pairs travel around the classroom, responding to each piece in a set amount of time. Lots of informal teaching occurs, and it also utilizes student choice (Fote, 2015).

CONCLUSION

And thus concludes our inside peek into the teacher's side of a student-centered classroom. Teaching a student-centered classroom requires a distinct mind-set that affects so much of what we do. It influences the way we approach our content, the way we view our students, and the way we teach and deliver. Ultimately, a student-centered classroom empowers students to view themselves as holders of knowledge—to reflect, critique, and contribute to the learning process.

Now, envision your own student-centered classroom. Imagine it in as much detail as you possibly can. How will it look like? What will you as the teacher be doing? What will your students be doing? Relish that memory, and use the five strategies mentioned above to help transform your teaching style and better prepare your students for the twenty-first century. Plan backward with the end assignment clearly in your mind. Design activities that promote students actively taking ownership of their learning. When teaching, always check to see what your students are actually learning and modify your teaching practices as needed. Build in time for students to evaluate each other's progress and understand and encourage collaboration. Lastly, always remember to infuse student choice whenever possible.

The student-centered classroom is now within your reach. Use the attached checklist at the end of the chapter to determine how to shift the dynamics of your classroom.

Cultivating a student-centered classroom is not an easy task and will take time to master. There will be battles in your classroom that you will lose. Despite all your planning and preparation, there will be days where your classroom may just become a nightmare. It is a natural part of the process. The artist in you must find a way to enjoy the journey of chipping away at the unnecessary and ineffective and embrace the beauty of the process.

CHECKLIST FOR UNDERSTANDING

Plan Backwards

1. Did the teacher make the final assessment of the unit clear to the students?
   Yes _____ No _____
   Evidence: _____
2. Can students articulate the goal of the unit? of the lesson?
   Yes _____ No _____
   Evidence: _____
3. Do the lessons in this unit help students complete their cumulative project?
   Yes _____ No _____
   Evidence: _____

Get Students to Drive Learning

1. Does the unit make student activity the focus of the lesson?
   Yes _____ No _____
   Evidence: _____
2. Is the teacher doing more of the talking in the lesson?
   Yes _____ No _____
   Evidence: _____

Check for Understanding

1. Did the teacher assess how well students understood the concept?
   Yes _____ No _____
   Evidence: _____
2. Does the teacher alter the teaching based on the level of student understanding, if need be?
   Yes _____ No _____
   Evidence: _____
3. Does this lesson provide students with opportunities to self-evaluate their own progress?
   Yes _____ No _____
   Evidence: _____

Allocate Time for Peer Assessment

1. Does this lesson provide students with opportunities to evaluate each other?
   Yes _____ No _____
   Evidence: _____

2. In the group activity, were students provided with clear instructions and a clear goal?
   Yes _____ No _____
   Evidence: _____

3. In the group activity, were students assessed on their performance and effort?
   Yes _____ No _____
   Evidence: _____

Encourage Student Choice

1. Did the teacher incorporate student choice and interest in the unit?
   Yes _____ No _____
   Evidence: _____

2. Does the unit provide space for students to share their experiences or expertise?
   Yes _____ No _____
   Evidence: _____

QUESTIONS FOR SELF-ASSESSMENT

1. How do your lessons help students complete the final assessment of the unit?
2. What activities will your students be doing in your unit? How are students driving the lesson or unit?
3. How will you check for understanding throughout the unit?
4. How does the unit include peer evaluation?
5. How does the lesson encourage student choice?

APPENDIX 1: EXTENSION MATERIALS

Additional Strategies for the Classroom

1. *RSA ANIMATE: Drive: The Surprising Truth about What Motivates Us.*

2. *Student-Centered Learning: It Starts with the Teacher* by John McCarthy (Edutopia.org).
3. *When Kids Can't Read: What Teachers Can D*o by Kylene Beers (specifically provides student-centered activities to improve literacy).
4. "Defining Assessment" by Grant Wiggins (Edutopia.org).
5. "Every Teacher's Guide to Assessment" by Amanda Ronan (Edudemic.com).
6. For more on media literacy, see NAMLE.net.

Taking Student-Centered Teaching to the Next Level

1. What if students controlled their own learning? | Peter Hutton | TEDxMelbourne.
2. The Power of Student Drive Learning | Shelly Wright | TEDxWestVancouver.
3. Barnes, M. (2013). *Role Reversal: Achieving Uncommonly Excellent Results in the Student-Centered Classroom.*

GLOSSARY OF TERMS

Backward design—lesson-planning theory by Grant Wiggins that promotes teachers to plan with the end of the unit in mind first.

Locus of control—the focus of the classroom that influences other decisions made in the classroom.

Teacher-centered classroom—a classroom in which the teacher is the person in power and makes all decisions about curriculum and classroom structure and manages student behavior.

Student-centered classroom—a classroom in which the teacher places students at the focus. He/she works with students to make decisions about curriculum and classroom structure and manages student behavior.

Learning environment—a place where children learn. Could be a classroom or extracurricular club or activity.

Knowledge creators—anyone who generates content and/or information that others may benefit from.

Knowledge holders—anyone who possesses content knowledge and/or information.

Reteach—to deliver the same lesson in a different way.

Peer assessment—an activity in which at least two or more students work together to demonstrate some level of understanding either by indulging in discussion, a group activity or by completing an assignment and checking each other's understanding.

Self-assessment—an activity in which a student analyzes and articulates his/ her level of understanding of a concept.

Student choice—student preference when it comes to genres, topics, types of activities, learning personalities, etc.

Surrender control—when the teacher allows space and time in the class- room for students to complete a specific task without expecting students to follow a specific way of doing it.

Community of learners—a group of people invested in advancing their knowledge and understanding.

Ownership—a feeling in which the learner begins to see a personal invested benefit in what he or she is learning.

REFERENCES

Barell, J. (2003). *Developing more curious minds*. Alexandria, VA: Association for Supervision and Curriculum Development.

Cammarota, J., & Fine, M. (2008). *Revolutionizing education: Youth participatory action research in motion*. New York, NY: Routledge.

Domine, V. (2009). *Rethinking technology in schools: A primer*. New York: Peter Lang.

Fote, L. (2015). Differentiating Instruction [workshop].

Freire, P. (1970). *Pedagogy of the oppressed*. New York, NY: Herder and Herder.

Jaleel, S., & Verghis, A. M. (2015). Knowledge creation in constructivist learning. *Universal Journal of Educational Research, 3*(1), 8–12.

King, A. (1993). From sage on the stage to guide on the side. *College Teaching, 41*(1), 30–35. Retrieved from http://www.jstor.org/stable/27558571.

Ladson-Billings, G. (1995). Toward a theory of culturally relevant pedagogy. *Ameri- can Educational Research Journal, 32*(3), 465–491. Retrieved from http://www. jstor.org/stable/1163320.

McKenna, B. (2014, January 28). New research shows effectiveness of student-cen- tered learning in closing the opportunity gap. Retrieved from https://ed.stanford. edu/news/new-research-shows-effectiveness-student-centered-learning-closing- opportunity-gap.

Mercado, C., & Moll, L. C. (1997). The study of funds of knowledge: Collaborative research in Latino homes. *Centro, 9*(9), 26–42.

Morrow L. M. (2001). *Literacy development in the early years: Helping children read and write* (4th ed.). Boston, MA: Allyn and Bacon.

P21. (n.d.). Partnership for 21st century learning. Retrieved from http://www.p21. org/.

Pedersen, S., & Liu, M. (2003). Teachers' beliefs about issues in the implementation of a student-centered learning environment. *Educational Technology Research and Development, 51*(2), 57–76. Retrieved from http://www.jstor.org/stable/30221162.

Reddit. (n.d.). Explain like I'm five. Retrieved from https://www.reddit.com/r/explainlikeimfive/

Roberts, K. (2015). Argument Writing [workshop].

Schulz, W., & Sibberns, H. (Eds.) (2004). *IEA Civic Education Study Technical Report*. Amsterdam: IEA.

SCOPE. (2014). Student-centered schools: Policy supports for closing the opportunity gap. Retrieved from https://edpolicy.stanford.edu/sites/default/files/scope-pub-student-centered-policy.pdf.

Tracey, D. H., & Morrow, L. M. (2012). *Lenses on reading: An introduction to theories and models* (2nd ed.). New York: Guilford Press.

Vygotsky, L. S. (1978). *Mind in society: The development of higher psychological processes*. Cambridge, MA: Harvard University Press.

Wallis, C., & Steptoe, S. (2006, December 9). How to bring schools out of the 20th century. Retrieved from http://content.time.com/time/nation/article/0,8599,1568429,00.html.

Wiggins, G. P. (1993). *Assessing student performance*. San Francisco: Jossey-Bass Publishers.

Chapter 4

Keys to Accessible Instruction for Students with Disabilities

Jennifer L. Goeke, Pohun Chen, and Niobel Torres

INTRODUCTION

In this chapter you will learn:

- a conceptual framework for inclusive teaching called Universal Design for Learning;
- three essential practices that advance the achievement of students with disabilities in inclusive classrooms:
  - explicit instruction,
  - strategy instruction, and
  - instructional scaffolding.

BACKGROUND AND CONCEPTUAL FRAMEWORK

As the movement toward including students with disabilities in the general education classroom was coming to prominence in the 1990s, educators and policymakers began exploring how students with disabilities would gain access to the general education curriculum, just as they were gaining physical access to general education classrooms through the Individuals with Disabilities Education Act (IDEA, 1997, 2005).

The Center for Applied Special Technology (CAST), a nonprofit organization with roots in assistive technology, was inspired by the concept of universal design in architecture, in which architectural objects designed proactively to meet the needs of individuals with disabilities had unintended benefits for many others. A classic example of universal design is curb cutting, where a ramp is built from the top of a sidewalk and gradually graded down to street level.

This adaptation was mandated by the Americans with Disabilities Act of 1990 to meet the needs of people with physical disabilities; however, curb cutting also benefited the elderly, children, cyclists, people moving objects with carts, and many others. Similarly, CAST envisioned universal design as an *educational* framework in which curriculum is designed from the outset with the needs of diverse learners (including students with disabilities) in mind. This proactive approach would lower barriers to curricular access, positively benefit other learners in the classroom, and allow all students to be engaged in respectful, appropriately challenging work (Orkwis & McLane, 1998). This approach was dubbed Universal Design for Learning (UDL).

As a conceptual framework, UDL offers a lens for planning and implementing inclusive teaching that centers and values diversity. Language regarding UDL was included in the reauthorization of the Individuals with Disabilities Act (IDEA, 2004) as a suggested model for providing effective instruction to students with disabilities. This represents a shift, even within special education circles, away from "retrofitting" a general educator's lessons with accommodations and modifications as an instructional afterthought and toward intentional planning for diversity from the outset.

This chapter helps novice teachers learn and apply three specific practices that have emerged from the special education research in recent decades. These practices are intended to help novices efficiently "train up" to reach learners with high-incidence disabilities (i.e., those with learning disabilities, emotional and behavioral disorders, mild cognitive impairment, etc.), who are the most likely to spend the majority of their school day within the general education class. Our list of inclusive teaching "essentials" from a UDL perspective includes:

1. Research over several decades has determined that most students need at least some *explicit instruction* in order to learn well (Clark, Kirschner & Sweller, 2012). In elementary school, this extends most notably to reading and mathematics instruction, in which learners must master essential component skills that build one upon the next. In middle and secondary school, this also applies to essential content and skills that all students must master as well as gaps in learners' basic skills and/or content knowledge.
2. Special education research, especially regarding adolescent learners, has determined that *strategy instruction* is an essential tool for developing independent, self-directed learners who can succeed in secondary and postsecondary settings. Making your instruction explicit *and* strategic is one of the best ways to intensify your teaching and accelerate the progress of learners with disabilities.
3. There are many learners with disabilities who can be successful within the general education curriculum if appropriate *instructional scaffolds* are

explicitly taught, practiced, and applied. The term "scaffolding" is tossed around frequently and casually among educators, but to be truly effective, scaffolds must be selected strategically, explicitly taught, monitored, and gradually faded at the appropriate time.

In the following sections, we describe each of these practices in detail and provide tools that can be used to plan and implement each practice. Teaching large, diverse groups of learners in a single classroom can be extremely challenging. As a novice teacher, it is important to use scaffolds (just as you would for your own students!) that can help build your ability to plan and implement these practices. You won't become an expert overnight, but through consistent, detailed planning, attention to implementation fidelity, and data-based reflection, you will become successful and you'll see the results in your students' learning.

EXPLICIT INSTRUCTION

The Idea in Brief

Explicit instruction (EI) is the application of teacher-directed instruction in contextually relevant and appropriate ways. Explicit instruction lessons are highly structured, typically with several parts that may include:

- a pre-instructional set, a "hook," or a "why";
- an explicit instructional procedure that follows the structure: I do—We do—You do; and
- closure that includes tangible assessment data (not a feeling or belief).

The Idea in Practice

In Mrs. Stein's seventh grade robotics class, students were learning about ratios and proportional relationships. On the basis of a pretest, Mrs. Stein knew that many students lacked the skills they would need to determine the size of the gears necessary to produce their robot's proper gear ratio. Students were also unfamiliar with the proportional relationship between force and torque that would enable them to calculate the maximum weight that their robots would be able to carry.

Since the skills that she wanted the students to learn were so well defined, Mrs. Stein taught these using explicit instruction. At the start of the lesson, Mrs. Stein posed a question: "How could students figure out what gear size to choose for their robot?" She then told students that their goal today was to set up ratios and solve proportional relationships. Mrs. Stein explained that learning these skills would help them with not only this specific problem, but also at home when cooking, when doing chores around the house, and in their future careers as scientists or engineers. Ms. Tyson then led a brief, active review of fractions, equivalence, and ratios. These were key pieces of prior knowledge that would enable the students to employ the problem-solving strategies that would be introduced later.

During instruction, Mrs. Stein modeled the equivalent fractions strategy using a think-aloud. She prepared a mnemonic that would help guide students in using the equivalent fractions strategy independently. While modeling each step of the strategy, Mrs. Stein would pause and ask herself a question. She would then direct students to an easel where the mnemonic step in question was highlighted, and she would say the step and perform it.

During guided practice, Mrs. Stein emphasized the steps of the strategy while doing two examples together, and during independent practice, they distributed flash cards with the steps for students to use as a prompt. Closure consisted of students independently solving a proportions problem using the equivalent fractions strategy. Mrs. Stein examined the closure data to determine whether students needed more practice with the strategy, whether they should be introduced to a new strategy, or whether they were ready to begin programming their robots.

What Is Explicit Instruction?

With all of the diverse learners present in inclusive classrooms, teachers must be prepared to address a wide range of learning needs. Over the past thirty years, educational theory has moved from a teacher-centered, information dissemination approach to a student-centered approach in which the teacher serves as a guide or facilitator. With this focus on constructed, self-directed learning, many students with disabilities and other struggling learners in inclusive classrooms have often been left at the *acquisition* level of learning (i.e., using their cognitive resources to learn and assimilate new content or skills) while class-wide learning activities quickly proceed to the *independent* or *application* level.

In many middle-school mathematics classes, for example, a problem is presented in the form of a lengthy paragraph full of complex academic vocabulary. Students are meant to intuit problem-solving methods to solve the problem through a small-group investigation. Many mathematics teachers never explicitly model or explain the complex problem-solving methods or algorithms that may be applied.

This method may be effective for learners with well-developed mathematical background knowledge, problem-solving strategies, and computational skills, and with effective literacy skills for reading the lengthy mathematics text and social skills for collaborating with peers in small groups. However, many students in inclusive classrooms lack some or all of these skills and face significant cognitive challenges (e.g., problems with working memory, auditory processing, attention, and so on). In content areas such as mathematics, language arts, foreign language, and science, foundational knowledge and skills are the basis for further academic success. Therefore, it is vital to ensure that all students master basic skills and content and have the cognitive "readiness" to participate in inquiry-based, self-guided instruction.

Despite the current emphasis on self-guided instruction, decades of educational research have shown that certain types of teacher-directed instruction produce gains in student achievement (Rosenshine, 1995). The form of teaching known as direct instruction (*big* D, *big* I; Engelmann & Carnine, 1991) initially involved the systematic (e.g., scripted) teaching of skills and strategies, controlled responses by learners, and systematic reinforcement of correct responses.

Over time, educators adapted this approach to a form of explicit teaching that retained a high level of teacher control but allowed more flexibility. This form of teaching became known as direct instruction (*little* d, *little* I; Rosenshine, 2009). Currently, the term "explicit instruction" is most often used to refer to models in which a teacher directly imparts content, skills, or strategies through a structured teaching procedure.

While there often appears to be tension between proponents of explicit instruction and proponents of self-guided learning, these two approaches need not be diametrically opposed. For example, a brief burst of explicit teaching (such as a five- to ten-minute mini lesson) may provide the cognitive "leg up" some learners may need to successfully approach a small-group investigation in math class. Explicit instruction can be applied strategically depending on the content, context, and individual student needs as a necessary and effective complement to more student-centered teaching approaches.

Explicit instruction is a process-driven model that makes explicit what is to be learned, why it is to be learned, and when and where the learning will be useful to students. Through explicit instruction, the teacher models skills and strategies through think-alouds, examples and nonexamples, and statements and restatements of goals ("I do"). The teacher then provides opportunities for guided practice ("We do"), scaffolding students' performance toward increasingly self-monitored and self-directed performance, until they can engage in the task on their own during independent practice ("You do"). Critical features of explicit instruction are explained in greater detail below.

Critical Features of Explicit Instruction

Because explicit instruction is unlikely to be effective unless implemented with fidelity, it is important to consider the following critical features:

1. *Briskly paced:* explicit instruction should be delivered at a brisk pace so that student attention and interest are maintained during teacher talk/think-aloud and guided practice. This extends to independent practice so that students are receiving constant feedback as they develop knowledge and skills.
   - Recommendations for teacher-led lesson time:
     - Elementary: 5–7 minutes
     - Middle school: 7–10 minutes
     - High school: 10–15 minutes
2. *Highly organized:* The lesson proceeds in an orderly progression from gaining students' attention and interest, to presenting new information (I do), to practicing new knowledge or skills with (we do) and without guidance (you do), to assessing progress.
3. *Teacher controlled:* Teacher direction enables a brisk pace to be set and students to focus on key knowledge and skills. It should be noted that although teacher control during explicit instruction is high, it does not mean that students are passive learners. Specific strategies are used to maintain student engagement and active application of the skill/content being taught.
4. *Focused on facts, skills, or strategies:* Explicit instruction is most useful and appropriate for two types of lessons: (a) when the goal is learning a well-defined body of information that all students must master; and (b) for teaching (or reteaching) component skills (i.e., skills, often in reading, writing, or mathematics, that build one upon the other). When the learning objective requires discovery or experiential learning, it may be more appropriate to design a lesson through inquiry, cooperative learning, or problem-based learning.
5. *Teaching students step-by-baby-step to the point of redundancy or overlearning:* Though enormously effective for students who need the reinforcement and repetition, redundancy (or overlearning) can be reached by some students very early, leading to boredom or frustration. Consider how to differentiate instruction to engage all students at the appropriate instructional level.
6. *Task analysis:* Planning explicit instruction can be challenging because it requires the teacher to break down an activity or skill he/she does automatically into its component parts in order to teach it effectively to students—a process known as "task analysis." It may help to put yourself in the student's shoes and try to imagine what it is like not to understand or to have never been taught how to do the task. Explicit instruction also requires patience—you will need to explicitly teach each step as you help students build *mastery* so that they can eventually perform the task as automatically as their peers.

Guidelines for Implementation

There are many models of explicit instruction, all of which include some combination of elements or "teacher moves" that have been identified through research as increasing student achievement. The elements in the Explicit Instruction Lesson Guideline (see Table 4.1) were adapted from Goeke (2009) and can be used to plan and evaluate Explicit Instruction lessons. Other effective models include Archer and Hughes (2010), the Madeline Hunter model (Hunter, 1994), Slavin (2003), and Huitt (2008). All explicit instruction models involve the key elements of (a) an introduction, overview, or preset; (b) teacher-led explanation and/or modeling, preferably in the form of a think-aloud; (c) guided and independent practice; (d) assessment; and (e) task-specific monitoring and feedback provided throughout the lesson as needed.

The Lesson Evaluation Guideline can be used to take a critical look at a particular lesson in which you would like to improve your use of explicit instruction. In the area for Your Notes, either mark that the component is present *or* suggest how the lesson could include the component (Table 4.1).

The Idea in Summary

Within an inclusive classroom, there is usually a broad continuum of learning needs represented by students with disabilities, ELLs, low-achieving students, average learners, and advanced learners, among others. This continuum requires students to engage in a variety of learning tasks, including acquiring new knowledge and skills, applying knowledge and skills in varied contexts for different purposes, and eventually becoming independent, self-directed learners. Aligned with these tasks are varied instructional approaches that can be applied by teachers to meet their students' needs.

Research over the last several decades has established that most students need at least some explicit instruction, especially when they are acquiring essential knowledge and skills. A critical aspect of this recommendation deserves attention: we do not advocate a steady diet of teacher-directed lecture. Overuse and abuse of teacher-directed instruction is not an effective use of instructional time for anyone. As with the other approaches discussed in this chapter, explicit instruction should be applied strategically depending on the content, context, and specific learning objective.

As one powerful instructional tool in your novice teacher toolkit, explicit instruction can help students acquire basic skills and content as they move along the continuum toward self-directed learning.

Table 4.1 Explicit Instruction Lesson Evaluation Guideline

How does the lesson plan indicate when and how the following will be provided:	Your Notes
Preinstructional Set • Students' attention is engaged and maintained. • The learning objective is clearly stated; all students understand the objective. • Description of the content, skills, strategy, and use ("a *what*, a *why*, and a *buy*")	
Prepare the Knowledge Base for Instruction • Students' prior knowledge is activated through an active strategy; connections to the current learning objective are made explicit. OR • Prior content/skills are explicitly reviewed; their connection(s) to the current learning objective are made explicit. OR • Key relevant vocabulary are pretaught using an explicit, contextual strategy.	
Instruction • The skill/strategy is explicitly modeled using a step-by-step process; key thinking processes and fix-up strategies are made explicit (I do).v • Students are engaged in guided practice that is active and directly aligned with cognitive modeling (We do) • All students' understanding is monitored using an active, data-driven strategy. • Students are engaged in independent practice that is directly aligned with cognitive modeling (You do).	
Closure • The lesson is concluded with an explicit closure activity that requires summarization, synthesis, analysis, etc.	
Active Participation • Multiple strategies are used to ensure that active participation by all learners is high throughout the lesson.	
Procedural Prompts/Strategies • Strategic visuals, prompts, mnemonics, or routines support student self-direction.	
Check Understanding • Student understanding is consistently monitored through a variety of *active* strategies (e.g., signaled response, choral response, communicator, etc.).	

Reflect on Explicit Instruction

- Am I applying explicit instruction appropriately and strategically as part of a varied set of instructional strategies?
- Who in my class may need a more explicit teaching approach, for what purposes, and how often? How will I monitor students' progress to know if my teaching is effective?
- How can I facilitate some time for explicit instruction within my total block of instructional time? If not all students need explicit instruction, what will they be doing?

Web Resource

Watch a video vignette in which explicit instruction and student exploration are used to increase independence. Catch and Release: Encourage Independence https://www.teachingchannel.org/videos/effective-teaching-technique (Time: 2:05).

STRATEGY INSTRUCTION

The Idea in Brief

Strategy instruction is a student-centered approach that teaches students how to identify the appropriate plan of action to tackle any given problem and how to implement that plan. Through strategy instruction, teachers help students become independent, *strategic* learners.

The Idea in Practice

Tyisha is a fourteen-year-old ninth grader. Her teacher, Mr. Armstrong, puts a strong emphasis on relating algebra to real-world situations that affect his students' daily lives. When Tyisha is given calculation problems to solve, she has no difficulty solving them. However, when given word problems that require her to set up the problem before solving it, she has a great deal of difficulty. This is frustrating to Tyisha because she knows how to perform the algorithm once the problem is written for her. Her teacher realizes that several students are having difficulty with this concept and has decided to teach them a strategy to help with the following task: write and solve the algebra equation in a real-life word problem.

Mr. Armstrong decides to teach the students a mnemonic strategy called STAR. STAR, a problem-solving strategy for algebra, stands for "Search, Translate, Answer, and Review." Mr. Armstrong knows that using a mnemonic device like STAR is useful if students are having difficulty pulling key information out of word problems in order to set up their equations. Students can use the STAR method in combination with algebra manipulatives (concrete application), pictorial representations (semiconcrete application), or written algebraic equations (abstract application). Mr. Armstrong ensures that students have mastered the concrete application of the STAR strategy using manipulatives before allowing them to move on to the semiconcrete or abstract phases.

What Is Strategy Instruction?

Strategy instruction is a student-centered approach that focuses on teaching students *how to learn* and *how to use what they have learned* to understand and solve problems (Deshler, Alley, Warner & Schumaker, 1981; Deshler and Lenz, 1989; Deshler & Schumaker, 1986). A learning strategy is a person's approach to learning and using information. Thus, strategy instruction helps students learn procedures for accomplishing a variety of academic tasks. By bringing awareness to the cognitive tools that strong readers, writers, and mathematicians rely on daily, students are explicitly taught strategies that they would never discover otherwise. Students who do not know or use effective learning strategies often learn passively and are more likely to fail in school (Mastropieri & Scruggs, 2010).

Strategy instruction is a two-part process that involves not just simply teaching students steps such as a mnemonic or acronym, but teaching the steps *and* teaching students how to use those steps proficiently and strategically to *mastery*. Strategies such as mnemonics or acronyms become *learning strategies* when students independently select the appropriate ones and use them effectively to accomplish tasks or goals. Strategy instruction has been identified as the instructional strategy most likely to benefit adolescent learners because of its focus on creating self-direction and independence. As adolescents move through the middle- and high-school grades, the content learning demands increase dramatically as well as the range and complexity of learning tasks. Learning strategies can help adolescent learners become independent as they face an increasingly complex set of academic demands.

What factors determine whether a student will succeed in a secondary content-area classroom? A survey of seventh and tenth grade teachers in Kansas, Indiana, and Florida indicated that nearly half of a student's report card grades depended on test performance. While such factors as attendance, punctuality, participation, and homework completion were also important, teachers made clear that test scores were the single most important factor in report card grades.

On average, teachers gave an average of eleven tests over the course of a single nine-week grading period. Therefore, students' academic survival is tightly linked to successful preparation for and performance on academic tests, especially the ability to remember and efficiently recall factual information. This can be problematic for students with learning disabilities, who have particular difficulties remembering academic content (e.g., Cooney & Swanson, 1987).

Applying a strategic approach to learning a new concept or skill is the hallmark of an expert learner. Effective strategy use is important for students who have disabilities and those who do not; all students can benefit from strategies that capable learners use. The goal of strategy instruction is to provide *all* students with the ability to be active learners, equipped with effective tools for strategic planning and independent learning.

How Are Learning Strategies Taught?

Many students with disabilities struggle with developing strategies for learning and remembering on their own. To ensure that students become truly independent, learning strategies cannot be taught as a "hint" or an "option." For learning strategies to become embedded in students' arsenal of strategic learning approaches, they must be explicitly taught *to mastery*.

To achieve mastery, students

- are provided with information on the usefulness of the strategy (buy-in);
- must acquire the ability to use the strategy fluently and independently;
- are taught to self-correct;
- must practice the strategy on controlled material at their independent level;
- regardless of level, until students have achieved mastery, new strategies should not be taught.

What Are the Types of Learning Strategies?

Scholars at the University of Kansas created a curriculum of learning strategies called the Strategic Instruction Model or SIM (Putnam, Deshler, & Schumaker, 1992; Swanson, 1999, 1993; see http://sim.kucrl.org/). Each SIM strategy targets a specific skill that students need to master to succeed in school from late elementary through college or university and beyond. SIM strategies are organized into categories, for example:

- *Learning how to learn:* For example, how to paraphrase critical information, picture information to aid in understanding and remembering, ask questions and make predictions while reading different kinds of texts, and identify unknown words in reading assignments.
- *Preparing for tests:* For example, develop mnemonics and other devices to help memorize facts and learn new vocabulary.

- *Expressing ideas and demonstrating knowledge:* For example, write sentences, paragraphs, and themes; monitor written work for errors; and confidently take tests.

Helping students understand what a task is asking them to do and select the appropriate learning strategy is part of helping them become active, independent learners.

Guidelines for Implementation

Strategy instruction is intensive (daily) and extensive (usually a minimum of four weeks, depending on progress toward mastery) and requires detailed, ongoing practice and feedback. When teaching a learning strategy, the following process should be followed with fidelity:

- Pretest and gain commitment.
  - Pretest students on the relevant task and select a strategy on the basis of student need (e.g., students must write a coherent paragraph but do not proofread their work, therefore the teachers choose the COPS strategy: Capitals, Organization, Punctuation, Spelling).
  - Elicit students' interest by linking the strategy to meaningful goals and different contexts in which the strategy can be applied.
- Describe the strategy.
  - Define each step.
  - Talk about how the steps are used at the mastery level.
- Model the strategy.
  - Demonstrate skilled use of the strategy.
  - Use think-alouds along with verbalization of each step.
  - Model errors, self-correction, and positive self-talk.
- Verbally practice the strategy.
  - Have students memorize the steps: Mastery is required!
  - Try using mnemonics, but keep working memory capacity in mind. Students may need to work on one step at a time until each individual step is mastered. As a result, learning a complete strategy may take several weeks, but the pay-off will be worth it!
  - Note: Graphic strategies might not require verbal practice.
- Controlled practice with feedback
  - Students use the strategy for the first time on EASY content that is at or below their current level.
  - Feedback should progress from teacher mediated to student mediated.
  - Since self-evaluation is critical at this stage, rubrics could be used as a tool.
  - Students who were unsuccessful should be retaught in small groups.

- Advanced practice with feedback
  - At this stage, students should progress to more advanced materials.
  - Feedback continues to move toward more student mediated.
  - There may be a decline in student performance because of more complex content.
  - Mastery of strategy use is required at this stage.
- Posttest
  - Use an instrument similar to pretest to allow students to see progress.
  - Share the results with the students in order to motivate them when it comes to the introduction of new strategies.
- Generalization
  - This should be your goal as students know when, where, and how to use the strategy.
  - Promote strategy use in novel situations that extend beyond the classroom; ask students to self-report when they have applied the strategy to a new context.

The Strategy Instruction Lesson Evaluation Guideline in Table 4.2 can be used to critically examine a particular lesson in which you would like to improve your use of strategy instruction. In the area for Your Notes, either mark that the component is present *or* suggest how the lesson could include this component (Table 4.2).

The Idea in Summary

Several key concepts are related to strategy instruction and that are important to remember. First, you are not only teaching the student what to do in order to complete an activity, you are giving him or her step-by-step instructions on how to tackle a problem. In this way, almost anything you teach can be taught as a strategy if you break it down into component parts, create a series of steps to help students remember the strategy, and teach them each step to mastery. Second, it is critical to teach the student how to self-monitor in order to know when the strategy is appropriate, whether or not the strategy is being used correctly, and when to be flexible in employing another strategy. Finally, teach the student how to identify pertinent information, plan, reason, and monitor his or her performance—students' ability to select and apply the appropriate strategy is the key to independence as a self-directed learner.

Reflect on Strategy Instruction

1. What learning strategies do *you* automatically use as a capable learner? Do you make lists, create songs or rhymes in your head, use visualization? How successful are these strategies for you?

Table 4.2   Strategy Instruction Lesson Evaluation Guide

Strategy Instruction Lesson Component	Your Notes
1. Pretest and Gain Commitment	
• Select a strategy on the basis of student need. • Pretest students on a task. • Get students to buy-in for the new strategy. • Link strategy to meaningful goals. • Establish local linkage to earlier strategy and the benefits they gained. • Describe different contexts (you can use this strategy when . . .)	
2. Describe	
• Describe the strategy (what each step stands for). • Talk about how the steps are used by experts.	
3. Model	
• Demonstrate skilled use of the strategy. • Use think-alouds along with verbalization of each step. • Model errors, self-correction, and positive self-talk.	
4. Verbal Practice	
• Memorize the steps (mastery is required). • Mnemonics are recommended (keep working memory capacity in mind and keep the cognitive burden manageable). • Graphic strategies might not require verbal practice.	
5. Controlled Practice with Feedback	
• Students USE the strategy for the first time. • Use EASY content (at or below current level.) • New strategy = easy content. • New content = easy strategy. • Feedback should progress from teacher mediated to student mediated. • Rubrics should be used for self-evaluation. • Meet and reteach small groups of unsuccessful students.	
6. Advanced Practice with Feedback	
• Students progress to more advanced materials (longer texts, more difficult problems, etc.). • Feedback continues to move toward more student mediated. • Student performance may decline at first because of more complex content. • Mastery of strategy use is required at this stage.	
7. Posttest	
• Use an instrument similar to pretest to allow students to see progress. • Show students results (powerful motivator).	
8. Generalization	
Goals: • Use of strategy in other settings. • Students know when, where, and how to use the strategy and the USE it! • Promote strategy use in novel situations—extend beyond your classroom.	

2. How can strategy instruction help teachers create access to challenging content for all learners within an inclusive classroom? How does this method fit with a Universal Design for Learning approach?

Web Resources

Watch an example of strategy instruction for actively reading textbooks, The SQ3R Reading Comprehension Strategy: http://inservice.ascd.org/actively-reading-textbooks/.

INSTRUCTIONAL SCAFFOLDING

The Idea in Brief

Instructional scaffolding is the process by which teachers provide and fade support so that students master skills and content for independent application. Teachers not only build scaffolds throughout their lessons, but also target scaffolding efforts toward specific students or groups of students.

The Idea in Practice

In Ms. Adarkwa and Mr. Igorovich's eighth grade science class, students are starting a unit on the atom. In planning for the first lesson on the size of an atom, Kristen and Mark discussed how they might structure the lesson. On the basis of their experience with students in previous years, Mark anticipated that there would be many students who would have difficulty conceptualizing sub-nanoscale objects. Kristen agreed, so the two teachers talked about areas where they could intentionally build scaffold points for students.

In the past, Ms. Adarkwa and Mr. Igorovich used an online animation to start a class discussion. It started with a coffee bean and zoomed in through several images of progressively smaller objects, eventually ending with an image of a carbon atom. The teachers knew from the previous year that some of the smaller objects were unfamiliar to students. This year, they decided that they would start with a set of larger and more familiar objects. They would then play off the discussion and have students perform a concept sort in a table. Students would compare and contrast the two sets of objects to see the size difference between the largest and smallest objects of each set. For some students who struggle with writing or self-starting, they decided that they would provide process scaffolding by giving them writing prompts. Overall, the functional scaffold (or table) described above would assist students in interpreting the animation and organizing the information.

The lesson would then transition to the scientific processes that enabled the study of atoms and the scientists who performed this work. As this section would be heavy on facts which would be necessary for the ensuing atomic model mini-design challenge, Ms. Adarkwa said that she would work on a graphic organizer (process scaffold) that would list each scientist along with the steps of the experimental procedures.

Along with the organizer, she would prepare a content scaffold in the form of a labeled diagram depicting the experiment. Mr. Igorovich would prepare explicit instruction of a mnemonic strategy to help students memorize the content. In addition to using a graphic organizer for the steps of the mnemonic strategy, Mr. Igorovich carefully chose think-aloud questions that would require students to repeat in order to self-monitor their progress with the strategy (metacognitive scaffold).

The two teachers agreed that this plan was a good start in scaffolding the lesson and that they would make further decisions after examining data from the lesson's exit tickets.

What Is Scaffolding?

The term "scaffolding" comes from the work of Wood, Bruner, and Ross (1976) and was developed as a metaphor to describe the type of assistance offered by a teacher or peer to support student learning. In the process of scaffolding, the teacher helps the student master a task or concept that the student is initially unable to grasp independently. Of central importance is allowing the student to complete as much of the task as possible, unassisted.

The teacher only attempts to help the student with tasks that are just beyond his current capability. Student errors are expected, but with teacher feedback and prompting, the student is able to achieve the task or goal. When the student takes responsibility for or masters the task, the teacher begins the process of "fading," or gradually removing the scaffolding, which allows the student to work independently. In other words, scaffolding serves as a developmental "bridge" that is used to build upon what students already know to help them arrive at something new (e.g., a new product, level of performance, form of problem-solving, conclusion, etc.).

Underlying scaffolded instruction is Vygotsky's (1978) theory of the Zone of Proximal Development (ZPD). Vygotsky suggested that there are two parts of a learner's developmental level: (a) their "actual developmental level" and (b) their "potential developmental level." The ZPD is defined as the distance between the actual developmental level and the potential developmental level. The ZPD can also be described as the area between what a learner can do by himself and what can be attained with the help of a "more knowledgeable other"—either an adult or peer. Vygotsky's theory prompted educators to apply the ZPD through the idea of scaffolded instruction.

As noted above in the section on explicit instruction, inquiry-based instructional approaches often progress quickly from a brief introduction or "big idea" to student-directed discovery or application. In inclusive settings, this is a logical place to insert scaffolding that might help diverse learners unpack the problem to be solved in a step-by-step manner, understand the expectations for their performance, or engage with peers in a productive content-based discussion.

In a middle-school language arts classroom, for example, the teacher, Ms. Eisen, typically teaches *mood* by reading an illustrative passage from a mentor text and then simply explaining through a think-aloud how the passage is an example of mood. Students then read their independent reading books to find and record an example of mood in their reading logs. Recently, however, Ms. Eisen came to understand that for many students in her inclusive block, the concept of mood is abstract and requires complex reading comprehension and inferential skills.

Rather than moving quickly from a brief verbal explanation to independent student application, she designed a three-step strategy to help students identify mood in a passage: (1) read a passage or chapter; (2) ask myself, "How did it make me feel?" Generate some words that illustrate that feeling; (3) find evidence in the text to support my answer. She taught the strategy explicitly by using the "I do—We do—You do" explicit instruction procedure and creating an anchor chart (visual prompt) listing the three steps. For independent practice, she gave students a process scaffold to organize their answers in their reading logs, as shown in Table 4.3.

Table 4.3 Organizational Scaffold

Passage or chapter (including page #s)	How did it make me feel? Write 1–3 mood words	Evidence from the text

Although *all* students took part in the ten-minute mini lesson on the mood strategy and could refer to the anchor chart for prompting, only *some* students were required to use the reading log process scaffold during independent practice. Ms. Eisen circulated through the classroom and prompted these students to insert the process scaffold in their notebooks. Through the additional scaffolding of explicit instruction of the step-by-step mood strategy, the mood strategy anchor chart, and the process scaffold, Ms. Eisen ensured that all of the learners in her inclusive block acquired, practiced, and moved toward mastery of identifying mood. Her scaffolds gradually assisted students to build an internal cognitive architecture for this concept.

As students gained mastery and began to internalize the three-step process for identifying mood, Ms. Eisen gradually withdrew the anchor chart and the process scaffold and students began writing their responses in narrative form. For some students, these scaffolds were faded sooner than for others. Ms. Eisen relied on assessment data from students' reading logs, exit tickets, and quizzes to determine which students still needed the scaffold and which students had internalized the mood strategy to mastery.

A key aspect of Universal Design for Learning is anticipating barriers in the general education curriculum for individual students and designing instruction that eliminates the identified barriers and provides access to all learners. The example above illustrates ways in which a teacher worked to eliminate barriers in the language arts curriculum and instruction to more effectively teach an important literary element.

An essential understanding related to this approach is the idea of "anticipatory practice"—using our knowledge of students (e.g., their learning characteristics, language, social skills, culture, etc.) combined with assessment data to design scaffolds that facilitate learning, rather than waiting for some students to fail, experience frustration, and practice errors before intervening with appropriate scaffolds (or not intervening at all). Occasionally, we will anticipate incorrectly: students whom we predicted would need a scaffold will sail through a task or problem unassisted; students we thought would be totally independent will rely temporarily on a scaffold. However, none of this is wasted effort.

Students' individual responses to scaffolded instruction provide essential assessment data about their learning and performance. Once an effective scaffold has been designed, it can be applied again and again in appropriate situations. Perhaps most meaningfully, through the implementation of scaffolded instruction, we communicate implicitly and explicitly that our approach to teaching is *inclusive* and that we will provide the supports necessary for all students to be successful. This can go a long way toward building the motivation, investment, and task-persistence of diverse learners in inclusive classrooms.

There are many different kinds of scaffolds. Table 4.4 describes types of scaffolds and their intended purposes for students. Although most inclusive teachers will say that they scaffold instruction for individual learners, this approach is implemented with varying degrees of effectiveness. Some teachers use the term scaffolding to mean any time they use questioning to try to guide students toward an answer. Others implement a variety of scaffolds, but never give students the opportunity to internalize them to the point of true independence.

Understanding specific types of scaffolds is useful for being able to apply scaffolds strategically and effectively, and then deliberately assessing their impact on student learning. No matter what type of scaffold you choose, to be truly effective, instructional scaffolding must include the following critical features:

- *Intentionality:* The task has a clear overall purpose. At times, scaffolding may be implemented to help students complete steps or "chunks" that contribute to completion of the whole task.
- *Appropriateness:* Scaffolding is applicable to instructional tasks within the student's Zone of Proximal Development, that is, problems that can be solved with help but that students could not successfully complete on their own.
- *Structure:* Cognitive modeling of a particular scaffold should be structured around an appropriate approach to the task and lead to a natural sequence of thought and language.
- *Collaboration:* The teacher's response to student work should reframe and extend the students' efforts to use the scaffold without rejecting what they have accomplished on their own (e.g., "I really like how you used the steps to check your own work. Can you go back one more time and make sure you hit every point?"). The teacher's primary role is collaborative rather than evaluative.
- *Internalization:* Scaffolding for a particular activity is gradually withdrawn as students internalize the process or task. It is important to use data to decide when a scaffold should be withdrawn. Withdrawing scaffolds too soon can lead to student frustration; leaving them in place too long can make students overly dependent. Give students the heads-up that the scaffold will not be available forever. Prompt them to use it at appropriate times and consistently reinforce independent use of the scaffold to promote internalization (Table 4.4).

Table 4.4 Types of Scaffolds

Scaffold	Ways to Use Scaffolds in an Instructional Setting
Functional	*Helps learners understand how to use and/or interpret:* • tutorials • instructions • explanations of representations
Process	*Helps learners understand how to do something:* • sequencing • mandatory, voluntary • linear, nonlinear, hierarchical • history of user's path
Content	*Helps the learner figure out an answer:* • hints • content information
Metacognitive	*Helps the learner to be aware of his/her own learning through reflection, monitoring, etc.:* • assessment of understanding (Do I know more/understand better now?) • progress reflection through the learning process
Interpersonal	*Helps facilitate social interaction:* • class management • turn taking • communication
Procedural	*Support the communication process.*

Guidelines for Implementation

As with explicit instruction and strategy instruction, scaffolding has specific implementation guidelines and should be implemented effectively.

1. Use your knowledge of the student and the curriculum.
   • Consider curriculum goals and the students' needs.
   • Select appropriate tasks.
2. Establish a shared goal.
   • Involve students in the planning of goals and activities.
   • Raise motivation and investment.
3. Begin with what the students can do.
   • Build on identified strengths and feelings of self-efficacy.
   • Tasks can be completed with little or no assistance.
   • Remember: The easiest way to scaffold is to reduce the complexity of the task. This can be accomplished in two ways:
     ○ Chunk information into smaller, digestible parts (i.e., teach a new main idea strategy using a very brief, simple paragraph first; assess frequently and gradually increase complexity of the paragraphs as students gain mastery of the strategy).

- ○ Start with an identification task (i.e., which one of these statements paraphrases the word problem correctly?) and gradually proceed to a production task (i.e., paraphrase the word problem in your own words).
4. Provide tailored assistance.
   - Choose from cueing, prompting, questioning, modeling, telling, or discussing.
   - Use as needed and adjust to meet students' needs.
5. Monitor progress toward the goal.
   - Ask questions and request clarifications.
   - Offer praise and encouragement.
   - Keep students focused on their goals.
6. Give feedback.
   - Teach self-monitoring strategies.
   - Summarize current progress.
   - Explicitly note behaviors that contributed to each student's success.
7. Assist internalization, independence, and generalization to other contexts.
   - Start fading support.
   - Provide opportunities to practice the task in a variety of contexts.
8. Help students to be independent when they have command of the activity.
   - Stop scaffolding support when students have demonstrated that they can perform the task independently.
   - Watch for clues from students that show when and how much teacher assistance is needed.

The Idea in Summary

In an inclusive classroom, students may need a continuum of instructional scaffolds to be successful. For one student, a simple verbal scaffold in the form of a few targeted questions may be sufficient for leading him or her toward independent performance. For others, consistent use of more structured scaffolds like visuals and prompts may be essential for their success. Scaffolding efforts will be successful only if students find them useful and teachers teach and reinforce students for their use.

Reflect on Instructional Scaffolding

- What scaffolds do I use consistently and for what instructional purposes?
- Am I following the guidelines for implementation effectively? Do my students internalize the scaffolds over time or do I withdraw them too rapidly?

Web Resource

Complete this online module: Providing Instructional Supports: Facilitating Mastery of New Skills at http://iris.peabody.vanderbilt.edu/module/sca/.

CONCLUSION

In this chapter, we presented three specific teaching approaches that can be used by novice teachers in inclusive classrooms to improve the performance of students with disabilities. These strategies have been demonstrated through research to positively impact academic achievement for students with disabilities. However, when applied effectively, it is likely that these approaches will also benefit other learners in the classroom.

These unanticipated benefits are a central feature of universally designed instruction. For example, explicit instruction is likely to benefit students with gaps in their basic skills, but may also benefit ELLs who need to see a skilled model of performance in order to fully understand the task. Instructional scaffolds like visuals will benefit students with working memory deficits by helping them remember all the steps in a learning activity; visuals are also likely to help students with attention deficits who have difficulty attending to and following multistep directions. In other words, when we plan instruction with the intention of meeting the needs of diverse learners in the classroom, we create a much higher likelihood that *all* students will succeed.

For novice teachers, learning how to implement each of these teaching approaches while also learning every aspect of what it means to be a new teacher can be daunting. It may be helpful to enlist some novice teacher colleagues who are also interested in improving their inclusive teaching and support each other toward effective implementation of these practices. Sharing resources and materials, reflecting on lesson successes and failures, and coanalyzing and interpreting student data can help create a supportive culture for inclusive teaching and learning. Work on one approach at a time and help each other toward mastery of that approach, just as you would with the learners in your classroom. You can use the worksheet in Table 4.5 to self-evaluate your progress and guide your supportive work sessions.

Finally, teaching students with disabilities within an inclusive setting is challenging. Meeting the learning needs of all students within a large group can sometimes feel like an impossible task. The best inclusive teachers acknowledge the diversity in their classrooms, get to know their students in a variety of ways, including through the use of systematic assessment data, and intentionally plan teaching that centers and privileges that diversity and prioritizes every student's growth and success (Table 4.5).

Table 4.5   Self Evaluation Checklist for Inclusive Teaching

Teaching Strategy	Strengths	Weaknesses
Explicit Instruction		
Strategy Instruction		
Instructional Scaffolds		
Summary of Instructional Goals/Next Steps:		

GLOSSARY OF TERMS

Mastery—a level of performance that must be attained before moving on to the next step or component of instruction.

Generalization—the transfer of learning to new situations.

Strategy—an individual's self-generated thoughts, feelings, and actions, which are systematically oriented toward attainment of their goals.

Scaffold—support given during the learning process which is tailored to the needs of the student with the intention of helping the student achieve his or her learning goals.

REFERENCES

Archer, A. L., & Hughes, C. A. (2010). *Explicit instruction: Effective and explicit teaching*. New York: Guilford Press.

Clark, R. E., Kirschner, P. A., & Sweller, J. (2012). The case for fully guided instruction. *American Educator*, (Spring).

Cooney, J. B., & Swanson, H. L. (1987). Memory and learning disabilities: An overview. In H. L. Swanson (Ed.), Memory and learning disabilities (pp. 1–40). Greenwich, CT: JAI Press.

Deshler, D. D., Alley, G. R., Warner, M. M., & Schumaker, J. B. (1981). Instructional practices for promoting skill acquisition and generalization in severely learning disabled adolescents. *Learning Disabilities Quarterly, 4*, 415–421.

Deshler, D. D., & Lenz, B. K. (1989). The strategies instruction approach. *International Journal of Learning Disability, Development and Education, 36*(3), 203–224.

Deshler, D. D., & Schumaker, J. B. (1986). Learning strategies: An instructional alternative for low-achieving adolescents. *Exceptional Children, 52*, 583–590.

Engelmann, S., & Carnine, D. (1991). *Theory of instruction: Principles and applications*. Eugene, OR: ADI Press.

Goeke, J. L. (2009). *Explicit instruction*. Upper Saddle River, NJ: Pearson Education.

Huitt, W. (2008). Direct instruction: A transactional model. *Educational Psychology Interactive*. Valdosta, GA: Valdosta State University. Retrieved [date] from http://www.edpsycinteractive.org/topics/instruct/instevnt.html.

Hunter, M. (1994). *Enhancing teaching*. Upper Saddle River, NJ: Pearson Education.

Mastropieri, M.A., & Scruggs, T. E. (2010). The inclusive classroom: Strategies for effective instruction (4th ed.). Upper Saddle River, NJ: Prentice Hall.

Orkwis, R., & McLane, K. (1998). A curriculum every student can use: Design principles for student access. ERIC/OSEP Topical Brief. Reston, VA: ERIC/OSEP Special Project. (ERIC Document Reproduction Service No. ED423654). Retrieved January 17, 2002, from http://www.cec.sped.org/osep/udesign.html.

Putnam, L. M., Deshler, D. D., & Schumaker, J. B. (1992). The investigation of setting demands: A missing link in learning strategy instruction. In L. Meltzer (Ed.), Strategy assessment and instruction for students with learning disabilities: From theory to practice (pp. 325–351). Austin, TX: Pro-Ed.

Scruggs, T. A., Mastropieri, M. A., & McDuffie, K. A. (2007). Co-teaching in inclusive classrooms: A metasynthesis of qualitative research. *Exceptional Children, 73*(4), 392–416.

Slavin, R. (2003). *Educational psychology: Theory and practice* (7th ed.). Boston: Allyn & Bacon.

Swanson, H. L. (1993). Executive processing in learning-disabled readers. Intelligence, *17*, 117–149.

Swanson, H. L. (1999). What develops in working memory? A life-span perspective. Developmental Psychology, *35*(4), 986–1000.

Rosenshine, B. (1995). Advances in research on instruction. *The Journal of Educational Research, 88*(5), 262–268.

Rosenshine, B. (2009). The empirical support for direct instruction. In S. Tobias & T. M. Duffy (Eds.), Constructivist instruction: Success or failure? (pp. 201–220). New York: Routledge.

Vygotsky, L. (1978). Interaction between learning and development. In *Mind and Society* (pp. 79–91). Cambridge, MA: Harvard University Press.

Wood, D. J., Bruner, J. S., & Ross, G. (1976). The role of tutoring in problem solving. *Journal of Child Psychiatry and Psychology, 17*(2), 89–100.

Chapter 5

Planning Instruction
for English Learners

Strategies Teachers Need to Know

Mayra C. Daniel

The changing demographics of school populations demand teachers meet top-down requirements while ensuring that the curriculum offers English learners (ELs) the medium they need to transact with text (Rosenblatt, 1978). This chapter focuses on ways with which teachers can strategically meet the educational needs of culturally and linguistically diverse students through *situated practice* (instruction adjusted for the context of the learners). It also leads the novice teacher through a conversation that begins with raising their awareness of the many responsibilities that are part of teachers' daily lives.

Grasping what is necessary to be an effective teacher of ELs then leads to the next two sections, Examining Biliteracy Development and Literacy and Bicultural Identity Development. The chapter also discusses how the bilingual brain uses language to learn new lexicons and takes the novice teacher on a journey to learn why lesson planning for ELs needs to begin with identification of language and content objectives. The conversation continues with strategies for instruction that include clear role definitions for the teacher and the student.

The strategies shared are based on research that has informed teachers' work for over thirty years in its implementation as the cognitive academic language learning approach (CALLA) (Chamot & O'Malley, 1994). Extension materials in Appendix 1 include a short list of current technology applications because CALLA lessons that teach ELs how to learn are effectively supported by the multimodal contributions to instruction provided by twenty-first-century technologies.

UNDERSTANDING TEACHERS' MANY RESPONSIBILITIES

This chapter will explore ways to help ELs achieve academic success. It will help them to "read the word" and "the world" (Freire & Macedo, 2005). This means that the novice teacher will ensure that the curriculum forms a linguistic and cultural bridge from ELs' life experiences to the content being taught.

For students to become learning partners, novice teachers have to consider that although they may be very knowledgeable content-area teachers, working with ELs requires them to be second-language teachers and cultural mediators. When teachers plan instruction, they can begin their instructional design by identifying the content and language objectives that will be the foci of their lessons.

Consider (1) if the ELs have the language they need to understand what they are reading (whatever the discipline and level of instruction may be) and (2) if they grasp the meaning of the words used as new concepts and evaluate their learning.

Examine the *affective domain* (ask if the classroom offers a welcoming environment) so that the students working to acquire English will feel safe asking questions. Know that language learning is expedited when learners feel safe to take risks. Convey to the students that mastering an additional language involves experimentation and being willing to make mistakes. Offer students avenues to increase their metalinguistic awareness (Garcia, 2009) and explicitly focus them on the language and content objectives that are identified in the lesson planning (Chamot & O'Malley, 1994).

Be aware that some of the students may communicate well orally using everyday English, because they have mastered *basic interpersonal communication skills* (BICS), but they may not have the discipline-specific language/ cognitive academic language proficiency (CALP) (Cummins, 1991) to succeed in social studies, biology, algebra, or other disciplines. Know that each learner offers a new and exciting canvas to explore. Set the goal to position the ELs as readers, writers, and artists working to develop new perceptions of who they are as they learn the nuances of a new language and the culture of its speakers and their place in the new society (Canagarajah, 1999).

EXAMINING BILITERACY DEVELOPMENT

Let's now look at how the bilingual brain works and what this suggests for teaching. Grosjean's (2008) work leads us to envision the bilingual brain as a single entity. The brain of a bilingual learner completes all tasks it undertakes using all the languages at its disposal. This means that while learners' storehouse of knowledge may be separated into different areas of their brains (such as in the left and right hemispheres, the amygdala, the frontal lobe, etc.), everything they know is involved in every thought they create, whether heard, spoken, read, or written.

Because students will simultaneously access and use all their languages to make sense of the English they are working to learn, it is important that teachers encourage them to *translanguage*: to move fluidly across their languages so that they will develop and share new understandings (Garcia & Wei, 2014). While examining what students do with their languages, consider if they will perceive classroom tasks to

- have a meaningful purpose,
- help them master English,
- encourage them to experiment with language forms, and
- convey the message that it is okay to make mistakes when working to communicate in English.

TEACHING LANGUAGES IN THE CLASSROOM

In your work, accept students' *hybrid language practices* (innovative use of one or more languages). This is part of natural second-language development. It is all right if teachers do not understand what all their students are saying to each other as they chat and work on classroom assignments. Encourage students to explore the ways by which their languages help them learn. Remember that what students know in one language does always help them to make meaning in other languages.

There may be students drafting compositions in Chinese, or Spanish, or Hindi first, rather than in English. Applaud this effort and know this will support multiliteracy development. Keep in mind that the end result of this drafting will be a paper prepared in two languages that can be shared in the classroom with classmates and with parents who may not speak English. Build a classroom library of books written in different languages. While students' home languages will provide them a base to develop English, classroom instruction will help them add to their *plurilingualism*.

In your work, fearlessly examine how language practices can be integrated in instruction, which will allow multilingual students to show what they know (Garcia & Wei, 2014). Trust the students to monitor their learning. Ask yourself these questions:

- How do I encourage students to use all their languages to access the message in narrative and expository texts written in English?

- How can I zero in on words and phrases that my students may not comprehend?
- What do I have to keep in mind to make content comprehensible for students at different levels of English-language proficiency?
- Can front-loading important information using graphics, videos, or other multimedia materials help my students understand math, science, etc.?
- What can I do to physically model the meaning of words that my students may find difficult? Can I adapt games like charades for my classroom context?

Tips on Language Practices in the Classroom

- As a teacher mentor your focus is to foster respect for all students' languages. You want to provide spaces that will foster unbiased acceptance of *hybrid language practices.*
- Disciplines: *Language Arts, Reading, History.*
- Level: fifth grade to high school
  - Observe language use as parents arrive at school to register their children.
  - Observe how the learners use language when completing small group work and during informal exchanges.
  - Write what you hear verbatim. If you are not bilingual, this task may be even more powerful in showing communication exchanges.
  - Quantify the number of exchanges that involve more than one language.
  - In what ways does the language you hear evidence translanguaging?
  - Analyze language use. Think and explain what you hear and how and why you interpret your findings as you do.

BILITERACY AND BICULTURAL IDENTITY DEVELOPMENT

Policies that control English instruction and bilingual education have shaped students' perceptions of the value society places on their bicultural identities (Cummins, 2009). When ELs are asked to speak only English at school, they are made to feel that their home languages are not valuable. They are then disadvantaged because they cannot negotiate meaning using all their languages. In your classroom, provide students opportunities to examine and question the *cultural norms* of citizens in the United States as they acquire English.

Share that you value their lives, stories, and their families' languages (Bartolomé, 1996). This will help the ELs feel safe to value their bicultural and bilingual identities. They will see that they have rights and that they are valued citizens of the classroom and the world (Canagarajah, 1999; Pennycock, 2007). In the vignette below, look for evidence of how the teacher (a novice teacher) shows her students that she respects their transnational experiences and their languages.

> *Claribel crossed the Rio Grande with the help of a coyote. During the crossing she witnessed situations she cannot forget. Her teacher decides that the after-school club for Latinas will offer students like Claribel a venue to begin to process and get past painful experiences. She shows the students a video about families who come to the United States from Mexico. When the students notice their teacher has a stack of notebooks on her desk, they ask if they can write their stories. Some students write in Spanish, while others do their best to compose in English, and then add images that will better express their thoughts.*

Claribel is a plurilingual learner because she has three languages at her disposal. Her languages serve her sociocultural needs in different ways when she communicates in her world. Before moving to the United States, her family lived in San Bartólo Coyotepec, a small community in the state of Oaxaca, Mexico. Thus, she speaks but does not write the indigenous language of her community, her formal schooling in Mexico was in Spanish, and she is now learning English in Arizona. Her teacher makes sure that her indigenous language is considered a resource in the monolingual English classroom.

Claribel's teacher is a social activist within her community. When she was completing her clinical hours as a teacher candidate, she noticed that after-school activities were used well by her supervisor as the basis of in-class literacy tasks. She strives to link the curriculum to the learners' communities and school experiences. She initiated the after-school club, recruited students, and plans activities that validate students' worlds. Consider the following questions about Claribel's story:

- How does the teacher validate students' realities and their identities?
- How does she extend traditional learning to after-school activities?
- What will you do to follow the teacher's example in your community?
- What will you do to show respect for students' home language?

Tips on Linking Instruction to the Students' Community

- Identify opportunities to *link instruction to the students' communities*. Set up the lesson by sharing with students the photos of the murals in the tourist community of Playa del Carmen, Quintana Roo, Mexico.
- Disciplines: *Art and Social Studies.*
- Level: fifth grade to high school.
- *Cultural Messages in a Community's Murals.* Plan a field trip for your high-school students. They can do it on their own or involve their families. Their

task is to photograph the murals and buildings in a Mexican American neighborhood of Chicago. Ask them to do the following:

- Discuss what the images reflect about the lives, struggles, and culture of the artists who created the murals. Explore the significance of the images in their community.
- Compare and contrast the images from their country of origin to images painted by Mexican American artists born and living in the United States. What do the images reflect about cultural identity?
- Look for and identify visible elements of homes and their surrounding landscapes that reveal the ethnicity of those who live in the homes. Ask your students if it is always possible to understand a family after a visit to their home.

ENGLISH LEARNERS, MULTILINGUALS, PLURILINGUALS

It is important to acknowledge that the educational community disagrees as to which term best describes the multilingual learner. Terms used continually change as educators strive to reflect an additive perspective of the person who is able to communicate in more than one language. The term "English learner" can be considered somewhat narrow as it implies that the student is learning only English and not becoming bilingual, trilingual, etc.

The term English learner may mislead teachers into thinking the student is a new immigrant to the United States, when in fact, many ELs are heritage language speakers born in this country. These students are labeled ELs because their immigrant parents and/or other close relatives interacted with them in a language other than English at home. Some of these learners are balanced bilinguals when they begin their formal schooling in the United States. Others may represent families where each parent has a different ethnic and linguistic background: the children communicate efficiently through these languages while having different levels of proficiency (they are plurilinguals).

Knowing the terminology used to describe students is important because educators need to be inquisitive researchers who examine each student's educational needs and plan lessons that support the learner. The reality is that every student has a unique linguistic and cultural background, and there are no shortcuts in lesson planning.

The vignette that follows is about Aidan, a seven-year-old bilingual boy growing up in a linguistically and culturally diverse urban area (author's grandson). He is an emerging bilingual bicultural child who engages in conversations using English and Spanish daily with family members. He has access to I-pad games, books, videos, and television in both languages. Many of the people in his life are college graduates. He is an independent reader who will tell his parents that he "needs a little down time to read." As you learn about his path to literacy, consider his family's role in his language development and the factors that are supporting his schooling. Identify how you would foster Aidan's bilingual development in a monolingual English classroom.

Be aware that not all learners experience Aidan's same level of familial educational support. Some immigrant parents, especially newcomers, need to focus on meeting basic needs such as paying the electric bill, putting food on the table, or finding a way to obtain permanent residency in the United States. As you read, consider what Aidan's life offers him and work to identify what can be done for your students. Think about ways you can share what you know about biliteracy development with parents who may be finding it very difficult to master English and who may not have completed a grade school education.

Consider what you can do for students like Aidan who at first glance do not appear to need extra instructional support.

On year one of Aidan's formal schooling, he was too young to enter kindergarten (K) in the public school system. His parents placed him in K in a private school, and he thrived in a classroom of ten children. Once he completed K he was invited to enter a dual-language Spanish-English program if he enrolled in K again. The principal assured his parents that he could participate in higher-level reading and math. He made friends, but the promise of academically appropriate instruction was not fulfilled. He loved the after-school carpentry and Lego programs. He read in the evenings and his mother bought him many books at his reading level. He developed into an avid and competent reader in his two languages. The next year Aidan changed schools again to begin first grade at a private monolingual English school. After one month, his parents were asked if they would agree to moving their son to second grade.

Aidan's story exemplifies the challenges to achieving biliteracy for ALL children growing up in multilingual environments. His story highlights the ways in which the community contributes to literacy, the power that parents have over children's education, and how informed teachers help parents make appropriate educational decisions.

Some questions to consider about multilingual learners growing up in the United States today and the power you have as a teacher are:

- Has this student's formal schooling been the sole contributor to his/her biliteracy development?
- Has the schoolhouse appropriately evaluated the student's language proficiency across his/her languages?

- Does the U.S. school system support emergent bilinguals?
- What happens to children whose parents cannot afford to make needed educational choices requiring they pay school tuition?
- What challenges do ELs face when their parents have not mastered English and find it difficult to help with homework?
- What can teachers do to inform and involve parents who do not speak English in their children's education?
- Parents unfamiliar with the expectations of the U.S. school system may not know where to turn for help. How will you help them mediate understandings across cultures?
- If you are a monolingual teacher, how will you evaluate students' biliteracy? How might families and community members help you?
- What will you do to ensure that the curriculum is at the right linguistic scaffold for your students?

PLANNING LESSONS FOCUSED ON LANGUAGE AND CONTENT OBJECTIVES

The work of O'Malley et al. (1985) took teachers to the awareness that second-language learners would benefit from explicit strategy instruction while acquiring (not learning) English in content-area classes. Their research documented that ELs needed instruction in learning how to learn. This research resulted in a rationale for planning lessons that has continued to inform developments of instructional methods: the Cognitive Academic Language Learning Approach (1994).

The strength of curriculum design based on CALLA is that its focus on cognitive theory places control of much of the learning processes on the student. It fosters the development of metacognition and gives teachers a vehicle to help students explore understandings of language and master academic content. This rationale gives the novice teacher the freedom to be innovative and to plan lessons that are not prescriptive.

RATIONALE FOR CALLA DESIGN AND IMPLEMENTATION

Planning CALLA lessons requires the novice teacher to take time to reflect on the content they will teach and the language students will need to understand. As the novice teacher teaches, the lessons will help ELs guide their learning through self-monitoring strategies. It is important to share content objectives for lessons, identify key language structures, and engage the ELs as cocreators because their opinions provide input to perfect the design of the lessons taught.

Components of an integrated CALLA unit of instruction include identification of major concepts to be studied, content and language objectives, preparation for instructional delivery and presentation, practice, evaluation, and expansion.

Many educators will teach through an integrated design that offers biliteracy and content-area instruction. Begin by guiding students to understand their meaning-making processes: their metacognitive, cognitive, and socioaffective skills. Teach them ways to think about their learning and direct its direction. Share that you want to understand their thinking processes and are not looking for perfection in their use of English, whether in writing or speaking. Students will feel supported when teachers foster a collaborative sociocultural environment.

Second, turn students into informed consumers and enroll them in helping the teaching process. Select age-appropriate synonyms to present the big ideas related to how and what they are learning. Notify students that while preparing lessons, what they know in content and in language is considered. Explain that the lessons are planned around two types of knowledge and that they have both: declarative (ability to explain what they know to another person) and procedural (ability to identify steps in a task and carry it out).

This way they will grasp that teachers want them to share what they know verbally and that it is even more important that they have time to practice new information so that they can make new ideas their own. Explain the role of practice in second-language acquisition by telling them they will be taught strategies that will help them know what to do, how to do it expediently, and ways to self-evaluate their progress. It is not necessary to specifically reveal to students that they are expanding their schemata (their approach to figuring out what to do to succeed in the classroom) as long as it is highlighted how their knowledge will transfer across languages.

STRATEGIES FOR EFFECTIVE INSTRUCTION OF ENGLISH LEARNERS

In the following section we will introduce a table of instructional strategies that can be used in the classroom, focusing on both student and teacher responsibilities and different approaches where the strategies can be applied. These strategies and their components will be further discussed following Table 5.1.

Table 5.1   Strategies for Instruction

Teacher's Responsibilities	Instructional Focus: Paths to Mastery	Students' Responsibilities
Teach concept and provide opportunities in the classroom for students to engage in exploration.	Strategy 1: Declarative Knowledge • Think-write-pair-share • Language experience approach • Graphic organizers • T-charts • Translanguaging for meaning	Share what they know.
Explain role of practice in learning.	Strategy 2: Procedural Knowledge • Think-pair-share • In the text questions • Concept maps	Engage in practice to master the skill.
1. Evaluate students' knowledge prior to lesson. 2. Explain what will be the focus of lesson content.	Strategy 3: Content Objectives • Anticipation guides Strategy 4: Identifying Links between Prior and Future Knowledge • Student friendly Rubrics • K-W-L charts • Contextualize Academic language	Make efforts to develop new knowledge.
1. Evaluate students' language. 2. Teach language by front-loading and during lessons.	Strategy 5: Language Objectives Identify cognates • Cloze passages • Word banks • Dictation • Model academic language in questions and short answers • Picture walks in content-area chapters • Sentence frames • Translanguage for understanding • Deconstruct academic language of texts	1. Work to identify what language is not comprehensible—verbs, vocabulary, descriptions in graphics, etc. 2. Ask for teacher help when needed.
Model and assign tasks.	Strategy 6: Language Functions • Jigsaw read and share • Prepare Power Point reports • Write questions at different levels of comprehension: in the text, beyond the text. • Identify and explore terms that have a different meaning when used in the context of a discipline; a kitchen table compared to the Periodic Table in chemistry.	Complete academic tasks that require analysis of written materials: compare and contrast, examine, evaluate, explain, justify, prepare graphs, order, classify, infer, convince, etc.
Plan standards-based lessons.	Strategy 7: Inform Learners Your Reasons for Consulting the Standards. • Explicitly identify content and language goals. • Write standard addressed on the board.	Be able to share value of lesson. Translanguage with classmates and students.
1. Teach strategies how to talk about the strategies they have learned. 2. Provide time to practice.	Strategy 8: Self-Monitoring Pre-lessons • K-W-L Strategy 9: Ongoing Self-Monitoring during Lessons • In the text questions • K-W-L Strategy 10: Self-Checks Post-lessons • Beyond the text questions • K-W-L	1. Name the strategy. 2. Explain its purpose and why it helps in learning. 3. Practice.

LANGUAGE FUNCTIONS IN SOCIAL
AND ACADEMIC CONTEXTS

Language serves its users in different ways across informal and formal contexts. The function of the phrase *Good morning!* is to greet and welcome. The words, accompanied by a smile or a nod, are easy to understand even when the speaker uses a language the listener has never heard. The language in academic texts conveys its message and informs the reader very differently from the way everyday communication does. Academic language specific to a discipline is not supported by the socio-cultural context unless teachers purposefully make its function a focus of instruction.

Content-area books at the elementary level may include pictures, while upper-level texts often include a few charts and diagrams. This creates more work for the student who is working to learn in a new language. Be aware that texts used across the content areas use language that is unique to the particular discipline. This is why understanding *academic language functions* requires more effort from the learners. ELs need their educators to model ways to engage in skilled interpretation, negotiations, and use language to carry out tasks such as explaining, justifying, and arguing.

In addition, teachers need to teach them that language fulfills different purposes (functions) and how meaning is conveyed differently in the study of science, math, and geography, etc.

CONTENT AND LANGUAGE OBJECTIVES

At school ELs use the four modalities of language in inter- and intrapersonal communication. Students' language proficiency will determine how well they can use English to develop an idea into a statement that a listener or a reader will understand. Always share the language objectives of lessons with students. Put these on the board and develop a routine that helps the ELs focus on the language they will need to understand as they listen, speak, read, and write in your class that day.

Depending on the state, teachers should also write the applicable state or national standard addressed in their lesson. When students know that their teachers are held responsible for their academic progress, and can discuss the language of the standards, they will support their efforts. Keep in mind that to master new content knowledge, students need to comprehend and use the metalanguage (academic language required to discuss the lesson topic). Teach nouns, verb tenses, prepositional phrases, and all other language the ELs will use to discuss the content that you are teaching. Students need help to master the functions of academic language across the content areas.

Purposefully raise learners' awareness of the metacognitive skills they already own and use to comprehend text as you teach them cognitive strategies that help them in their future learning. Teachers can facilitate this ongoing *self-monitoring* process when establishing the classroom routine of using a K-W-L chart. Students will come to know the value of always thinking about what they knew before the lesson (their prior knowledge), hypothesize where the teacher may be taking them (the lesson's instructional goals), and once the lesson reaches its end, consciously evaluate what they have learned and what else may be relevant (future learning).

Consider sheltering some of the classroom language (using simpler vocabulary to ensure the learners understand). Remember that sheltered English will make it easier at the moments during lessons when the language is simplified, but know that your ELs need more than this. They need to know how to express themselves using the metalanguage (technical language of academic texts). It is essential to hold the same high expectations for ELs' academic success as all other students. In lessons give ELs "language to talk about language" (Brisk, 2015, p. 42).

Help the ELs to examine language: to deconstruct and construct the language in the texts they are reading. For example, classrooms might use concept maps to help the ELs deconstruct the dense language of content-area texts. When deconstructing a paragraph from a text, students break it apart into sentences, phrases, and incomprehensible vocabulary. As students explore the meaning within the sentences and ask questions about what the author is stating, the task will, step by step, lead your ELs to higher levels of comprehension.

DECLARATIVE AND PROCEDURAL KNOWLEDGE

Effective instruction aims for students to be able to share an explanation of what they know before, during, and after a lesson. To reach the end goal, instruction has to lead learners to know the steps required to complete the classroom tasks so well that they will not only know what to do, but also feel comfortable asking their teacher for help as they uncover questions and pinpoint where they need more help. In all learning, ELs use the knowledge that is stored in their long-term memory to make sense of new information and to assist their short-term memory decipher the input they need (the message within what they are hearing, seeing, or reading) to complete schooling tasks.

Students demonstrate their *declarative knowledge* when they access their schemata (prior knowledge) to explain their understandings (state what they have mastered). Learners use *procedural knowledge* when they complete tasks efficiently (they have the requisite mastery to know what to do). Using

CHECKLIST FOR PLANNING INSTRUCTION FOR ENGLISH LEARNERS

1. All languages are recognized to merit use in the classroom.
   Yes _____ No _____
   Provide concrete evidence _____

2. Instruction supports the histories of culturally diverse learners.
   Yes _____ No _____
   Provide concrete evidence _____

3. Multi-modal instructional methods empower the students.
   Yes _____ No _____
   Provide concrete evidence _____

4. Instruction scaffolds both the concepts and the language the students need to understand discipline specific information.
   Yes _____ No _____
   Provide concrete evidence _____

5. High expectations for students' academic success are evident.
   Yes _____ No _____
   Provide concrete evidence _____

6. Students are taught strategies for learning.
   Yes _____ No _____
   Provide concrete evidence _____

7. Small group tasks provide opportunities to us academic language in context. Provide concrete evidence _____

8. Student friendly rubrics help guide the learning.
   Yes _____ No _____
   Provide concrete evidence _____

9. Content assessments allow students to demonstrate their learning while in the process of acquiring English.
   Yes _____ No _____
   Provide concrete evidence _____

10. Students' parents actively contribute to the curriculum.
    Yes _____ No _____
    Provide concrete evidence _____

11. Respect is evident in the classroom community.
    Yes _____ No _____
    Provide concrete evidence _____

the analogy of riding a bicycle, if I know how to ride I do so without thinking about it (procedural knowledge). The knowledge that I have allows me to teach a friend to ride. This teaching requires that I use my declarative knowledge to lead my buddy through the steps of pedaling, changing gears, and putting on the break.

In the classroom, teachers will help the ELs develop procedural and declarative knowledge while using English when provided with opportunities to practice what is being taught and dedicating time for them to share and show what they are learning to their classmates. Cognitive strategies for learning allow students to explore new information and experiment as they work to understand novel input. At the same time the learners are completing their work, they convert some of the new input (that resides in the short-term memory) to permanent storage in their brains.

SELF-REFLECTION

Whether you are a novice teacher, a teacher educator, or a teacher candidate involved in early clinical experiences, examine your observations and heartfelt reactions as you decide if the following components of instruction are an integral part of your lessons.

CONCLUSION

When working with multilingual students who represent a plethora of cultural and linguistic diversity, it is impossible to use one instructional paradigm as a fail-proof method. This chapter addressed teachers' responsibilities when working with diverse students and understandings of how to promote literacy for culturally and linguistically diverse learners. We know that teachers serve as role models and cheerleaders, as well as literacy and content-area experts.

As we go forward, it is crucial that we remember how students learn languages. We must first remember that in our classrooms, we must evidence our conviction that translanguaging is a natural and positive component of meaning-making processes.

Second, in our instruction we want to show our students the value of our explicitly teaching those strategies for learning. Students need us to remind them that academic success involves developing cognitive, metacognitive, and socio-affective skills. In addition, we want to share with our students that interpersonal communication skills are necessary for them to learn, for us to teach, and for everyone to succeed in life.

Third, if we believe that educators are jack-of-all-trades, we will engage in an ongoing process of exploring what we can do better and what new tools are available to us. When we collaborate with stakeholders we create win-win situations for everyone involved. I now leave you with one big idea that will help you advocate for learners and for teachers: strive to develop your interpersonal skills so that you will be able to expertly justify your practice.

APPENDIX 1: EXTENSION MATERIALS

Books That Address Teachers' Practice

Brisk, M. E. (2015). *Engaging students in academic literacies: Genre-based pedagogy for K-5 classrooms.* New York NY: Routledge.

Cloud, N., Lakin, J., Lininger, E., & Maxwell, L. (2009). *Teaching adolescent English language learners: Essential strategies for middle and high school.* Philadelphia, PA: Caslon Publishing.

Daniel, M., & Mokhtari, K. (2015). (Eds.). *Research and instruction that makes a difference in English learners' success.* Lanham, MD: Rowman and Littlefield Publishers, Inc.

Technology Applications

1. To increase students' knowledge of current events while helping them develop literacy, go to: http://www.newsela.com. At this site you will find information that you can use for all content areas. Articles are modified with language that younger audiences will understand. Newssela includes articles written in five different lexile levels for each article, with comprehension questions for students at the end of each.

2. An easy-to-use free application is Edmodo: https://www.edmodo.com. This is a classroom blog that is password protected for schools. Once your create the blog, only students and parents whom you invite participate. Edmodo is effective for learners of any ages.

3. Google Dictionary (3.0.19) addresses comprehension during reading. It allows students to click on words within a website for an immediate definition. It also has biographical information of well-known people and places.

4. You can create a *flipped classroom* using many different types of applications. This is an effective instructional option that teachers use to develop materials for students at different levels of English-language proficiency. In the flipped classroom there are fluid boundaries between teacher and student roles. You create and upload materials for the learners to read and/or listen to and react to. These provide scaffolds to learning before class. In the flipped classroom you provide websites, videos, or YouTube

segments for students to view. You post questions to help students begin to reflect on the topic that will be covered in class instruction. This approach gives students whatever time they need to go through your postings and be better prepared for what you will teach in the classroom.

GLOSSARY OF TERMS

Acquiring versus learning a language—in second-language acquisition (SLA), the learner may first focus on what he/she does not know and may feel stress at having to explain the meaning of the language before using it. The goal in SLA is for students to subconsciously access the language and use it without stopping to decide if the words selected are appropriate. Thus, acquisition implies mastery.

Affective domain—student's comfort level in the classroom. This is evidenced in the learner's openness to participation and risk-taking in the learning context. In welcoming classrooms students feel free to make errors and develop positive self-esteem.

Basic interpersonal communication skills (BICS)—everyday language such as *Good morning!, Where is the bathroom?, One order of French fries please.*

Cognitive academic language proficiency—academic language that is often discipline specific, not needed for everyday conversations, and poses greater challenges to a language learner.

Conscientization—a teacher or a student who operates at the level of conscientization is a person who feels a need to do more than observe events in the world. This is the person who takes action, who cautiously but with determination, feels compelled to make a difference within his/her circle of influence.

Cultural norms—the implicit and explicit components of a culture and how these influence behaviors and interpersonal interactions within and outside the person's cultural group.

Hybrid language practices—as ELs use language to share ideas, they may include short phrases in more than one language. When talking to speakers of more than one language, the student may change languages in the middle of sentences in an effort to be understood by everyone involved in the conversation. The teacher may not understand how learners negotiate meaning across languages, but it is essential to respect the hybrid language practices we observe.

Phenotype—an individual's skin color may represent the person's genetic makeup but not his/her ethnicity. Visible phenotype often leads to incorrect assumptions. The essence of a person is not what is visible but how the individual chooses to self-define.

Plurilingualism—speakers of more than two languages may identify themselves as plurilinguals. This means that although a person may not have reached high levels of academic language in all their languages, their knowledge allows them to carry out important interpersonal functions within different communities of people.

Situated practice—teaching and learning is not the same across all contexts. Effective teachers adjust their instruction to the realities of students' lives with a keen eye on what may be facilitating or preventing the learners from experiencing academic success.

Translanguaging—an approach to explaining processes of second-language acquisition that is holistic and situated in current language learning philosophies. Translanguaging is an understanding of what language learners do in their multilingual worlds as they use all the languages at their disposal for intra- and interpersonal communication.

Zone of proximal development—Vygotsky explained the zone in two ways. First, because instruction scaffold appropriately is neither too easy nor too difficult for the learner, it results in effective learning. Second, when students work within the social world of their classroom, the level of learning is raised by the collaborative exchanges that occur.

REFERENCES

Bartolomé, L. (1996). Beyond the methods fetish: Toward a humanizing pedagogy. In P. Leistyna, A. Woodrum, and S. Sherblom (Eds.), *Breaking free: The transformative power of critical pedagogy* (pp. 229–252). Cambridge, MA: Harvard Educational Review.

Brisk, M. E. (2015). *Engaging students in academic literacies: Genre-based pedagogy for K-5 classrooms*. New York, NY: Routledge.

Canagarajah, S. (1999). *Resisting linguistic imperialism in English teaching*. Oxford: Oxford University Press.

Chamot, A. U., & O'Malley, J. M. (1994). *The CALLA Handbook: The cognitive academic language learning approach*. Reading, MA: Addison Wesley.

Cummins, J. (1991). Language development and academic learning. In L. Malave & G. Duquette, *Language, culture, and cognition*. Clevedon: Multilingual Matters.

Cummins, J. (2009). Pedagogies of choice: Challenging coercive relations of power in classrooms and communities. *International Journal of Bilingual Education and Bilingualism, 2*(3), 261–271.

Daniel, M. C., & Cowan, J. (2012). Exploring teachers' use of technology in classrooms of bilingual students. GIST *Education and Learning Research Journal, 6,* 97–110.

Daniel, M., & Huizenga-McCoy, M. (2014). Art as a medium for bilingualism and biliteracy: Suggestions from the research literature. *GIST Education and Learning Journal* (8), 171–188.

Freire, P., & Macedo, D. (2005). *Literacy: Reading the word and the world.* London: Taylor and Francis.

Garcia, O. (2009). *Bilingual education in the 21st century.* West Sussex, UK: Wiley-Blackwell.

Garcia, O., & Wei, L. (2014). *Translanguaging: Language, bilingualism, and education.* London, England: Palgrave MacMillan.

Grosjean, F. (2008). *Studying bilinguals.* New York, NY: Oxford University Press.

John-Steiner, V. (1995), Cognitive pluralism: As sociocultural approach. *Mind, culture, and activity, 1*(2), 2–11.

O'Malley, J. M., Chamot, A. U., Stewner-Manzanares, G., Russo, R. P., & Kupper, L. (1985). Learning strategy applications with students of English as a second language. *TESOL Quarterly, 19*(2), 557–584.

Pennycock, A. (2007). *Global Englishes and transcultural flows.* London: Routledge.

Rosenblatt, L. M. (1978). *The reader, the text, the poem: The transactional theory of the literary work.* Carbondale, IL: Southern Illinois University Press.

Vygotsky, L. S. (1986). *Thought and language.* Cambridge, MA: MIT Press.

Section II

CURRICULUM DEVELOPMENT

Chapter 6

Engaging Students through Interdisciplinary Lessons and Units

Melanie Bloom and Sandra Rodríguez-Arroyo

The purpose of this chapter is to encourage K through 12 language and *content-area* teachers to discover the potential that interdisciplinary lessons and units have to increase student engagement, as well as strengthen student connections and interests to other disciplines. Through examples, application ideas, and activities, novice teachers will gain concrete strategies for developing interdisciplinary connections and applying those connections to their lessons and units.

WHAT IS INTERDISCIPLINARY TEACHING?

Santau and Ritter (2013) define "interdisciplinary instruction" as "presenting knowledge of constituent disciplines and their relations, connections to other domains, and uses in the everyday world" (p. 260). This conceptualization of interdisciplinary instruction is not new. Progressive education scholars, from as early as the 1920s, referred to interdisciplinary curriculum as "core" and promoted the idea of "combining two or more disciplines, pedagogical approaches, groups of people, or skills" (Mathison & Freeman, 1998, p. 1).

John Dewey, the most famous progressive educator, was a strong advocate for an integrated curriculum and believed that it was a method for students to develop critical thinking and actions to "enable them to participate as informed citizens in a democracy" (Mathison & Freeman, 1998, p. 5). However, sociopolitical events in the 1950s and the economic crises of the 1980s brought with them lots of suspicion and several curriculum initiatives were either censored or eliminated to avoid "frills" that could have been the cause of lower student achievement.

However, the recent decades have seen a resurgence of interdisciplinary or cross-curricular planning that could be associated with two education philosophies: *whole language* and literacy in the content areas. As defined by Edelsky, Altwerger, and Flores (1991), whole language "is a professional theory, an explicit theory in practice. . . . Whole language weaves together a theoretical view of language, language learning, and learning into a particulars stance on education" (p. 7).

With this theoretical foundation, whole language instruction focused on a holistic view of language teaching that recognized language as embedded in all areas of knowledge; therefore, language skills should not be excluded from any area of teaching. Even though whole language was criticized due to its lack of direct teaching of grammar and phonics, its main tenets have influenced the instructional practices of teachers who started their careers in the late 1980s and 1990s. In addition to whole language, literacy in the content areas and its focus on incorporating literacy skills (reading, writing, speaking, and listening) into content areas such as science and math to learn the "language of the field" have strongly influenced the use of interdisciplinary *thematic units* of instruction.

The focus on literacy in the content areas is strongly influenced by national reports and professional teaching standards that emphasize the importance of learning and using the language of the field. Nonetheless, as Draper and Siebert (2010) remind us, "Content area teachers still remain resistant to implementing reading and writing instruction in their classrooms" (p. 20).

The following vignette from a high-school science teacher is an example of a missed opportunity to integrate language and authentic experiences/materials in a cell structure lesson.

Matt is a high-school biology teacher. He has an infectious personality that his students enjoy. As he begins his class, Matt jokes with his students and puts them at ease. Matt then proceeds to introduce the topic for the class: cell structure. As the class progresses it becomes apparent that Matt prefers lecturing on cell components and functions. The students follow his lecture using black and white drawings of a human and a vegetable cell and identify each part. At one point, Matt stops the lecture to dramatize how the mitochondria work harder during exercise, like in PE class, and the students respond very well to this example. This is the only connection that Matt makes to another subject area while he teaches this lesson, before moving to the lab area of the classroom to identify human and vegetable cells using a microscope.

Matt's lesson is very typical in science classrooms, as teachers need to cover this and other important topics in a limited amount of time. Nonetheless, teachers are also encouraged to use authentic texts and real-world experiences to connect the curriculum to students' lives. To accomplish this, teachers like

Matt can explore materials outside their discipline to forge these connections. For example, the book *The Immortal Life of Henrietta Lacks* by Rebecca Skloot is currently being used in many classrooms around the nation to connect learning about the cell structure with cancer research, discrimination, civil rights, ethics, and more (see Appendix 1). If Matt took the time to work with a colleague, he could brainstorm ways to make the teaching of the cell structure more connected to real-life current and historical issues.

Scholars in the field have suggested that there is a continuum of inter-disciplinary instruction ranging from more traditional disciplinary-focused approaches to integration of content topics into language instruction or vice versa. For example, in our field of second-language instruction, on the far end of the continuum exists *content-based instruction* (Brinton, Snow & Wesche, 1989), in which teachers adapt their content-area classes using language learning strategies through the *sheltered instruction observation protocol* (Echevarria, Vogt & Short, 2013), or they collaborate among themselves to develop interdisciplinary thematic units (Fogarty, 1991; Kysilka, 1998; Loepp, 1999; López, 2008) (Figure 6.1).

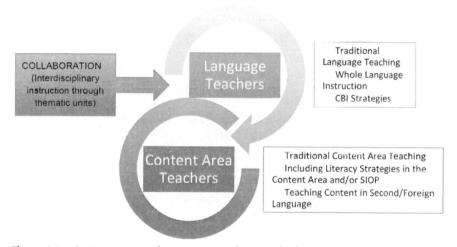

Figure 6.1   Content Area and Language Teachers Methods.

FOSTERING INTERDISCIPLINARY TEACHING

Interdisciplinary teaching takes time to plan and implement, but at the elementary level the results are evident in all subjects. The following vignette provides evidence of this:

Laura is a first grade teacher who presented a thematic unit on recycling. During her social studies lesson she had her students sing a song on the importance of taking care of the planet. She then proceeded to check her students' background knowledge of recycling and asked if they recycled at home. The students then watched a short movie from National Geographic on why recycling is important and how it helps to avoid global warming.

After watching the movie, Laura asked the students to discuss the main idea of the movie. After contributing their answers, Laura used a graphic organizer to explain how to organize trash, and she introduced words such as glass, aluminum, paper, plastic, and cardboard. The students divided up into groups and were assigned to sorting stations with recyclable and nonrecyclable materials. Throughout the unit Laura also made sure that the students could use what they were learning about recycling in other content areas. For example, during the language arts class she read aloud a nonfiction reading from Scholastics News on Earth Day about the importance of conserving our natural resources, and during her math lessons, Laura used the same recyclable materials she had used before to teach addition problems.

Unlike Matt, Laura was able to tie the recycling theme to all of her instructional activities, as well as consider her students' lived experience with recycling. By emphasizing these interdisciplinary connections and the impact of recycling efforts in their own community, Laura simultaneously personalized the unit and addressed the state standards across the disciplines. Some might argue that Laura can do this more effectively given her teaching context, as she is the only one responsible for instruction in the first grade. At the secondary level, if the teacher is not familiar with other content areas it can be challenging, but it is possible when teachers collaborate with each other and other experts in the field. Take for example the case of Jill:

Jill is an ESL (English as a second language) teacher at a local middle school. As she brainstormed topics of interest with her English language learners (ELLs), she noticed they were curious about the name of their school, Lewis and Clark. Therefore, students started to read about the incredible journey of Meriwether Lewis and William Clark. The readings mentioned how when Lewis and Clark traveled through the Great Plains, they described it as a sea of grass that contained hundreds of grasses, shrubs, and tree species supporting huge herds of grazing animals. Lewis and Clark were describing prairie lands. The students were then curious about prairies and wondered if they could visit one.

Jill contacted Nebraska Parks and Recreation and a local university to help her find more information on prairies. Jill took her students to visit a prairie in the area and worked on research projects to raise awareness of the importance of conserving prairies. During the semester, each student took pictures at the prairie, selected his/her favorite picture, developed a Tagxedo (an online word cloud) with at least twenty-five words describing the prairie, wrote captions of his/her pictures, and presented his/her work at a gallery walk at the school. They also decorated bird feeders to sell and then donated the proceeds to the Prairie Conservation Fund.

In this vignette we see that Jill did much more than teach English to her middle-school students; her interdisciplinary unit included social studies, photography, art, and environmental science. In addition to being an inter-disciplinary unit, it is also one that emerged from students' inquiry about the area of the country in which they live and learn.

As exemplified in the above vignettes, the current view of integration is "associated with the growth in a child-centered curriculum that takes into account the whole child, including physical, emotional, social and cognitive needs" (Mathison & Freeman, 1998, p. 5). It is this emphasis on students that makes interdisciplinary teaching worth trying.

WHAT IS STUDENT-CENTERED INSTRUCTION?

Student-centered instruction is a term that is commonly used to refer to a wide variety of student-centered activities such as *inquiry-based instruction,* problem-based learning, performance-based assessments and so on. However, as an instructional philosophy in practice it can be a "complicated and messy idea" (Neumann, 2013, p. 172). It can refer to a range of approaches from allowing students choice in the selection of assignments, to collaborating with students to make curricular decisions, to allowing students themselves to drive the direction and creation of the curriculum.

This approach is often contrasted with *teacher-centered instruction* in which the teacher is solely responsible for the organization of the class-room, the structure of daily lessons, the learning outcomes as well as their assessment. Does this mean that there can be no teacher-centered lessons in student-centered instruction and no student-centered activities or assignments in teacher-centered instruction? No, individual lessons or assignments in both types of instruction may vary, but their fundamental approach to students, to unit and lesson planning, and to assessment are distinct.

What Difference Does Student-Centered Instruction Make?

Research on student-centered schools and classrooms has been conducted in nearly every content area and at every level of instruction. We can look at student-centered instruction from a macro, school-based level, or a more micro level, within a particular classroom. Some districts or schools have adopted schoolwide student-centered instruction for which this instructional perspective serves as the pedagogical foundation of the school's curriculum.

For example, Stanford's Center for Opportunity Policy in Education (Friedlaender et al., 2014) recently released a research brief that describes the impressive outcomes of four California high schools that predominantly serve low-income students of color through a student-centered curriculum. This research found that these students outperformed their peers at other institutions on state assessments, the completion of college preparatory courses, graduation rates, and college acceptance and persistence.

Student-centered instruction in the content classroom can also impact student learning and engagement. For example, Grimes and Stevens (2009) describe the results of an elementary math class before and after they introduced a student-centered approach to *differentiated instruction* that determined student readiness to learn. They note that both the low-performing and the high-performing students in the class benefited from the approach, observing dramatic improvement in test scores and also more positive attitudes toward math!

Connecting Student-Centeredness to Interdisciplinary Instruction

Some of you might now be asking yourselves, how is student-centeredness connected to interdisciplinary instruction? By tapping into our students' prior knowledge, as well as their learning needs and interests, we not only personalize the curriculum to our student group, but also inherently create interdisciplinary connections as students' interests are not determined by discipline as we saw in Jill's ESL class.

Tips on Creating Interdisciplinary Connections

- At the beginning of the year, have students write a "Top 10 List" about themselves that includes the top ten most important things that others should know. Use these lists throughout the year to make connections to students' interests.
- Introduce a new thematic unit with a K-W-L chart in which the students begin by exploring what they already know about the theme and what they want to know. Identify common interdisciplinary connections from the students' charts.
- Establish dialogue journals with your students in which you write back and forth on the basis of either a prompt or reflections from class, depending on your students' age and literacy skills.
- Interview the students in your class about their likes and interests. Potential questions include:

- What activities do you participate in outside of school (i.e., sports, recreational activities, volunteer activities, etc.)?
- What's your favorite subject in school? Why do you enjoy it?
- What types of school activities do you enjoy the most? Why?

Once you have an idea of your students' interests outside of your content area, you can begin to make connections to those areas through unit and lesson planning as well as assignment creation. Let's consider the case of Ashley, a secondary Spanish teacher working in a rather homogeneous school in a small town outside of Omaha, Nebraska. Ashley wanted her students to develop a more personal connection to the Spanish language and the cultures of the Spanish-speaking world:

> *Using the concept behind Genius Hour (see Appendix 1), Ashley developed a year-long, student-centered project she called "Passion Projects." She began the project by having students work in small groups brainstorming topics that they were passionate about. Each group then selected a topic that best fit the interests of their group. She then presented the students with the American Council on the Teaching of Foreign Languages (ACTFL) World-Readiness Standards for Learning Languages (2015) of communication, cultures, connections, comparisons, and communities. Over the course of the academic year, the student groups investigated their passion, actively tying the theme to each one of the ACTFL standards.*
>
> *At the end of the year, student groups presented the results of their research to the rest of the class. As an example, one student group which was passionate about food chose the taco as its topic. The students investigated the historical and cultural origins of the taco discovering when, why, and how the taco came to be. To investigate the taco in their local community, they developed a rubric for evaluating a "good taco" which included categories such as authenticity and flavor. They ate tacos at ten area restaurants rating the tacos at each with the rubric they created. They also used their Spanish-language skills to communicate at many of the restaurants. Finally, they developed a glossary of taco-related vocabulary.*

Ashley knows that it is hard for her students to feel personally invested in the study of another language and culture. She used students' own interests to motivate them through the completion of an ambitious year-long project. Connecting the project to the ACTFL standards also allowed her students to connect to other disciplines. For example, the students investigating the taco connected to social studies and math as well as explored their local community through the project. Finally, as the project extended across the academic year, it was used to frame formative assessments and the final presentation served as a summative assessment of all five ACTFL World-Readiness Standards.

Tips on Using Student Interests

- Use student interests to connect students to your content area.
  - *Language arts*: Students at various instructional levels can complete "All about me" charts or simple self-descriptions.
  - *Math*: Create simple polls of students' likes and calculate totals or averages.
  - *Science*: Take a walk around the playground or a sports field and have students record questions about the world around them. What are they curious about? Why is the sky blue? Why do some birds fly in a V formation? How does a weed-killer kill weeds but not grass?
  - *Social studies*: Pose questions such as "Why do we like the things we do? Is it personal? Cultural? Historical?"
- Broaden student interests by moving across disciplines.
  - *Elementary*: Use favorite student books that contain counting or measuring concepts to connect language arts and math.
  - *Middle grades*: For a sports-oriented math class, math and physical education teachers can collaborate to report results and player statistics of games and races completed during PE class.
  - *High school*: For an artistically inclined German class, collaborate with art teachers and theater teachers to create sets and scenes to be performed in German.

STEP-BY-STEP PROCESS

What follows is a suggested step-by-step process that novice teachers who are new to interdisciplinary instruction can follow to develop integrated units and lessons. (For more information on these steps, see Vogt [1997] and Appendix 1).

1. Select a theme for the unit. There are many ways of selecting a theme, but we encourage you to find a theme on the basis of student interests and school curriculum.
   a. *Start with your standards and pacing guides.*
      Example. Laura noticed that her school district added the topic of recycling and reusing as part of the science curriculum, but the guide didn't specify *how* to teach it. Therefore, she decided to use this topic not only in her first grade science class, but also in social studies, language arts, and math.
   b. *Have students brainstorm topics they are passionate about.*
      Example. As we were able to see in Ashley's example, she started her "Passion Projects" by having students work in small groups brainstorming topics that they were passionate about.

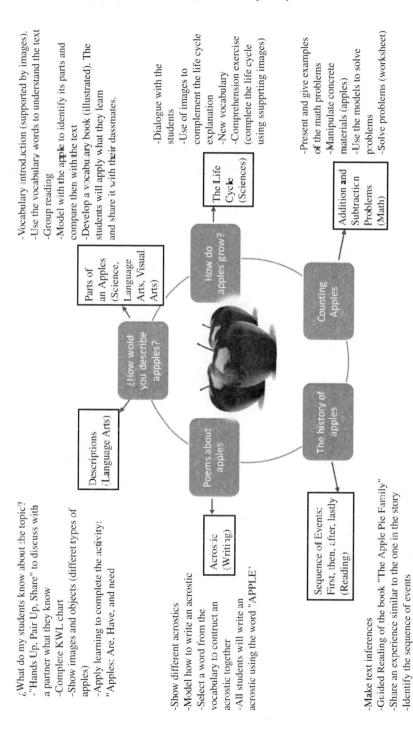

¿What do my students know about the topic?
- "Hands Up, Pair Up, Share" to discuss with
  a partner what they know
-Complete KWL chart
-Show images and objects (differet types of
apples)
-Apply learning to complete the activity:
"Apples: Are, Have, and need

-Vocabulary introduction (supported by images).
-Use the vocabulary words to understand the text
-Group reading
-Model with the apple to identify its parts and
compare then with the text
-Develop a vocabulary book (illustrated). The
students will apply what they learn
and share it with their classmates.

-Dialogue with the
students
-Use of images to
complement the life cycle
explanation
-New vocabulary
-Comprehension exercise
(complete the life cycle
using susprting images)

-Present and give examples
of the math problems
-Manipulate concrete
materials (apples)
-Use the models to solve
problems
-Solve problems (worksheet)

Parts of
an Apples
(Science,
Language
Arts, Visual
Arts)

How do
apples grow?

The Life
Cycle
(Sciences)

Addition and
Subtraction
Problems
(Math)

Counting
Apples

¿How wold
you describe
appples?

Descriptions
(Language Arts)

The history of
apples

Poems about
apples

-Show different acrostics
-Model how to write an acrostic
-Select a word from the
vocabulary to contruct an
acrostic together
-All students will write an
acrostic using the word "APPLE"

Acrostic
(Writing)

Sequence of Events:
First, then, after, lastly
(Reading)

-Make text inferences
-Guided Reading of the book "The Apple Pie Family"
-Share an experience similar to the one in the story
-Identify the sequence of events
-Develop their own story adequately using the sequence of events

Figure 6.2 World of Apples.

CHECKLIST TO IMPLEMENT INTERDISCIPLINARY LESSONS

1. Do you assess the needs and interests of your students?
   Yes _____ No _____
   Provide some concrete evidence _____

2. Do you take your students' needs and interests into account in lesson and unit planning?
   Yes _____ No _____
   Provide some concrete evidence _____

3. Do you actively make connections between content and your students' lives?
   Yes _____ No _____
   Provide some concrete evidence _____

4. Do you implement integrated thematic units?
   Yes _____ No _____
   Provide some concrete evidence _____

5. Do you connect your thematic units to content area state and national standards?
   Yes _____ No _____
   Provide some concrete evidence _____

6. Do your daily lessons connect to at least one other content area outside of your own?
   Yes _____ No _____
   Provide some concrete evidence _____

7. Do your lessons and thematic units link to your students' prior knowledge?
   Yes _____ No _____
   Provide some concrete evidence _____

8. Do your assessments encourage students' to connect to other disciplines?
   Yes _____ No _____
   Provide some concrete evidence _____

9. Do you actively collaborate with teachers outside of your own content area?
   Yes _____ No _____
   Provide some concrete evidence _____

10. Do you reflect on the implementation of your unit and make changes for future lessons?
    Yes _____ No _____
    Provide some concrete evidence _____

2. Brainstorm connections to other content areas, standards, extracurricular activities, etc.

Example. Diana started her "World of Apples" thematic unit preparing a "Unit Web," so she could see the content-area connections to her theme as she continued planning her unit (See Figure 6.2).

3. Start designing your unit researching new concepts and developing lesson plans with a timeline for implementation. Whenever possible collaborate with peers from other content areas.

Example. In the Prairie Thematic Unit example, we read how Jill included activities related to science and the environment, photography, and art. For her to do so, she took a training course through Nebraska Parks and Recreation and subscribed to their magazine *Nebraska Parks*. Jill also collaborated with the head prairie biologist, a professional photographer, and an art teacher at her school.

4. Search for authentic materials, preferably realia (objects from real life). Most interdisciplinary units are developed on students' interests. As such, use the context around you to find your instructional materials.

Example. Instead of using pictures of recycling materials Laura used real objects and her students sorted them.

5. Implement thematic unit. As you implement your thematic unit you may notice that you need more or less time for certain topics or you may include more materials and/or connections to other content areas.

Example. Jill's Prairie Project evolved over the years to incorporate additional content areas, such as photography. In addition, her focus on prairie-related language evolved as well to focus on higher-level scientific terminology.

6. Reflect on interdisciplinary thematic unit implementation. It is important for both teachers and students to reflect on the implementation of new thematic units. Through the assessment process, teachers discover what their students have learned from these units, but it is also important to take into consideration what worked and what did not work from the students' perspective. Thus, teachers should consider surveying their students or assigning reflection activities following a new interdisciplinary unit. Suggestions for teachers' self-reflection are included in the following section.

SELF-REFLECTION

Consider video-recording an interdisciplinary lesson that you have planned or have a colleague or supervisor observe your lesson. After viewing the lesson or receiving feedback from your colleagues, reflect on the following questions:

- How did you engage students by tapping into their interests today?
- What other content areas did you connect with?
- How did you connect to other disciplines?
- What human or other resources did you use to make interdisciplinary connections?
- How did your students respond to the lesson?

CONCLUSION

The purpose of this chapter was to provide novice teachers with background information on interdisciplinary instruction as well as to present concrete examples of interdisciplinary instruction in action. Although interdisciplinary instruction is not a new curricular initiative, it is one that continues to be relevant, especially in state and national instructional standards in many content areas. Thus, interdisciplinary instruction is often standards based, but we should not stop with the standards. True interdisciplinary instruction is a collaborative effort among students, teachers, and area professionals. It is our hope that from this chapter you find strategies that are relevant to your particular teaching context.

APPENDIX 1: EXTENSION MATERIALS

Genius Hour

"Genius hour" is an educational movement that encourages students to explore their interests in new and creative ways within the educational context. Teachers incorporating a genius hour in their classes should set aside sixty minutes per week for students to work on content area-related projects that they are passionate about. For more information on genius hour and how it might fit in your teaching context, see: http://www.geniushour.com/.

Digital Storytelling

Digital storytelling is a unique way for students to personalize their assignments by telling their own stories while developing both traditional and digital literacy skills. In addition, students can explore the visual and dramatic arts through the use of their own voices and digital images. Although designed for school library media specialists, the following website is very helpful for anyone interested in developing a http://courseweb.lis.illinois.edu/~jevogel2/lis506/index.html.

Tagxedo

Word clouds are an excellent way to teach vocabulary from different content areas; this particular online program does so with visuals created with the words of your choice. Visit the Tagxedo website for more ideas: http://www.tagxedo.com/.

A Collection of Thematic Units

Looking for more specific examples of interdisciplinary thematic units to use with your students? Graduate students at Lesley University have published numerous complete interdisciplinary units online, many containing a community engagement component as well. Although designed specifically for middle-school students, many of these units could be tailored to fit high-school students given their focus on adolescent interests. Several units could also be adapted to suit upper-elementary students: http://www.lesley.edu/middle-school/service-learning/examples/.

Online Workshop on Interdisciplinary Instruction

For a step-by-step online workshop that takes educators through the definition of interdisciplinary learning, examples of interdisciplinary instruction, expert-answered questions and advice on implementation, check out the following website: http://www.thirteen.org/edonline/concept2class/interdisciplinary/.

Video on Integrated Studies

For an introduction to Integrated Studies as well as for access to in-depth articles and videos, take a look at the following Edutopia video: http://www.edutopia.org/integrated-studies-introduction-video.

Themes for Interdisciplinary Units

If you need ideas to develop an interdisciplinary unit, the educational website given below provides integrated thematic unit learning resources. Click on the left menu for several examples and supporting materials: http://www.in2edu.com/thematic_topics/thematic_units_topics_index.html.

The Immortal Life of Henrietta Lacks

The Immortal Life of Henrietta Lacks by Rebecca Skloot is a great resource for high-school content area and language teachers to integrate their subjects.

The following websites include resources for both teachers and students to learn more about the topics included in the book:

Author's website: http://rebeccaskloot.com/the-immortal-life/teaching/.

Information about HeLa cells: http://ric.libguides.com/c.php?g=62138&p=400592.

Science lessons developed using the book: http://sciencenetlinks.com/lessons/immortal-life-henrietta-lacks/.

GLOSSARY OF TERMS

Content area—is now the preferred term used among teachers to talk about what was formerly commonly referred to as subject. While academic subjects are typically specific areas of study such as reading, math, science, or Spanish, content area is a bit broader term that allows educators to refer to language arts, STEM, or performing arts, for example. Thus, some content areas by themselves are interdisciplinary.

Content-based instruction (CBI)—Brinton, Snow, and Wesche (1989) define CBI as "the integration of particular content with language aims" (p. 2). As with whole language, CBI emphasizes students' interests and needs, authentic and meaningful use of the language, and students' background experiences (Brinton, Snow & Wesche, 1989). Even though the content material guides the instruction, language learning is still the primary goal of CBI; however, the barriers between language and content classes are crossed to expose students to academic language skills.

Differentiated instruction—also known as differentiated learning, differentiated instruction refers to responding to students' needs by varying instruction to match those needs. According to Tomlinson (1999), teachers can differentiate instruction according to the content to be learned, the instructional process, and the product/s created to assess learning. We can also differentiate according to student characteristics such as their readiness to learn, their interests, and their learning profile (Gregory & Chapman, 2002). Differentiation does not mean "watering down" curriculum, as teachers must maintain high expectations for all students. Like student-centered instruction, differentiation involves respecting students' background knowledge and learning styles, responding to students' needs and honoring students' differences (Theisen, 2002).

Inquiry-based instruction—is often defined on the basis of the content area as some areas view inquiry as discovery, while others introduce inquiry as problem-solving (Aulls & Shore, 2008). Regardless, inquiry-based instruction across content areas often involves posing questions, investigating the answer/s to those questions, problem-solving, and project-based learning. In their definition of inquiry-based instruction, Aulls and Shore (2008) also note that the process of sustained inquiry is extremely student centered as it requires internal motivation, self-efficacy, and determination. Thus, students must be as committed, if not more committed than, the teacher to the inquiry process.

Interdisciplinary instruction—is the act of making natural connections between traditional disciplines through instruction. Meeth (1978) suggests that in interdisciplinary instruction, the contributions of two or more disciplines are used to address a real-world issue or problem. This could refer to a wide array of types of integration. For example, it could refer to the integration of knowledge and skills within one content area, such as reading, writing, and speaking in language arts. However, more broadly, it could encompass two or more content areas that may be unified under one thematic unit, an inquiry cycle, or a student-centered project.

Sheltered Instruction Observation Protocol (SIOP)—the authors of the SIOP model define it as an "approach for teachers to integrate content and language instruction to students learning through a new language" (Echevarria, Vogt & Short, 2013, p. 16). When they first developed the model in the early 1990s, it was intended as a research and supervisory tool to be used to observe teachers as they implemented sheltered instructional strategies. The SIOP model has since developed into a teaching approach that encourages content-area teachers to adapt their instruction for language learners after considering the language expectations of each area. The SIOP model includes thirty features under eight components: lesson preparation, building background, comprehensible input, strategies, interaction, practice and application, lesson delivery, and review and assessment. Contrary to CBI, the primary goal of the SIOP model is learning the content area knowledge by becoming conscious of the language of the field.

Student-centered instruction—also referred to as learner-centered instruction, student-centered instruction is an educational philosophy that considers each student in a classroom as an individual with individual instructional needs. Precisely what student-centered instruction looks like in the classroom is up for some debate as, for example, Chung and Walsh (2000) found in their review of the literature forty separate definitions of student-centered instruction. In general student-centered instruction allows students to make decisions that direct their own learning rather than putting all of the responsibility for learning on the shoulders of the teacher. Student-centered instruction can be met with student resistance for two reasons: it may differ significantly from the instructional approach that students are used to and they must take more responsibility for their learning process (Weimer, 2002).

Teacher-centered instruction—the teacher remains solely responsible for the curriculum. He or she determines what will be learned, how it will be learned, and how it will be assessed. The students have little input in either the content or the structure of the learning. Thus, the teacher maintains an authoritative position and relinquishes little of that authority to the students, who play a more passive role.

Thematic units—unifying lessons around a central theme is one way to naturally achieve interdisciplinary instruction. Thematic units integrate many content areas that relate to a single overarching theme. For example, a world language teacher might construct a unit on water quality around the world. This unit would naturally incorporate learning new vocabulary as well as reading and writing about water quality issues in the target language. In addition, the unit would incorporate environmental studies, and students could explore environmental as well as social issues that affect water quality in developing and developed countries worldwide. They could learn outside of the classroom by testing a local water source for contaminants and/or volunteering to clean up a local pond, stream, lake, river, or beachfront area.

Whole language—is an educational philosophy rather than a specific method or approach to language and literacy instruction. According to Kenneth Goodman (1986), the whole language philosophy establishes certain principles for the processes of reading and writing, such as the main goal of each is the construction of meaning, and we learn to read and write through reading and writing. He also notes that the whole language philosophy creates a supportive classroom environment that is respectful of the whole student and the whole teacher and encourages educational risk-taking. This philosophy is often distorted or whittled down to a simple approach to language arts that considers top-down versus bottom-up processing. As Edelsky, Altwerger, and Flores (1991) note, whole language is not the sum of a checklist of whole language activities; it is a theory-driven practice.

REFERENCES

American Council on the Teaching of Foreign Languages. (2015). *World-readiness standards for learning languages*. Alexandria, VA: ACTFL.

Aulls, M. W., & Shore, B. M. (2008). *Inquiry in education, volume I: The conceptual foundations for research as a curricular imperative*. New York: Lawrence Erlbaum Associates.

Brinton, D. M., Snow, M. A., & Wesche, M. B. (1989). *Content-based second language instruction*. New York: Newbury House.

Chung, S., & Walsh, D. J. (2000). Unpacking child-centeredness: A history of meanings. *Journal of Curriculum Studies, 32*(2), 215–234.

Draper, R. J., & Siebert, D. (2010). Rethinking texts, literacies, and literacy across the curriculum. In R. J. Draper, P. Broomhead, A. P. Jensen, J. D. Nokes, & D. Siebert (Eds.), *(Re)Imagining content-area literacy instruction* (pp. 20–39). New York: Teachers College Press.

Echevarria, J., Vogt, M., & Short, D. J. (2013). *Making content comprehensible for English learners: The SIOP model.* Boston, MA: Pearson.

Edelsky, C., Altwerger, B., & Flores, B. (1991). *Whole language: What's the difference?* Portsmouth, NH: Heinemann.

Fogarty, R. (1991). Ten ways to integrate curriculum. *Educational Leadership, 49*(2), 61–65.

Friedlaender, D., Burns, D., Lewis-Charp, H., Cook-Harvey, C., & Darling-Hammond, L. (2014). *Student-centered schools: Closing the opportunity gap.* Stanford Center for Opportunity Policy in Education. Stanford, CA. https://edpolicy.stanford.edu/sites/default/files/scope-pub-student-centered-research-brief.pdf.

Goodman, K. (1986). *What's whole in whole language?* Portsmouth, NH: Heinemann.

Gregory, G., & Chapman, C. (2002). *Differentiated instructional strategies: One size does not fit all.* Thousand Oaks, CA: Corwin Press, Inc.

Grimes, K. J., & Stevens, D. D. (2009). Glass, bug, mud: A self-assessment system enables teachers to differentiate elementary mathematics instruction, which boosts both student learning and students' sense of themselves as mathematicians. *Phi Delta Kappan, 90*(9), 677–680.

Kysilka, M. (1998). Understanding integrated curriculum. *The Curriculum Journal, 9*(2), 197–209.

Loepp, F. L (1999). Models of curriculum integration. *The Journal of Technology Studies, 25*(2), 21–25.

López, M. V. (2008). La integración de lengua y contenidos en E/L2 en el ámbito escolar: Modelos e implicaciones. In S. Pastor Cesteros and S. Roca Marín (Eds.), *La evaluación en el aprendizaje y la enseñanza del español como lengua extranjera/segunda lengua: XVIII Congreso Internacional de la Asociación para la Enseñanza del Español como Lengua Extranjera (ASELE): Alicante, 19-22 de septiembre de 2007* (pp. 370–378). Servicio de Publicaciones.

Mathison, S., & Freeman, M. (1998). *The logic of interdisciplinary studies.* Albany, NY: National Research Center on English Learning & Achievement.

Meeth, L. R. (1978). Interdisciplinary studies: A matter of definition. *Change: The Magazine of Higher Learning, 10*(7), 10.

Neumann, J. W. (2013). Developing a new framework for conceptualized "student-centered learning." *The Educational Forum, 77*(2), 161–175.

Santau, A. O., & Ritter, J. K. (2013). What to teach and how to teach it: Elementary teachers' views on teaching inquiry-based, interdisciplinary Science and Social Studies in Urban Settings. *The New Educator, 9*(1), 255–286.

Theisen, T. (2002). Differentiated instruction in the foreign language classroom: Meeting the diverse needs of all learners. *LOTE CED Communiqué, 6,* 1–8.

Tomlinson, C. (1999). *The differentiated classroom: Responding to the needs of all learners.* Alexandria, VA: Association for Supervision and Curriculum Development.

Vogt, M. E. (1997). *Cross-curricular thematic instruction.* Reading/Language Arts Center. Houghton Mifflin Company. Retrieved from http://www.eduplace.com/rdg/res/vogt.html.

Weimer, M. (2002). *Learner-centered teaching: Five key changes to practice.* San Francisco, CA: Jossey Bass.

Chapter 7

Shaping Effective Learning through Student Engagement

Susan Wray

The purpose of this chapter is to explore the importance of *student engagement* and to discuss specific approaches that promote student engagement in support of the learning process. Student engagement is often cited as the most important component in the promotion of student learning, and yet it is often misunderstood. The lack of student engagement leads to limited learning at a deep and purposeful level. Additionally, it can contribute to challenging student behavior resulting in the need to redirect students. Having to deal with behavioral issues takes away from the substance of the learning experience and reduces the amount of time devoted to the learning process for all learners.

There are a number of issues that are important to address when thinking about how to enhance student engagement. While many chapters in this book include strategies that ultimately enhance student engagement, this chapter will focus specifically on two key approaches: planning for student engagement and creating a positive classroom community. Explanations and examples of each approach will be provided along with teaching tips and resources to help further understanding and application.

DEFINING "STUDENT ENGAGEMENT"

In this chapter "student engagement" will refer to the "degree of attention, curiosity, interest, optimism, and passion that students show when they are learning or being taught, which extends to the level of motivation they have to learn and progress in their education" (Student Engagement, 2016, The Glossary of Education Reform). It is hard to imagine that anything worth learning and retaining is accomplished without interest, curiosity, and purpose—engagement. Think back to the last time you learned something new. Perhaps it was how to use the new SmartBoard just installed in your classroom. Or perhaps you are learning to ride a horse. Regardless of the topic, interest was at the core. You had an interest. There was a purpose. So, too, should be the experience of students in our classrooms.

Working with and teaching disengaged students is considered one of the biggest challenges in education. Much has been written and studied on student engagement, including how to engage students in the learning process, the importance of student engagement and its impact on student learning, and specific teaching and curricular connections. Specifically, "Student engagement has been built around the hopeful goal of enhancing all students' abilities to *learn how to learn* or to become lifelong learners in a knowledge-based society" (Gilbert, 2007, p. 1). Essentially, student engagement is a seminal foundation of the overall learning experience and requires attention by both the teacher and the student.

Key elements of student engagement as described in the research literature include: instructional approaches that require student-student interactions (e.g., cooperative learning, peer teaching) (Guthrie & Wigfield, 2000); teacher warmth and responsiveness (Bergin & Bergin, 2009; Fredericks et al., 2004); and cognitive engagement and thought processes needed to attain more than a minimal understanding of the course content (Finn & Zimmer, 2012).

The best evidence for student engagement is what students are saying and doing as a consequence of what the teacher is doing, or has done, or has planned. And while students may be physically active (e.g., using manipulative materials in mathematics or making a map in social studies), it is not essential that they be involved in a hands-on manner in order to be engaged; it is, however, essential that they be challenged to be "minds-on" (Danielson Framework, 2013).

There are different types of engagement, including intellectual, social-emotional, and physical, and while all curricular plans might not address each of these types of engagement, the implementation over time of well-planned classrooms and curricula do. Intellectual engagement refers to the ability to understand the content being taught. Some students are not engaged due to the content being too difficult, while others are not engaged because the content is too easy. Moreover, often it is the content itself that contributes to students' disengagement.

Social-emotional engagement refers to the desire to engage in the social process of learning, rather than the discussion, the collaboration, the relational work with specific individuals that the lesson requires. Physical engagement is the act of actually doing the work as planned within the lesson, and those less engaged resist the kinesthetic learning process that might require movement, role-playing, and the use of specific tools/manipulatives.

These categories of engagement help us consider why a student might not be as engaged in the learning experience as had hoped.

Engagement can be observed and internal. *Observed engagement* is that which can be seen, heard, or measured such as students' time on-task, participation in class discussion and activities, and completion of homework. *Internal engagement* refers to the relevance and purpose of learning that the student places on the learning process and school overall. While more challenging to measure, internal engagement is equally if not more important than engagement that can be observed since it connects to intrinsic student motivation.

When students are engaged in learning, they are not merely "busy," nor are they only "on-task." Rather, they are intellectually active in learning important and challenging content. The critical distinction between a classroom in which students are compliant and busy and one in which they are engaged is that in the latter students are developing their understanding through what *they* do. That is, the students are engaged in discussion, debate, answering "what if?" questions, discovering patterns, and the like; thus, they are invested in their own learning.

PROMOTING STUDENT ENGAGEMENT THROUGH EFFECTIVE PLANNING

So, how do we enhance student engagement? One of the best approaches is through thoughtful curricular planning that attends to the key components of student engagement so as to promote maximum student learning. Some students will be naturally interested in the topic being taught; others less so. The day-to-day evolution of the school year reveals that student interest ebbs and flows as the subjects and experiences of the school curriculum change and evolve.

Effective planning means that you consider your students' interests, learning styles, the pacing of the lesson, and the learning process when planning short-term/long-term lesson plans/units. Additionally, effective teachers also consider the impact that the physical space has on the students' learning and overall engagement and make adjustments as needed. Here are some key elements to consider when planning for enhanced student engagement.

Activities and Assignments

When planning lessons and curricular units, the activities and assignments are the centerpiece of student engagement since they determine what it is that students are asked to do. Activities and assignments that promote learning and student engagement require student thinking that emphasizes depth over breadth and encourages them to explain their thinking.

When planning, be sure to differentiate your teaching and learning approach allowing for whole group, small group, and independent work over time. Additionally, plan for moments of conversation and movement within the lesson so as to provide opportunities for students to increase their engagement—physically and mentally—with the content and the learning process.

Grouping of Students

How students are grouped for instruction (whole class, small groups, pairs, individuals) is one of the many decisions teachers make every day. There are many options: students of similar background and skill may be clustered together or the more advanced students may be spread around into the different groups. Alternately, a teacher might permit students to select their own groups or they could be formed randomly. Regardless of the grouping strategy you employ within your lesson, it is important to consider how it will contribute to learning of the content and how it will enhance student engagement with the content and learning process.

Tips on Approaches to Teaching and Learning

Post this in your room as a way of reminding yourself and your students of the different approaches to teaching and learning in which your classroom engages. Refer to them when planning and implementing lessons.

There will be times when

- we all do the same thing,
- some do different things,
- we all work together,
- you work alone, and
- you choose for yourself.

Instructional Materials and Resources

The instructional materials a teacher selects to use in the classroom can have an enormous impact on students' experience. Though some teachers are obliged to use a school's or district's officially sanctioned materials, it is highly recommended that you regularly selectively supplement the curriculum with other materials that are better suited to engaging students in deep learning.

For example, you can use primary source materials in social studies. Other examples of using other sources in your teaching involve using your students' experiences as sources for stories, writing prompts, and morning message while teaching English language arts (ELA) lessons; creating your own math word problems using students names and a familiar context; or having your students write their own math word problems to be solved by their peers.

Tips on Incorporating Students into Learning

Incorporate your students into the learning scenarios.

- Write math word problems that include the names of your students.
- Write math word problems with familiar contexts—the school play, the football game.
- Have your students write their own math problems for their peers to solve.
- Use student stories and experiences (with permission, of course) and write them into ELA examples, morning message, etc.

Bringing the students into the learning in an authentic way can enhance their interest in the content.

Structure and Pacing

No one, whether an adult or a student, likes to be either bored or rushed in completing a task. Keeping things moving, within a well-defined structure, is one of the signs of an experienced teacher. Incorporating awareness of timing and length of time on a particular task while planning lessons helps to ensure that students remain engaged throughout the lesson. And since much of student learning results from their reflection on what they have done, a well-designed lesson includes time for reflection and closure.

The following student story illustrates a child who would benefit from a classroom that embraced different approaches to learning and the impact that limited engagement can have on student learning.

My name is Sam. If I have to sit still for one more minute, I think I'll just explode. The teacher gets really crabby when I move around or tap on the desk, but I just can't stay as still as she wants me to. When I try to stay still all the time, it seems like that's all I can think about, and so I miss what she's telling us, and then that makes me get behind some more and that makes me feel worse and that makes me need to move even more. The teacher gets mad when I move around. She tells me to stay still, and I get embarrassed or mad or something, and it makes me have to move more. I like it in PE when we get to do things and talk to people. I wish we could have PE twice every day. I wish I knew why we had to learn all

this stuff anyhow. It seems like a lot of lists of things that people have to sit still
to learn. Maybe why I don't do well in school is because I can't sit still to learn.

Rather than require Sam to sit still for long periods of time, his teacher would
better serve his needs by allowing him moments of movement throughout
the day. Why not allow Sam to stand up while completing his work? If this
doesn't bother the other students and Sam is able to remain focused for a
longer period of time, what is the harm? Planning for movement within the
day for all students—stretch breaks, yoga, free movement breaks—will not
only benefit Sam and his need to move but will most certainly help others.

Movement provides a brain break and students often return to the lesson
refreshed and refocused. And finally, many schools are doing away with or
eliminating altogether outdoor recess, which means that students do not have
any time for unstructured movement. If this is the case where you teach, you
must take responsibility for incorporating movement in your classroom, and
not only the kind that is quiet and sedate. Kids need to move, as is evidenced
by Sam's story, and good teachers recognize this and plan for it within the
day and week.

Creating a Positive Classroom Community

Interestingly some teachers don't see the importance of spending time on
creating a strong classroom. Rather, in this era of testing and accountability,
some believe that focusing on the content should be primary and that spending time on creating a strong classroom community is a waste of instructional
time. However, there are many reasons why a teacher would want to and
should spend time "creating community" in a classroom.

First, it creates a safe place for learning. It helps more easily intimidated
students feel comfortable asking questions and participating in discussions.
It can help students who aren't traditionally high achieving feel like they too
have a valued role in the classroom. Creating community promotes positive
social-emotional development. It encourages cooperation, not just competi-
tion. Finally, students are more likely to buy into rules and values if they feel
part of the community that created the rules and values. If you establish the
right atmosphere and the right procedures in the beginning of the year, you
will likely have more time during the rest of the year to devote to academics.
It's an up-front investment that can yield great returns.

Establish Classroom Norms and Expectations

Deciding how you and your students will live and work together throughout
the school year is an essential component to creating a positive classroom

community. Some teachers call this creating a list of class rules; others call it creating a class agreement or charter. Whatever the name it is important for you and your students to create a list of expectations that everyone agrees to follow so that the classroom can run and function smoothly. Even very young children can engage in this activity. Create them together, negotiate what is most important, and write them in a way that everyone can access and understand. Post them in a location that is easily seen and referenced when needed.

Establish and Practice Classroom Procedures and Routines

A successful classroom learning environment is ready: the work is ready, the room is ready, the teacher is ready, and the students are ready. Classroom procedures are tasks and actions that are concerned with how things are done in the classroom. The foremost problem in the classroom is not the lack of discipline but the lack of procedures and routines.

Categories for procedures include how to complete academic work, personal responsibility, time-specific tasks, and movement in the classroom and school. When creating and implementing routines, consider which ones need to be taught the first day/week of school and which ones can be introduced over a longer period of time. You'll also want to consider whether all procedures should be predetermined or whether some are created as needs arise.

Once these decisions have been made be sure to teach the procedure, don't just tell your students about the procedure. In other words, have your students practice what to do when they enter the classroom first thing in the morning. Continue to practice, monitor, and reinforce each routine over time until the process is second nature. And finally, revisit procedures throughout the school year as some new ones might arise.

Physical Space

How you organize the physical space of the classroom has a huge bearing on how students engage in the learning process and the day overall. One aspect to consider is the seating arrangements. If a classroom is organized for efficient work habits and access for all students, they will feel more actively engaged in classroom activities. There are many ways of arranging the desks in a classroom and many philosophies about why one arrangement is better than another. The bottom line is this: the best arrangement is the one that fits the teacher's and students' learning styles, fits the classroom dimensions, feels comfortable to the students, and promotes learning. There are four common seating arrangements to consider.

Desks in groups: The groups can be in two, four or six, with six usually the high number. When a group is larger than six, it interferes with the group dynamics and students splinter off into smaller informal groups of two or three. If grouping for cooperative work is the goal, then the number of students in the group should equal the number of tasks or jobs for cooperative work. For early childhood classrooms it is suggested that frequently used materials—pencils, erasers, crayons, rulers, glue sticks, pencil sharpeners—be arranged centrally at each group. This limits students getting out of their seats, thus cutting down on off-task behavior.

Horseshoe shape: In this arrangement, two rows of desks are facing each other from opposite sides of the room and one row faces forward toward the whiteboard. This allows for communication between all members in the class and is perfect for class sizes of twenty or fewer students.

L-shape arrangements: Two desks are placed at a right angle to two other desks. This desk configuration creates groups of four students that can work together cooperatively. In a small space, the L shape may be tessellated through the room with no space between the groups. This allows for a wide center aisle in an otherwise crowded room.

U-shape arrangement: The desks are arranged in a U across the room, allowing all the students to see each other. This arrangement benefits student-to-student conversation and encourages everyone to participate. The U-shape arrangement is similar to the horseshoe shape and is also an excellent choice for classes that hold meetings, thus encouraging community development.

The following vignette illustrates how different learning styles impact student engagement:

> *Marcus is an active second grader. Whether tapping his pencil, adjusting his seat, sharpening his pencil, "shooting baskets" with his trash, or walking through the room, Marcus seems to be in constant motion. During independent work, Marcus's constant motion is often evidence that he is off-task. This is particularly the case when his teacher is working with a small group at the group table. The teacher interrupts the small group on a regular basis to try to get Marcus refocused on his independent work. Marcus's teacher made a sketch (below) of the classroom and recognized that there were several distractions that might encourage Marcus to be off-task. The teacher is planning to rearrange the classroom and/or Marcus's seating position (starred) to help him meet the following goals in four weeks:*
>
> - *Increase the quantity of time on-task during independent work.*
> - *Increase the number of independent assignments completed.*
> - *Decrease the number of interruptions to the small group instruction.*

Clearly this experienced teacher is aware of the impact an effective seating arrangement can have on student learning. She continually evaluates and adjusts the classroom arrangement on the basis of feedback she gets from observing student behavior and quality of work.

Getting to Know Each Other

Offering opportunities for the members of the classroom to get to know each other throughout the school year is an essential component of creating a *positive classroom environment*. When students and teachers know each other well, the greater is the chance that all members of the classroom will support each other as they learn and live together. Obviously, organizing some "getting to know you activities" early in the school year makes great sense and many good teachers regularly incorporate this into their practice. It is also important to incorporate opportunities for students to continue to deepen their understanding of each other throughout the year.

Tips on Creating a Positive Atmosphere

Goal: To allow students to share something positive and create a more positive, uplifting atmosphere.

Procedure: As often as you are able (once a week, once a month, everyday!), allow students to volunteer to share something positive. This can be good news or something good that's happened to them, but just this alone does not always invite enough students to share. Try using one of the four options listed below.

1. Share some good news that's happened for you or someone you know.
2. Tell us who or what you are thankful for.
3. Say a kind word or appreciation for someone else in the class. The comment must be sincere and cannot be about the person's physical characteristics or possessions.
4. Make us laugh. Jokes or stories must be clean and classroom appropriate. (If not very many students take you up on this option, you might want to bring in a book of child-appropriate jokes and funny stories to get the ball rolling.)

Other issues to consider when planning the physical space of the classroom include:

• Keep high traffic areas free of clutter. This includes group work areas and access to the pencil sharpener, trash cans, water fountain, all desks, bookshelves, and computer stations. Making sure that the physical space is

easily navigated by all students, especially those with physical disabilities, is key to ensuring access to learning by all students.
• Be sure students can be seen easily by the teacher and that all students can see the teacher and all instructional spaces within the room. Everyone should have a clear line of sight around the room at all times in all locations.

Creating a comfortable learning space is a way to be proactive about preventing and controlling problems between students in the classroom. If students feel crowded, stress levels may rise and arguments may occur. Plan now for a pleasant, relaxing, and safe classroom.

CONCLUSION

The purpose of this chapter was to discuss and explain how effective planning and the creation of a positive learning environment can enhance student engagement. All good teachers work to develop learning experiences that motivate their students to want to learn, to persevere when the learning becomes more challenging, and to revel in their successes. Attending to increased student engagement within your classroom is a task that requires continual review and reflection. This chapter does not offer all methods of how to increase student engagement, rather it offers information on two widely used approaches that, when done well, are effective tools to enhance student learning.

EXAMPLES OF CLASSROOM PROCEDURES

1. Dismissal at the end of the period or day
2. Quieting a class or gaining students' attention
3. Start of the period or day
4. How students ask for help
5. Distribution of and access to materials
6. Location of supplies and how they are to be accessed by students
7. Handing in homework
8. What to do when students complete their work
9. Working in and moving within centers
10. Leaving and entering the classroom
11. When students are tardy or absent
12. How students indicate that they understand or have questions
13. Moving in the halls

CHECKLIST TO ENHANCE STUDENT ENGAGEMENT: EFFECTIVE LESSON PLANNING

1. Are the topics selected relevant to your students' lives?
   Yes ____ No ____
   Provide some concrete evidence _____

2. Does the unit topic incorporate multiple subjects?
   Yes ____ No ____
   Provide some concrete evidence _____

3. Does the lesson contain a variety of learning experiences?
   Yes ____ No ____
   Provide some concrete evidence _____

4. Does the lesson offer authentic performance based assessment?
   Yes ____ No ____
   Provide some concrete evidence _____

5. Are you providing multiple pathways to learning?
   Yes ____ No ____
   Provide some concrete evidence _____

6. Do you attend to the learning styles of your students?
   Yes ____ No ____
   Provide some concrete evidence _____

7. Do you offer various ways for your students to demonstrate their learning?
   Yes ____ No ____
   Provide some concrete evidence _____

8. Are learning goals and how to reach them clearly articulated to your students?
   Yes ____ No ____
   Provide some concrete evidence _____

9. Do your students have choice as to how they learn the content?
   Yes ____ No ____
   Provide some concrete evidence _____

10. Do you offer different approaches to learning based on student readiness?
    Yes ____ No ____
    Provide some concrete evidence _____

11. Do you provide challenge or extension activities for those students who demonstrate their ability to move beyond the primary scope of the lesson?
    Yes ____ No ____
    Provide some concrete evidence _____

CHECKLIST TO ENHANCE STUDENT ENGAGEMENT: CLASSROOM COMMUNITY DEVELOPMENT

1. Have you considered the best seating arrangement that will enhance student learning and engagement?
   Yes _____ No _____
   Provide some concrete evidence _____

2. Do you regularly evaluate the arrangement of the physical space and make adjustments as needed?
   Yes _____ No _____
   Provide some concrete evidence _____

3. Have you created a list of classroom expectations with your students?
   Yes _____ No _____
   Provide some concrete evidence _____

4. Do you make adjustments to the list of classroom expectations as needed?
   Yes _____ No _____
   Provide some concrete evidence _____

5. Do you introduce and practice essential classroom routines?
   Yes _____ No _____
   Provide some concrete evidence _____

6. Do you adjust and reinforce classroom routines as needed throughout the school year?
   Yes _____ No _____
   Provide some concrete evidence _____

7. Do your students have the opportunity to get to know each other and regularly share their experiences with their peers?
   Yes _____ No _____
   Provide some concrete evidence _____

APPENDIX 1: EXTENSION MATERIALS

Video Resources

1. https://www.teachingchannel.org/videos/strategies-for-engaging-students. This video is about a strategy called "The Wingman" that is designed to keep the student who might not participate normally to stay engaged during the lesson.

2. http://www.edutopia.org/practice/improving-learning-all-students-multi-tiered-approach.

   This video also highlights the importance of differentiating instruction in order to keep all students engaged and up to speed. The school in the video features a three-tiered approach to differentiating instruction. Tier 1 is common instruction, tier 2 features supplemental instruction, and tier 3 is for students who need intensive intervention.

3. https://www.teachingchannel.org/videos/engage-students-meaningful-work-hth.

   This video features a school that promotes student engagement by creating "project-based learning." Students learn about an issue and the curriculum is designed on the basis of their interests and what they would like to learn more about. "They are engaged in the process of learning and they care about what they are creating.... What they are producing becomes important."

4. https://www.teachingchannel.org/videos/real-world-math-examples.

   This video features teachers designing a lesson that connects that material to real-world experiences. They teach a math lesson while highlighting why the material is important and how what they are learning can apply to real-world situations. This real-life connection strengthens student engagement.

5. https://www.teachingchannel.org/videos/student-motivation-techniques.

   In this short video the teacher discusses how making material meaningful to students is important. She also discusses that instruction should make connections with their own lives so that students will see the benefit in their learning and remain engaged.

6. http://www.edutopia.org/stw-assessment-authentic-student-engagement-video.

   This video showcases a sixth grade science teacher trying to promote student engagement. He has his students act as teachers and create their own "giant cell" so they can interact with the material more intimately. Because of the creativity and connections to their own lives, the students were extremely engaged.

WEBSITE RESOURCES

Student Engagement: offers advice and suggestions for enhancing student engagement in the classroom.

- http://www.edutopia.org/blogs/tag/student-engagement.
- http://www.teachersfirst.com/content/knowyou/index.cfm.

- https://www.teachingchannel.org/blog/2012/09/10/14-ways-to-cultivate-classroom-chemistry/.
- http://www.edutopia.org/blog/back-to-school-strategy-building-community-anne-shaw.

Effective Seating Arrangements: offers scenarios and options for considering various seating arrangements in the classroom.

- http://iris.peabody.vanderbilt.edu/wp-content/uploads/pdf_case_studies/ics_effrmarr.pdf.

GLOSSARY OF TERMS

Student engagement—degree of attention, curiosity, interest, optimism, and passion that students show when they are learning or being taught, which extends to the level of motivation they have to learn and the progress made in their education.

Internal engagement—the relevance and purpose of learning that the student places on the learning process and school overall. This form of engagement can be aligned with internal motivation in that it comes from the students' own desire to learn and engage with the subject matter rather than being told to pay attention by others. Internal engagement can be aligned with intrinsic motivation.

Observed engagement—that which can be seen, heard, or measured such as time on-task, participation in class discussion and activities, and completion of homework.

Effective planning—consideration of your students' interests, learning styles, the pacing of the lesson, and the learning process when planning short-term/long-term lesson plans/units. Additionally, effective teachers also consider the impact that the physical space has on the students' learning and overall engagement and makes adjustments as needed.

Positive classroom environment—consideration of what teachers can do in their classrooms that will develop the skills, attitudes, and dispositions in students so they can be active and engaged participants in a democracy.

REFERENCES

Bergin, C., & Bergin, D. (2009). Attachment in the Classroom. *Educational Psychology Review*, *21*(2), 141–170.

Danielson Framework. (2013). The Danielson Group. Retrieved from https://www.danielsongroup.org/framework/.

Finn, J. D., & Zimmer, K. S. (2012). Student engagement: What is it? Why does it matter? In S. L. Christenson, A. L. Reschly, & C. Wylie (Eds.), Handbook of research on student engagement (pp. 97–131). New York, NY: Springer.

Fredricks, J. A., Blumenfeld, P. C., and Paris, A. (2004). School engagement: potential of the concept: state of the evidence. *Review of Educational Research, 74,* 59–119.

Gilbert, J. (2007). Catching the Knowledge Wave: Redefining knowledge for the post-industrial age. Education Canada, 47(3), 4–8. *Canadian Education Association.* www.cea-ace.ca.

Guthrie, J. T., & Wigfield, A. (2000). Engagement and motivation in reading. In M. L. Kamil, P. B. Mosenthal, P. D. Pearson, & R. Barr (Eds.), Reading research handbook (Vol. III, pp. 403–424). Mahwah, NJ: Erlbaum.

Student Engagement. (2016). The Glossary of Education Reform. Retrieved from http://edglossary.org/student-engagement/.

Chapter 8

Developing Academic Literacy

What Novice Teachers Can Learn from the Case of Teaching Latino/Bilingual Learners Science and Mathematics

Sandra I. Musanti and Sandra Mercuri

We believe that when teachers focus on developing students' academic literacy in the content areas, it contributes to strengthening the achievement of underrepresented minorities in the STEM field. This chapter will provide you with ideas to develop academic literacy through mathematics and science instruction.

It is important to keep in mind that each content area such as mathematics, science, social studies, arts, music, and others has its own particular way to use language to communicate meaning. This means that students need to become familiar with the *discourse* practices common to each discipline to be able to understand and communicate knowledge.

Let's think of a simple example. Very young children learn to use and read words such as *more, less, same, observation, data,* and *experiment*. These words are ubiquitous. We found them used across disciplines and contexts. Children, especially bilingual or multilingual children learning English, need multiple opportunities to learn the specific ways in which language is used across disciplines. This means that teachers need to help students understand the specific ways of listening, speaking, *reading,* and *writing* in different content areas.

In this chapter we define "academic literacy" and describe meaningful strategies for students to participate in varied ways of doing and talking mathematics and science. We focus on teaching situations that involve students who speak a language other than English at home or who can be identified as *bilingual learners*. The number of bilingual learners in the country's classrooms is growing. The National Center for Education Statistics (NCES, 2015) indicates that an estimated 4.4 million or 9.2 percent of students in public schools are classified as ELLs. Then, it is important that all teachers become familiar with strategies that foster academic literacy for all students but especially those who are learning content through a second language.

This chapter presents different strategies to develop academic literacy illustrated through vignettes from classroom instruction designed for Latino bilingual learners showing: (a) challenging K-2 mathematics instruction that fosters problem-solving and communication of mathematical thinking through multiple ways of representation, and (b) challenging three to five science instruction that *scaffolds* critical thinking through an integrated process of talking, reading, and writing about science.

In addition, in this chapter you will learn how the strategies described could be adapted for diverse populations to foster academic literacy development in science and mathematics, and we will highlight some tips to foster academic literacy across content areas. We will focus especially on understanding how teachers can use students' cultural and linguistic resources to support conceptual understandings across the curriculum.

THE LANGUAGE OF SCHOOL

To be successful and to fully participate in classroom activities all children need to acquire the "language of school," a complex type of English that includes a wide range of competencies. "As students develop competence in using every day, social English to interact, they must also acquire the *academic language* associated with each specific content area" (Egbert & Ernst-Slavit, 2010, p. 4).

Typically, academic language is associated almost exclusively with specific vocabulary that students need to learn to do well in the different content areas. However, academic language involves developing multiple competences at three levels: vocabulary or word level, grammar or sentence level, and discourse or text level (Table 8.1).

UNDERSTANDING ACADEMIC LITERACY

Most teachers when thinking of literacy think of reading and writing. Recently, different authors have indicated that academic literacy involves reading and writing skills but also the abilities of listening, viewing, thinking, speaking, and expressing through multiple representational systems (Gottlieb & Ernest-Slavit, 2014; Short & Fitzsimmons, 2007). Academic literacy requires the development of advanced levels of proficiency in the

Table 8.1 Elements of Academic Language

Levels	Definition	Examples
Vocabulary/ Word Level	*General Academic Vocabulary*: Words used across content areas	Analyze, explain, contrast, compare similar, interconnected, reasoning, explanation
	Specialized Content Vocabulary: Terms associated and mostly used in specific content areas	Mathematics: hypotenuse, cardinal and ordinal numbers Science: photosynthesis, experiment, osmosis Language Arts: spelling, grammar Social Studies: continents, latitude, altitude, democracy, constitution, amendment Music: overture, melody, tempo
	Signal Words: Used to establish connections between ideas	"because" or "consequently" identify cause-and-effect relationship "finally" and "first," indicate a sequence
Grammar/ Sentence Level	It relates to the syntax and the mechanics of writing sentences and paragraphs. Some features relate to specific content areas.	Mathematics: formulas, use of prepositions (divided by) Science: use of imperative in experiments instructions Social Studies: use of multiple forms of past tense
Discourse/ Text Level	Different types of text used across content areas	Mathematics: story problems, proofs Science: experiment instructions, science report, science journaling Social Studies: cartograms, folktales, historical documents Language Arts: autobiographies, novels, plays

Adapted from Freeman & Freeman (2009); Slavit & Ernst-Slavit (2007); Egbert & Ernst-Slavit (2010); Gottlieb & Ernst-Slavit (2014).

four *language domains*: reading, writing, listening and speaking and visual literacy skills (NGA & CCSSO, 2010).

Developing academic literacy also requires that students can understand and effectively use the specific forms of oral and written communication that vary from subject to subject. In addition, it comprises the knowledge of multiple *genres* of text, as well as purposes for text use. For instance, in science, students need to become familiar with how to write experiments' instructions; in social studies, students will write historical reports; and in music, students will become familiar with music notations.

Then, developing academic literacy involves students acquiring academic language in terms of specific vocabulary, types of sentence patterns used in different types of texts, and the characteristics of the texts or discourse associated with different subjects. Recently, changes in the way we communicate through visual media make it essential for students to understand visual images in connection with accompanying text, as well as being able to visually represent different types of knowledge.

As students move through the elementary grades in school, they are asked to use language in increasingly more demanding ways. This language requirement puts bilingual learners at a disadvantage and, in the long run, diminishes their opportunities for academic success. To succeed in school *all* students need advanced levels of proficiency in the four language domains of reading, writing, listening, and speaking, as well as in viewing and visually representing knowledge. Teachers will need to develop strategies that support students' use of language in different situations, for varied purposes, and with different audiences (Egbert & Ernst-Slavit, 2010).

An instructional approach that considers the cultural and linguistic differences that students bring to the classroom, requires that teachers understand the language demands that learning content in a different language impose to children.

The concept of academic literacy was well summarized by the Adolescent ELLs Literacy Advisory Panel:

- Includes reading, writing, and oral discourse for school
- Varies from subject to subject
- Requires knowledge of multiple genres of text, purposes for text use, and text media
- Is influenced by students' literacies in contexts outside of school
- Is influenced by students' personal, social, and cultural experiences

(Short & Fitzsimmons, 2007, p. 8)

Tips on Academic Literacy in Lesson Planning

Think of a lesson you have planned or taught in a content area such as mathematics, science, and social studies and reflect back on the following questions:

- How was academic literacy addressed in your lesson?
- Did your lesson consider multiple ways of representing knowledge? How?

Based on what you have read so far about academic literacy, what could change in this lesson to better address academic literacy?

From this perspective, teaching across disciplines needs to emphasize the need for students to participate in literacy events contributing to the development of new knowledge, ways to challenge current practices, and the use of language for advance literacy practices (Schleppegrell & Colombi, 2002). Following Conley (2012), we identify a series of principles to develop content-area literacy:

- Create opportunities for collaboration through interdisciplinary curricular units of exploratory learning.
- Provide students with multiple opportunities for practice for listening, speaking, reading, writing, interpreting visual media, and visually representing text.
- Focus student attention on words and patterns as they read and write about or discuss the content they are learning.
- Teach students to become critical thinkers by evaluating each other's contributions about a particular content or evidence presented on their investigations.

UNDERSTANDING THE LANGUAGE DEMANDS OF CONTENT LEARNING

Learning academic literacy occurs when teachers design instructional strategies that provide students with multiple and varied opportunities to participate in ways of doing and communicating knowledge in the content areas and to share new knowledge through multiple ways of representation (Schleppegrell, 2004). The *language demands* of learning in the content areas are typically invisible for mainstream teachers, especially for teachers teaching content in middle or high school because they are not used to see language as content of instruction (Harper & de Jong, 2004).

Let's think about an example. Helen, a novice third grade teacher, has learned that using a K-W-L chart is a "good" teaching practice. She has planned to use the K-W-L chart during her social studies lesson to guide students through a reading about the basic structure of government in the local community, state, and nation, while making connections to their previous knowledge on the topic. Being aware of the language demands that this task entails, she needs to consider the language skills that bilingual students need to effectively participate in the activity. With this in mind, she asks questions to scaffold student's brainstorming of ideas and language use:

What I *K*now
- Tell me everything you know about _____.
- What made you think of that?

What I *W*ant to Know
- What do you want to learn about this topic?
- What do you think you will learn about this topic from the text you will be reading?
- What would you like to learn more about idea X?

What I *L*earned
- Students answer the questions in the W section.
- Students list interested facts they found.
- Students consult other resources to answer the questions they did not find in the text.

To complete and interpret these questions, students need skills that will enable them to identify and state facts and propose ideas and ask questions (Harper & de Jong, 2004). These tasks could be very cognitively demanding for students who are learning content in a second language. It is important that instructional activities in the different content areas make explicit the different reading and writing demands and discourse conventions of the disciplinary domains (Schleppegrell, 2004).

Tips on K-W-L Implementation

Consider a situation where you are teaching the concept of extreme weather conditions:

- Select a reading to introduce the concept and build background knowledge of your students using a K-W-L chart.
- Using similar questions like the ones presented in the previous example, complete the K and W part of the chart with your students.
- Consider the language demands of the selected reading, and on the basis of your assessment, decide on the vocabulary that you will have to front-load to make the reading event accessible to all learners in the class.
- Think of a strategy that you can use to introduce the vocabulary.
- Read the text, discuss it with students, and ask them to complete the L part of the chart in groups on the basis of the information gathered from the book.
- Reflect: In what ways did the strategic use of the scaffold support your students' access to the content and facilitate their language use?

The content areas or disciplines are social constructions that involve particular ways of representing and communicating knowledge using distinct discourses and different levels of *linguistic complexity*. As an example, despite the extended belief that mathematics is a universal language, some mathematical ideas are represented differently in different countries. For instance, the procedures taught in the United States for the long-division algorithm might be very different from those that students learn in schools in their home countries.

Promoting Literacy through Challenging K-2 Mathematics Instruction

Communicating mathematically and making sense of mathematics problems could be challenging for young children, particularly children who are in the process of learning the language of instruction. To help students develop mathematics academic literacy, teachers need to see language and mathematics as jointly constructed and not separate. Developing mathematics vocabulary either in English or in the students' first language is important. However, effective practices should be anchored in a more complex understanding of literacy and focus instruction on providing multiple opportunities to listen, develop, and communicate orally and in writing mathematics reasoning and not just vocabulary development (Moschkovich, 2007). To achieve this, teachers at all grade levels can develop strategies to

- use *language as a pedagogical resource* by building on students' bilingual language skills;
- promote challenging problem-solving and communication of mathematical thinking through multiple ways of representation (modeling, drawing, using symbols, writing, oral explanations); and
- explicitly teach the language of mathematics, semantic reasoning, and the specific symbols.

Bilingual learners come to school with a wide range of linguistic resources. When learning mathematics or other content areas, bilingual learners not only use their English and home language skills, but also draw from both sets of social and academic languages. When designing mathematics instruction that values communication, teachers must consider bilingual learners' language skills and foster participation in both "everyday" and "mathematical" interactions (Moschkovich, 2007; Slavit & Ernst-Slavit, 2007). There are ways of saying and communicating ideas in mathematics that are influenced by culture and language.

Tips on Student Language

Observe and reflect on student language resources and teacher instructional strategies during a mathematics lesson. You can observe a peer or watch a video of a lesson online. Mathematics lessons' videos can be found at http://www.insidemathematics.org. While observing a lesson:

• Identify instances when students use their home language to communicate mathematically.

Does the teacher use strategies such as questioning to ask for clarification, building on student responses and revoicing student's explanations. Mathematics learning requires the development of academic literacy skills that support students in the process of making-meaning of content through activities that consider students' culture and language (Celedón-Pattichis & Musanti, 2013). For instance, when teaching mathematics teachers can design word problems that connect students' familiar practice of storytelling in their native language to mathematics problem-solving (Turner, Celedón-Pattichis, Marshall & Tennison, 2009).

The following vignette illustrates how Analía, a second grade teacher in a bilingual classroom, presents students with a challenging partitive division mathematics problem. Analía has noticed that several students in her classroom struggle to understand the structure of some mathematics problems, and they have difficulties identifying relevant information to use while solving the problem. Her objectives for this lesson were to work on more effective ways to solve this type of problems and to model how to interpret the language of the problems providing tools to support students' semantic reasoning.

For this lesson, Analía purposefully selected a problem that involves a multiple of 5 to encourage grouping by fives. Yesica had 45 cookies. She is going to share them with 8 friends. How many cookies does each girl get? After writing the problem on the board, teacher and students read the problem as a whole group.

> *TEACHER: Raise your hand. First, what information is important to solve the problem? What information is important and necessary to know to find the answer?*
>
> *STUDENT 1: Yesica had 45 cookies*
>
> *TEACHER: Good [underlining the information in the problem]. What else is important?*
>
> *STUDENT 2: How many cookies does each girl get?*
>
> *TEACHER: The question! [Teacher underlines the problem question on the board.]*

TEACHER: [Turns to face students] What else is important? Can we solve this problem with this information?

STUDENTS: Nooo!!!!

TEACHER: Another piece of information is missing.... We need more information. What is it?

[Several students raise their hands. Teacher chooses one student.]

STUDENT 3: Share with 8 friends

TEACHER: What does it mean "she will share with 8 friends"?

STUDENT 1: That Yesica is going to count that she is going to have cookies.

TEACHER: Is that right? Then how many girls are there in total?

STUDENTS: Nine!!!!

TEACHER: Yes, nine. Now do we have all the information we need?

STUDENTS: Yes!!

TEACHER: Now, you can think with your group what is the fastest way to find the answer.... We already know how to count by two's, five's, ten's.... Think with your group how you can find the answer and what is the fastest way. Represent in your poster how you did it.

To solve this problem, students need to identify key information and to infer that they need to divide 45 between 9 girls. The problem implies that Yesica will get cookies too. This problem might challenge all students, but it could be particularly difficult for bilingual students who are still not familiar with the specific ways to use language in mathematics, that is, the mathematics discourse. In this case, the language demand requires them to interpret the idea of "sharing" as involving Yesica. This lesson shows how important it is to scaffold the use of language that students need to tackle challenging mathematics problems. The vignette shows three important ways in which this teacher is promoting mathematics academic literacy.

First, the teacher asked students to identify important and necessary information to solve the problem. This is an important skill that requires students to make sense of the word problem. The narrative structure of problem scaffolds students' thinking and provides the clues to identify essential information. Analía modeled the process writing on the board what students identified as relevant information using different ways to represent the information with symbols and in writing.

Second, the teacher helped students to make sense of mathematics language. For instance, she asked them to explain the mathematics meaning embedded in the sentence, "She will share the cookies with 8 friends." A common mistake students made was to identify the numbers in the problem without consideration to the text and how the meaning changed that numeric value.

Third, the teacher challenged students to compare different ways to solve this problem, asking them to find the fastest strategy. This is an important problem-solving skill that all students need to develop. To support this process Analía asked students to represent and explain the different ways by which they could solve the problem and compare the strategies in terms of efficiency.

For instance, students were able to identify that as there were 45 cookies and 9 girls, Yesica could distribute 5 to each until she ran out. Analía asked them to demonstrate this strategy to prove if it would work using different ways to represent their solution. She encouraged students to work in groups and come up with at least two different ways to show how they solved the problem, either by drawing their solution, using numbers and algorithms, or by writing their explanation.

The use of multiple ways to represent problem-solving strategies is an important skill that students need to develop. After solving the problem, each group shared the different ways they used to solve the problems with the whole class. Students were asked to explain the solution. To scaffold oral communication of mathematics thinking, teachers can use different types of questioning to

- make sense of the problem: ask questions to help students retell the problem or describe the problem in their own words and to identify important information.
- demonstrate or probe how they solved the problem and explain their reasoning: ask questions to explain how they reach a solution or describe a strategy. Would you explain to me how you figured this out? How did you count? Why? Which way of solving this problem is faster?

An important practice to develop academic literacy requires the implementation of strategies that promote teachers' and students' mathematics talk using multiple ways to communicate students' thinking and problem-solving strategies (Chapin, O'Connor & Anderson, 2009).

Tips on Closing the Math Achievement Gap

Go to Closing the Math Achievement Gap site: http://www.uwosh.edu/coehs/cmagproject/cogn/word_prob.htm

- Explore the word problem examples for the grade level you are teaching or you would like to teach. Compare and contrast with the word problems in

the mathematics curriculum you are using or a teacher you have observed is using.
- Try to identify similarities and differences.
- Choose a type of problem and write examples of problems that integrate your knowledge of your students' cultural background.

Promoting Academic Literacy through Challenging Three to Five Science Instruction

As we explained above, the type of academic literacy that is required for school-related tasks involves not only the development of listening, speaking, reading, and writing skills, but also the development of more abstract and demanding language. For example, the academic language of science

The following text sample is from a third grade bilingual learner. The sample is about the rainforest. In groups or with a partner:
- First, identify what type of text the sample is based on the different type of science genres described above.
- Second, discuss the academic language features used by the student.
- Lastly, provide a series of strategies or steps you could use to further develop the student's writing of the sample provided.

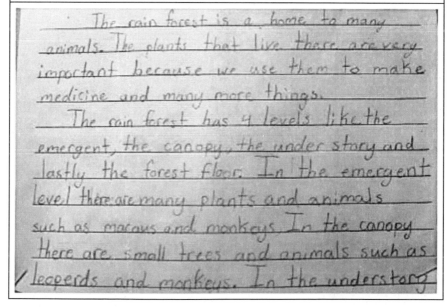

The rain forest is a home to many animals. The plants that live there are very important because we use them to make medicine and many more things.

The rain forest has 4 levels like the emergent, the canopy, the under story and lastly the forest floor. In the emergent level there are many plants and animals such as macaws and monkeys. In the canopy there are small trees and animals such as leoperds and monkeys. In the understory

Figure 8.1   Text Sample.

uses technical words and complex grammatical structures with a high density of information that makes the reading of science text challenging for all students and, more in particular, for bilingual learners (Snow, 2010). It is important that teachers design instruction to help bilingual students learn the content knowledge and the academic language of science—including critical thinking—through an integrated process of talking, reading, and writing about science (Mercuri & Ebe, 2011; Lee, 2005).

One way to provide opportunities for the development of *scientific literacy* while creating opportunities for exploration is to plan *interdisciplinary units of inquiry* (Freeman, Freeman & Mercuri, 2005). These units of inquiry are guided by an essential question and integrate literacy throughout including activities for students to read and write different types of texts. For example, Freeman and Freeman (2009) explain that there are different genres in science for students to read or write:

- Procedural text: reading and writing instructions for an experiment. Students use the imperative tense.
- Procedural recount: recording and describing what has been done in an experiment. Students use the past tense.
- Science report: organizing information by dividing a phenomenon into its parts or steps or by listing its properties. Students use the present tense.
- Scientific explanation: describing how and why a scientific phenomenon occurs, dealing with interactions of factors and processes rather than a sequence of events.

Working with bilingual learners through these different types of texts presents a challenge for teachers today. Students have to access academic content through their second language while they are still developing that language (Short & Fitzsimmons, 2007). Research has shown that students' first language should be used to support content understanding in their second language and to facilitate the transfer of language skills. One approach to using students' first language as a pedagogical resource is by designing instruction that integrates strategies such as *Preview/View/Review* (P/V/R) (Mercuri, 2015). When using this strategy, the teacher usually starts by introducing the topic in students' first language, then develops the lesson content in the main language of instruction, and finalizes the lesson with a review of the main ideas or an integration of ideas in students' first language.

For instance, in a third grade interdisciplinary unit on ecosystems, María starts by introducing the topic by reading the book *Dentro de la selva tropical* (Inside the Rainforest) by Willow and Jakes (1993). This activity contributes to enhancing students' understanding about the topic of the lesson and also

Table 8.2 Key Academic Vocabulary

When planning your next unit of inquiry, use the following table to identify key academic vocabulary		
Type of Vocabulary	Definition	Examples
General Academic Vocabulary	Words used across content areas	Analyze, explain, contrast, similar
Specialized Content Vocabulary	Terms associated and mostly used in specific content areas	Mathematics: hypotenuse Science: photosynthesis
Signal Words	Words that establish different type of connections or relationships between ideas	"because" or "consequently" identify cause-and-effect relationship "finally" and "first" indicate a sequence

Source: Adapted from Freeman & Freeman (2009) and Slavit & Ernst-Slavit (2007).

to enriching their academic vocabulary in Spanish through the descriptive language used throughout the book (Table 8.2).

In her research synthesis on ELLs and science education, Okhee Lee (2005) explains that "subject area instruction should provide a meaningful context for English language and literacy development, while advancing English skills provides the medium for engagement with academic content" (p. 492). An important aspect of developing the language of science is a focus on words and sentence patterns as they read and write about or discuss the content that they are learning (Conley, 2012).

The following vignette illustrates how Natalia, a fifth grade teacher in a border town of Texas, creates opportunities for students to develop science content knowledge and academic language through effective academic literacy practices when teaching the steps of the scientific methods.

TEACHER: What is your experiment about?

STUDENT 1: It's about slime

STUDENT 2: Our independent variables are the types of glue, our dependent variable is the slime effect we will create.

STUDENT 1: Our hypothesis is if we use Elmer's glue then it will create a slimier effect because it's denser than the other HEB glue we will use... and our procedure is...

STUDENT 2: Okay... first we put the glue in the container and mix it... well, first we put a tablespoon in the container and second one tablespoon of borax in the same container, third red food coloring in the same container and then we dissolve it with water...

STUDENT 1: We dissolve it with 10 ml of water and then we mix them, and finally slime should start to form.

TEACHER: Great... show me the results... what happened?

STUDENT 2: This one... (pointing at the first container) was the clear HEB glue... and it came out more compact...

TEACHER: And the other container?

STUDENT 1: The other one looks like gum, you can stretch it more, look... (pointing at the second container).

TEACHER: Then, was your hypothesis correct?

STUDENTS 1 and 2: Yes. The Elmer's glue creates a slimier effect.

This vignette shows students' use of academic language to explain the experiment and their findings. Students use specific science vocabulary, general academic terms, and signal words to describe the experiment, which shows their academic language development (Freeman & Freeman, 2009; Gottlieb & Ernest-Slavit, 2014). For example, students use content-specific vocabulary such as *dependent, independent variables*, and *slime effect*.

In addition, the students are using general academic terms that appear across different content areas. Some of those terms are *experiment, hypothesis, procedure, dissolve*, and *compact* and are not commonly used by bilingual learners in everyday language. Students are using signal words to explain the procedure to justify their claims (i.e., *first, second, third, then*, and *finally*), and to construct sentences traditionally used in scientific discourse to present hypothesis. For example: "Our hypothesis is *if* we use Elmer's glue *then* it will create a slimier effect because it's denser than the other HEB glue we will use."

Tips on Designing Activities for Lesson Review

On the basis of the lesson that Ms. Huarte taught about the rainforest described above, consider strategies for checking for understanding and language use such as:

- Completing the L part of a K-W-L charts on the topic of study
- Using an oral exit ticket on a concept to provide clarification
- Doing a whole-class picture match activity to check for understanding
- Using a soft ball for "wonder questions" about a topic
- Using the games "*Simon Says*" or "*I have, Who has*" to practice academic vocabulary.

Design a short activity for the review segment of the lesson. Keep in mind that the activity should be a checking for comprehension of what the students have learned during the lesson in English. After designing the activity consider the following questions:

1. How does the activity integrate the content students learned and the language development of skills that students are working on?
2. Does the activity consider linguistic differentiations according to students' different language proficiencies?

The way they integrate the vocabulary to support their explanations of the experiment results demonstrates both conceptual understanding and academic language development. In addition, the interaction between teacher and students is an example of scaffolded instruction that focuses on students' productive participation in scientific practices and discourse to support the development of scientific literacy (Zembal-Saul, McNeill & Hershberger, 2013).

As seen in the vignette, science provides a context for the meaningful learning of language structures and functions, and these linguistic processes become the medium for analysis and communication of scientific knowledge. Language and content knowledge build on each other and support the development of scientific literacy.

ACADEMIC LITERACY AS AN INTERDISCIPLINARY APPROACH

All teachers, Analía, Maria, and Natalia, apply their understanding of academic literacy to other content areas. All plan instruction through interdisciplinary units, identifying themes and developing lessons in different content areas that contribute to the understanding of the overall topic while developing proficiency in the different language domains. For instance, María designed a culminating activity for the unit on the tropical forest so students could integrate and demonstrate the knowledge gained through an art project.

For this project María expected their students to visually represent their understanding using geometric figures to create the different layers of the tropical forest, including animals and plants. In addition, students needed to present their art projects giving them the opportunity to practice their oral language skills to interpret visual images as well as text, and to further develop their speaking abilities.

She designed this project so that all students, no matter what their English *language proficiency* is, could express their understandings through different ways of representing knowledge. She knows that this is an excellent opportunity to develop academic literacy through art forms, integrating students' first language and cultural knowledge.

Tips on Developing Unit Projects

- Develop a culminating project for a unit that you have taught or plan to teach.
- Include in the project an aspect of social studies, art, or math that you want your students to present to demonstrate the knowledge gained through the unit.
- Develop a handout that provides examples for students to demonstrate the connections they can make across content areas and topics.
- Identify in the handout what the students will do to further develop their four language domains: listening, speaking, reading, and writing.

SELF-REFLECTION

Reflect back on what you consider was an effective mathematics or science lesson you planned and taught. Try to identify two reasons why you consider this lesson successful and write them down.

a. To complete this reflective exercise, now, make a mental picture of the classroom, the different groups of students, and what you know about these students in terms of language diversity and cultural diversity. Ask yourself questions, such as:
  - What did you notice in relation to students' cultural diversity?
  - What did you notice in relation to students' language diversity?
  - What did you notice in terms of students' language resources (social language skills, academic language skills, first-language use, second-language use)?
  - What did you notice in terms of students' literacy experiences?
b. Now it is time to look back at the reasons you have identified as critical for a good mathematics or science lesson and consider how they relate to what you have noticed about your students' culture, language, and literacy experiences.
  - How could you integrate this knowledge in your lesson planning?
  - What specific changes in terms of activities, content, and language support will you apply to this lesson?
  - How will these changes improve students' content understanding and academic literacy development?

While answering these questions you might want to consider the following checklist to develop academic literacy across content areas.

CHECKLIST TO ADVANCE ACADEMIC LITERACY ACROSS CONTENT AREAS

To make sure you are including strategies that foster academic literacy development in the different content areas, use the following checklist.

1. I design instruction through units of inquiry to promote more contextualized and exploratory learning.
   Yes _____ No _____
2. I include activities to scaffold understanding of basic and complex concepts of the different content areas.
   Yes _____ No _____
3. I consider the language demands of the content in relation to my students' language proficiency.
   Yes _____ No _____
4. I consider the cultural and linguistic resources that my students bring to the classroom.
   Yes _____ No _____
5. I include activities that foster collaboration and interaction between teacher and students, and students and students.
   Yes _____ No _____
6. Students have meaningful opportunities to communicate their reasoning both orally and in writing.
   Yes _____ No _____
7. Student have multiple opportunities to represent their understanding through different media (print, visual, interactional, & electronic).
   Yes _____ No _____
8. Students have opportunities to develop and use academic language (words, sentence patterns, and different types of text).
   Yes _____ No _____
9. Students are encouraged to use their first language when needed as a resource for learning.
   Yes _____ No

CONCLUSION

To close the achievement gap that exists among underrepresented minorities such as Latinos, African American, and Native American students, we need instruction that advances the development of academic literacy across content areas. To be successful, all students need to develop the language of school, that is, the *social language*, to communicate effectively with others and the academic language that includes the vocabulary, syntax, and discourse styles of particular content areas. The chapter highlights the importance of understanding that academic literacy is much more than reading and writing, and we redefined it as integrating four language domains (listening, speaking, reading, and writing) as well as literacy skill to interpret and generate visual representations such as images and graphics.

This chapter describes an example of how to design mathematics instruction in K-2 settings that includes challenging problem-solving and fosters academic literacy. The example shows how teachers can draw on students' first-language competencies, and how to support students' use of multiple ways to represent solutions while promoting mathematics talk. The chapter also shows how to plan science lessons around interdisciplinary units to develop academic literacy while integrating the process of talking, reading, and writing about science and developing students' academic vocabulary and knowledge of different science texts (i.e., how to write hypotheses or the steps of an experiment).

Finally, this chapter provides important ideas to develop academic literacy across content areas. It is important to remember that to contribute to academic development teachers need to consider a variety of factors such as student prior knowledge, the ability to read and use vocabulary for different purposes, the language demands of each task, the linguistic complexity of the reading materials, and the nature and complexity of what the students are expected to do, say, or write. Specifically, we highlight the importance of integrating students' cultural and language resources and previous literacy experiences through instructional approaches such as teaching through interdisciplinary units of inquiry.

In addition, whenever possible, teachers should integrate strategies that tap into students' first language as a resource for learning. For instance, they should use strategies such as Preview/View/Review, presenting content in students' first language to build on students' linguistic competence and background knowledge. Finally, it is important to be aware of the language demands that learning content can impose on bilingual learners and to generate scaffolding strategies that promote multiple opportunities for students to represent and share their understanding both orally and in writing using different media (drawings, symbols, interactions, and text).

APPENDIX 1: EXTENSION MATERIALS

Building a Discourse Community in the Classroom

Bilingual learners need multiple opportunities to participate in meaningful mathematics and science conversations. Some authors have argued that teachers need to create discourse communities in their classroom, where students can actively participate in sharing and producing mathematical knowledge. To achieve this, teachers need to implement strategies to facilitate classroom discussions. These are some sources with valuable examples and tips:

- *Talking the Talk: Tips for Engaging Your Students in Scientific Discourse*: TeachingChannel.org offers this blog authored by Alissa Berg that addresses key instructional points from the Next Generation Science Standards (NGSS). "This blog briefly explains the difference between traditional classrooms talk and 'productive talk' and includes tools and strategies for generating and facilitating the latter in your classroom." Available at: https://www.teachingchannel.org/blog/ausl/2014/04/21/talking-the-talk-tips-for-engaging-your-students-in-scientific-discourse/.
- *Math Solutions* website: The site has several videos and free resources that illustrate lessons that foster math talk.
  - *What does academically productive talk look like?* This is a blog entry that defines math talk as a strategy to promote deeper learning and provides tips to implement it in the classroom. http://mathsolutions.com/free-resources/what-does-academically-productive-talk-look-like/.
  - *"Math Talk in Action—First Grader"* (A first grade teacher in a two-way bilingual school helps her students listen to and repeat a classmate's thinking): http://mathsolutions.wistia.com/medias/09lyt1vbry.

Teaching for Scientific Literacy

Developing scientific literacy is critical for individual and social growth. The Next Generation Science Standards (NGSS, 2013) state that literacy development is critical to construct science knowledge. "Any education in science and engineering needs to develop students' ability to read and produce domain-specific text. As such, every science or engineering lesson is in part a language lesson, particularly reading and producing the genres of texts that are intrinsic to science and engineering" (NRC *Framework*, 2012, p. 76).

- Project 2061 is a long-term research and development initiative focused on improving science education so that all Americans can become literate in science, mathematics, and technology. This project is sponsored by the American Association for the Advancement of Science (AAAS). We encourage you to explore this site and the publications, research, and teaching materials they have developed. For instance, you will find the *Atlas of Science Literacy* with conceptual strand maps—and commentary on those maps—that show how students' understanding of the ideas and skills that lead to literacy in science, mathematics, and technology might develop from kindergarten through twelfth grade. http://www.aaas.org/program/ project2061.

- The National Science Teacher Association (NSTA) has a series of books and resources that will support teachers at all grade levels in the teaching of science. Some of those resources are free. Check the link below for free resources from the NSTA. https://www.nsta.org/publications/freebies. aspx.

Articles, Books, and Websites

- K-5 Mathematics Teaching Resources: This site provides an extensive collection of free resources, math games, and hands-on math activities aligned with the Common Core State Standards for Mathematics: http://www.k-5mathteaching resources.com.
- You can find interesting examples and lesson materials such as a virtual mathematics word wall in many different languages at: *The Algorithm Collection Project*—a website developed by Daniel Clark Orey, PhD professor emeritus, California State University, Sacramento: http://www.csus.edu/ indiv/o/oreyd/ACP.htm_files/Alg.html.
- Books to enhance teachers' understanding of how to teach for scientific literacy:

  Zembal-Saul, C., McNeill, K., & Hershberger, K. (2013) *What's your evidence? Engaging K-5 students in constructing explanations in science.* Upper Saddle River, NJ: Pearson Education.

  Thier, M., & Daviss, B. (2002). *The new science literacy: Using language skills to help students learn science.* Portsmouth, NH: Heinemann.

  Grant, M., & Fisher, D. (2010). *Reading and Writing in science: Tools to develop disciplinary literacy.* Thousand Oaks, CA: Corwin Press.

Videos

These are some videos available online that provide valuable ideas on how to develop literacy across the content areas.

Literacy across the curriculum: This video demonstrates how literacy is part of all aspects of school life. https://www.youtube.com/watch? v=R088edAQYzc.

Academic literacy in mathematics education: This video shows an example of how a teacher supports literacy development through mathematics teaching in a third grade classroom. https://www.youtube.com/watch?v=sCpDXuo NpTQ&index=1&list=PLdhfCYg5nUa1-v_EJSwk-pA2dRSA3blRh.

A Focus on Math: Áhi'iltaa, *Math in Cultural Context*: This short film illustrates the use of Dine' (Navajo) Language and Culture in the math curriculum in the STAR School 3-to-3rd project. This is the second in a series of three short films demonstrating how and why the STAR School's 3-to-3rd (age 3 to grade 3) project focuses on math. STAR is located on the southwestern edge of the Navajo Nation and serves a majority indigenous population. Available at: https://www.youtube.com/watch?v=nQCItldgzw0.

What is science literacy? This video shows the importance of developing critical thinking and science literacy. https://www.youtube.com/watch?v=BaM662xrlp8.

Exploring STEM concepts with younger students. This video was produced by Dr. Diana Wehrell-Grabowski. It shows how young children learn about STEM concepts, communication skills, and collaboration while building with blocks. In addition, teachers and students were introduced to numerous children's literature that reinforces STEM concepts. https://www.youtube.com/watch?v=HglYz0h2n2E.

GLOSSARY OF TERMS

Academic language—academic language is the language used to learn at schools and to develop knowledge in different disciplines. It includes a range of competences to process and produce meaning across language domains (listening, speaking, reading, and writing) and specific linguistic traits of each discipline including types of texts or discourse, grammatical features, and specific vocabulary. Academic language is produced in a specific sociocultural context. We use academic language to acquire new understandings and skills, to develop knowledge, and to communicate knowledge to others (Slavit & Ernst-Slavit, 2007).

Bilingual learners—recently, authors such as García and Kleifgen (2010) have raised important questions over the labeling of students as English language learners (ELLs). Specifically, they argue that ELLs are in fact "emergent bilinguals." This means that they become bilingual throughout their schooling experience and as they acquire English, communicating and interacting using their home language as well as English to make sense of the world and to learn. In this chapter, we prefer to identify students in this situation as bilingual learners to be inclusive of the wide range of experiences and development of bilingual skills.

Discourse—the different ways in which we use language to convey multiple connected ideas in a way that is specific to different fields of culturally and historically located meanings. Discourse is most simply understood today as a sort of unit of language organized around a particular subject matter and meaning. For an enhanced explanation, see: http://csmt.uchicago.edu/glossary2004/discourse.htm

Genre—the Merriam-Webster dictionary defines "genre" as "a category of artistic, musical, or literary composition characterized by a particular style, form, or content." That is the socially defined ways in which different types of texts are used to participate in particular contexts to serve specific purposes (WIDA Consortium, 2012). Text genres vary across disciplines and could include written or oral text. For instance, social studies and science are characterized for the predominance of expository (informational) texts, and fiction texts are typical in language arts and literature. Examples of genres are journals, biographies, poetry, picture books, textbook, novel, science article, dialogue script, debate, and many more.

Interdisciplinary units of inquiry—when planning interdisciplinary units, the subject areas are connected. Interdisciplinary thematic units are organized around big or essential questions that provide integration between the different themes and help to connect with students' lives and experiences. Students learning in different subject matters will connect to this big topic and help them answer the big question. This approach also provides more meaningful opportunities to learn academic language (Freeman, Freeman & Mercuri, 2005).

Language as pedagogical resource—students language/s are a resource for learning. Students access, construct, and communicate knowledge through language. This is especially important for bilingual learners who are still developing their second language. Understanding students' first language as a legitimate and necessary resource for learning is a step toward designing instruction that provides the best access to conceptual understanding (Musanti & Celedón-Pattichis, 2012).

Language demands—language demands relate to the complexity and variations of academic language across disciplines and the cognitive challenges it imposes on students to understand the content. When considering the language demands of a learning task, teachers need to pay attention to the receptive language skills (e.g., listening, reading) or the productive language skills (e.g., speaking, writing) that the students need to engage in and complete the task. Each content area might involve different language demands in terms of specific or technical vocabulary, grammatical features, the use of symbols, constructing explanations, critiquing reasoning of others, asking questions, identifying problems, and accessing different types of texts, among others.

Language domains—language includes different modalities related to the receptive function (listening and reading) and expressive function (speaking and writing).

Language proficiency—students' abilities to process language (through listening and reading) and to produce (through speaking and writing) language.

Linguistic complexity—"The organization, cohesion, and relationship between ideas expressed in the variety and kinds of sentences that make up different genres and text types in oral or written language at the discourse level" (WIDA Consortium, 2012, p. 114).

Preview/view/review—preview/view/review allows teachers to make the second language more comprehensible by giving an introduction, or preview, in the students' first language, then teaching the content in the second language using a number of techniques to make the input comprehensible, and finally reviewing after the lesson in the students' first languages (Freeman, Freeman & Mercuri, 2005; Mercuri, 2015).

Reading—reading is a complex process that involves making meaning from print.

Scaffolding—scaffolding refers to teaching that provides the support to build on students' previous experiences, skills, and knowledge through the use of strategies such as simplified language, teacher modeling, use of visuals and graphics, and hands-on learning to foster language development and student learning (WIDA Consortium, 2012).

Scientific literacy—is defined as the knowledge of science content and processes with an added ability to articulate and communicate inquiry procedures and science understandings orally and in writing. This definition of scientific literacy includes two abilities central to the development of scientific literacy: producing scientific explanations and argumentation both orally and in writing (Zembal-Saul, McNeill & Hershberger, 2013).

Social language—the everyday language use in interactions outside and inside school (WIDA Consortium, 2012).

Writing—writing is a form of communication that allows students to express ideas, events, and feelings, and to convey meaning through print.

REFERENCES

Celedón-Pattichis, S., & Musanti, S. I. (2013). Grade 1: "Let's suppose that...": Developing base-ten thinking with Latina/o emergent bilingual learners. In M. Gottlieb and G. Ernst-Slavit (Eds.), *Academic language in diverse classrooms: Promoting content and language learning. Grades K-2, Mathematics*. Thousand Oaks, CA: Corwin Press.

Chapin, S. H., O'Connor, C., & Anderson, N. C. (2009). *Classroom discussions: Using math talk to help students learn, grades K–6* (2nd Ed.). Sausalito, CA: Math Solutions.

Conley, M. (2012). *Content area literacy: Learners in context*. Boston, MA: Pearson.

Egbert, J. L., & Ernst-Slavit, G. (2010). Access to academics. Planning instruction for K-12 classrooms with ELLs. Boston, MA: Pearson.

Freeman, D., & Freeman, Y. (2009). *Academic language for English learners and struggling readers*. Portsmouth, NH: Heinemann.

Freeman, Y., Freeman, D., & Mercuri, S. (2005). *Dual language essentials for teachers and administrators.* Portsmouth, NH: Heinemann.

García, O., & Kleifgen, J. A. (2010). *Emergent bilinguals: Policies, programs, and practices for English language learners.* New York, NY: Teachers College Press.

Gee, J. P. (1999). *An introduction to discourse analysis: Theory and method.* New York: Routledge.

Gottlieb, M., & Ernest-Slavit, G. (2014). *Academic language in diverse classrooms: Definitions and contexts.* Thousand Oaks, CA: Corwin Press.

Harper, C., & de Jong, E. (2004), Misconceptions about teaching English-language learners. *Journal of Adolescent & Adult Literacy, 48,* 152–162. doi: 10.1598/JAAL.48.2.6.

Lee, O. (2005). Science education with English language learners. *Review of Educational Research, 75*(4), 491–530.

Mercuri, S., & Ebe, A. (2011). Developing academic language and content for emergent bilinguals through a science inquiry unit. *Journal of Multilingual Education Research, 2,* 81–102.

Moschkovich, J. N. (2007). Examining mathematical discourse practices. *For the Learning of Mathematics, 27*(1), 24–30.

Musanti, S. I., & Celedón-Pattichis, S. (2012) *"They need to know they can do math"* Reaching for equity through the native language in mathematics instruction with Spanish speaking students. *Journal of Bilingual Education Research & Instruction, 14*(1), 80–94.

National Governors Association Center for Best Practices (NGA) & Council of Chief State School Officers (CCSSO). (2010). *Common Core State Standards for English language arts and literacy in history/social studies, science, and technical subjects.* Washington, DC: Authors.

National Research Council. (2012). *A framework for k-12 science education: Practices, crosscutting concepts, and core ideas.* Washington DC: National Academies Press. Retrieved from http://www.nap.edu/catalog.php?record_id=13165.

NGSS Lead States. (2013). Next generation science standards: For states, by states. Retrieved from http://www.nextgenscience.org/.

Scarcella, R. (2003). *Academic English: A conceptual framework.* Santa Barbara: University of California Linguistic Minority Research Institute.

Schleppegrell, M. J. (2004). *The language of schooling: A functional linguistics perspective.* Mahwah, NJ: Lawrence Erlbaum Associates.

Schleppegrell, M. J., & Colombi, C. (2002). *Developing advanced literacy in first and second languages: Meaning with power.* Mahwah, NJ: Lawrence Erlbaum Associates.

Short, D., & Fitzsimmons, S. (2007). *Double the work: Challenges and solutions to acquiring language and academic literacy for adolescent English language learners—A report to Carnegie Corporation of New York.* Washington, DC: Alliance for Excellent Education.

Slavit, E., & Ernst-Slavit, G. (2007). Teaching mathematics and English to English language learners simultaneously. *Middle School Journal, 39*(2), 4–11.

Snow, C. (2010). Academic language and the challenge of reading for learning about science. *Science, 23*(328), 450–452.

Turner, E., Celedón-Pattichis, S., Marshall, M., & Tennison, A. (2009). "Fíjense amorcitos, les voy a contar una historia": The power of story to support solving and discussing mathematical problems with Latino/a kindergarten students. In D. Y. White and J. S. Spitzer (Eds.), *Mathematics for every student: Responding to diversity, grades pre-K-5* (pp. 23–41). Reston, VA: National Council of Teachers of Mathematics.

U.S. Department of Education, National Center for Education Statistics. (2015). *The Condition of Education 2015* (NCES 2015-144), English Language Learners.

WIDA Consortium. (2012). *Amplification of the English language development standards, Kindergarten–Grade 12*. Wisconsin: Author.

Willow, D., & Jackes, L. (1993). *Dentro de la Selva Tropical*. Watertwon, MA: Charlesbridge Publishing.

Zembal-Saul, C., McNeill, K., & Hershberger, K. (2013) *What's your evidence? Engaging K-5 students in constructing explanations in science*. Upper Saddle River, NJ: Pearson Education.

Chapter 9

Using Traditional Assessments to Effectively Inform Your Teaching

Nicole Barnes and Charity Dacey

One of the most difficult, exasperating, and least-liked aspects of teaching concerns the assessment and grading of students. If you have not encountered this difficulty during your observations or student teaching, you will soon. Assessments are the tools teachers use to gather information about their students' knowledge and skills. Like a master carpenter, teachers need lots of different tools and the expertise to select the right tools. Selecting the right tools helps to ensure that teachers make accurate inferences about students' thinking and their own instructional practices. When assessments are used in this way, they become useful for teachers.

There are many different types of assessments that can be used for different purposes. In this chapter we focus on how teachers create and use traditional assessments, which teachers rely on as a major part of their assessment system. *Traditional assessments* are the paper-and-pencil tests that were likely used in your own K–12 school experiences.

Learning how to construct and use traditional assessments to improve teaching is a valuable skill needed to be a successful teacher. Inevitably, when student learning is not taking place on the trajectory that teachers planned for or at the pace that they anticipated, teachers must ask which parts of this scenario are beyond my control and which parts am I responsible for? By creating assessments that give teachers insight into students' thinking and the nature of their misconceptions, teachers can begin to use the information from these assessments to adjust their planning and instruction in informed ways. This is referred to as *assessment-informed teaching*.

WHAT ARE TRADITIONAL ASSESSMENTS?

As mentioned above, traditional assessments are those paper-and-pencil tests that are widely used in K–12 schools and generally include a combination of selected-response and constructed-response items. *Selected-response items* require students to choose the correct answer from among the responses listed. Examples include true/false, matching, and multiple choice. Teachers use selected-response items because they involve a minimum amount of writing, allowing teachers to assess a broad range of content relatively quickly. *Constructed-response items* require students to construct or write their answer. Short-answer and essay items are considered constructed-response items.

Planning for a Traditional Assessment

Traditional assessments are useful when teachers trust that they are an accurate representation of students' thinking and understanding: we refer to this as "validity." The *Standards for Educational and Psychological Testing* (American Educational Research Association [AERA], American Psychological Association [APA], & National Councils on Measurement in Education [NCME], 2014) define validity as "the degree to which evidence and theory support the interpretations of test scores entailed by proposed uses of tests" (p. 9). Let's break this down together.

First, validity refers to the inferences that teachers conclude from assessment results. Therefore, the test itself is not valid or invalid. Instead, validity pertains to the interpretations that teachers draw about their students' performance and how that information is used. Teachers need to ensure that the inferences they make about students' knowledge and skills, and upon which they make assessment decisions, are accurate and fair.

Second, teachers' interpretations should be supported by evidence. The more evidence teachers have to support their interpretations, the greater is the validity. In other words, validity is a matter of degree and varies along a continuum depending on the quality and quantity of evidence. Third, when determining validity, teachers need to take into account the proposed use of the test. A test that is appropriate in one context or for one use may not be so for another. Let's consider an example:

> *Ms. Engles is a history teacher at Park Slope High School. She wants to use an assessment to determine which students should be enrolled in her advanced placement (AP) history course. Ms. Engles has noticed that students who read well are more likely to do better in her course. She decides to use a test of students' reading fluency to determine which students to enroll. Are Ms. Engles' actions appropriate?*

The correct answer is "no," because interpretations about students' readiness to advance to these higher-level courses would not be valid as this is not the proposed use of this test. Ms. Engles's interpretation of students' differences in reading fluency is not valid for determining which students should be enrolled in her AP history course.

A Tool to Enhance Validity

The *Table of Specifications* (TOS) is a tool that teachers use to enhance validity (Fives & DiDonato-Barnes, 2013). Figure 9.1 shows an example of a TOS used to construct a unit test on Native American culture for a fifth grade social studies class. This two-way chart aligns instructional objectives (Column B), the cognitive level at which each objective was taught (Columns F & G), and the amount of class time spent teaching that objective (Columns C & D) to determine the number and type of assessment items to include on a test (Notar, Zuelke, Wilson & Yunker, 2004).

There are two decisions that a teacher needs to make before constructing the TOS. First, she must determine the number of test items (questions) she wants to have on the test. Here, she has decided to include ten items. Second, the teacher needs to determine how many of those questions will be selected or constructed response.

In this example, the teacher has decided to include seven selected-response and three constructed-response items. The number of items and item type to include on any given test is a "professional decision made by the teacher based on the number of objectives in the unit, his/her understanding of the students, the class time allocated for testing, and the importance of the assessment" (Fives & DiDonato-Barnes, 2013, p. 4). Let's review Figure 9.1 together.

The information for Columns A, B, and C come directly from the teacher's lesson plans and notes. Column D is the percentage of total class time spent on each objective which is calculated by taking the minutes spent on the objective divided by the total minutes, multiplied by one hundred. To determine the number of test items that the teachers should use for *each* objective, he or she multiplies each value in column C by the total number of items on the test (recall that the teacher decided ahead of time to construct a ten-item test).

In some instances, the teacher's calculations do not result in whole numbers. When this happens the teacher rounds up or down to determine the number of test items to include. In Figure 9.1, there are two instances (i.e., Objective 7 and 10) in which the teacher rounded down to zero, meaning that she did not spend enough class time teaching that content for it to warrant an item on this test.

Fifth Grade Social Studies
Chapter 1: Native American Culture

A	B Instructional Objectives	C Time Spent on Topic (Mins)	D % of Class Time on Topic	E Number of Test Items per Topic	F Cognitive Level	G Item (#, Cognitive Level, and Type)
Day 1	1. Identify different dwellings for different Native American tribes and their locations	15	10.00%	1.00	Low	1 Low Level Multiple Choice
	2. Summarized how Native Americans used different weapons for hunting and defending	15	10.00%	1.00	Low	1 Low Level Short Answer
Day 2	3. Identify Crazy Horse Whitefield as a leader of the Oglala Lakota tribe	10	6.70%	.67 (round to 1)	Low	1 Low Level Multiple Choice
	4. Evaluate the impact of the Battle of Little Bighorn	20	13.30%	1.33 (round to 1)	High	1 High Level Multiple Choice
Day 3	5. Describe the importance of Native American symbols and pictographs	15	10.0%	1.00	Low	1 Low Level Multiple Choice
	6. List ways in which Native Americans used symbols in sand paintings	10	6.70%	.67 (round to 1)	Low	1 Low Level Short Answer
	7. Identify the contributions Native American symbols and pictographs to other art movements	5	3.30%	.33 (round to 0)	Low	None
Day 4	8. Interpret information in a bar graph.	15	10.00%	1.00	High	1 High Level Multiple Choice
	9. Gather and organize information using a bar graph.	15	10.00%	1.00	High	1 High Level Short Answer
Day 5	10. Identify the challenges Native Americans faced interacting with the American Government	5	3.30%	.33 (round to 0)	Low	? Your Turn
	11. Analyze the importance of the role different groups of Native American tribes played in American History	10	6.70%	.67 (round to 1)	High	? Your Turn
	12. Explain how different Native American tribes adapted to and made use of the resources available to them.	15	10.00%	1.00	High	? Your Turn
		150	100.00%	10		5

Figure 9.1   Fifth Grade Social Studies.

In Column F, the teacher classifies each objective according to the level of cognitive processes it requires of students. Building off the work of Benjamin Bloom, Anderson et al., (2001) suggested a six-level hierarchy of cognitive processing. The TOS presented in Figure 9.1 limits the levels of cognitive processing to high and low levels for practical reasons (see Kastberg, 2003). A teacher classifies an objective as low level if it requires students to engage in recall, identification, or comprehension. Alternately, objectives that require students to engage in application, analysis, evaluation, and synthesis necessitate higher-level cognitive processes and therefore are classified as high level.

Now it's time to pull everything together in Column G. After you have had a chance to review the first nine examples, try examples 10, 11, and 12 on your own.

Constructing Traditional Assessments that Yield Information about Student Thinking

Teachers decide whether to write their own assessment items or to use/adapt items that are provided by commercial publishers. Either way, items need to be written or rewritten in such a way as to elicit information about students' thinking that so they can be used to improve teaching. In this section, we present how to construct selected-response and constructed-response items that yield information about students' understanding. We start with selected-response items. Since multiple-choice items are the most used selected-response item, they will be the focus here.

Let's take a look at an example together from a high-school English assessment on Edgar Allan Poe's poetry.

Question: The Raven deals with

A. *a man reading a book*
B. *a killer crow who pecks out innocent victim's eyes*
C. *a man whose wife died and was buried by the seashore*
D. *all of these*

One thing you should notice about this item is that the answer choices do not provide the teacher with a range of information about students' thinking. Answer response A and B are far-fetched, obviously incorrect answers. If students select one of these answer choices the teacher can conclude that they do not understand the poem, but they don't provide the teacher more information about the nature of the students' misunderstanding. Moreover, once students rule out either A or B, they can automatically conclude that answer choice D is incorrect as well. As such, by process of elimination, students can select the correct answer choice (i.e., C), without actually knowing much about the poem, which is problematic.

Furthermore, given this limited information about students' thinking, there is not much the teacher can do in response to further *differentiate instruction*. He or she can reteach the poem to all those students who selected answer choices A, B, or D and allow those students who selected answer choice C to complete a different task. However, the answer choices do not differ enough to give the teacher information about students' misconceptions that would allow the former to tailor instruction in more meaningful ways. Let's take a look at an alternate example.

Question: The poem "The Dream" relies on its poetic structure and devices to provide a tone to the reader. Based on your understanding of the poem, which statement is most correct?

A. *The ABAB format and use of light imagery gives the poem an uplifting and positive tone.*

B. *The use of dark imagery and the repetition of the "long a" and "long e" sound give the poem a foreboding tone.*

C. *The move from dark to light imagery combined with ABAB structure gives the poem a hopeful tone.*

D. *The ABAB format and the repetition of the "long a" and "long e" sound give the poem a sad tone.*

Can you notice the difference between this item and the one presented previously? Here, the answer choices target misconceptions and common errors so they provide the teacher with information about students' developing learning. For example, if students select answer choice B, this suggests that they have a gross misunderstanding of the poem. If students choose answer choice D, it indicates that they have some understanding of the poem, but are missing a major point. If students select answer choice A, it reveals to the teacher that students have a good understanding of the poem, but were missing a minor (but important) point. Finally, if students choose answer choice C, this indicates to the teacher that students have a good understanding of the poem.

Note that none of the answer choices are obviously incorrect; instead, each answer choice provides the teacher with information about students' understanding, ranging from minor to major misconceptions. This detailed feedback gives the teacher key information about her students' understanding. On the basis of the results, she may decide to revisit aspects of her instruction, reteach particular concepts in nuanced ways, or provide additional practice to ensure that students have mastered all necessary skills.

While selected-response items require students to select their answer from a range of choices provided by the teacher, constructed-response items have students write or "construct" their own response to the prompt. Teachers typically use constructed-response items because they are conducive to measuring higher-order thinking skills (i.e., analysis, evaluation). However, it is important to remember that these items are just as likely as selected-response items to be lower level if they require lower level thinking processes such as recalling facts or summarizing information.

Tips on Ensuring Higher-Order Thinking

- First make sure the content is aligned with the learning goals and think through what evidence would help you conclude students have mastered the objectives.
- Avoid simple recall of facts from class; instead focus on ways to ensure students can manipulate their knowledge in order to provide an argument.
- Find similar but new material to be analyzed; ask students to apply concepts to something they have recently read or seen.
- Consider if students could benefit from trying to evaluate the same situation from a different perspective.
- Remember that selected-response items can be equally effective at assessing higher-order thinking skills if thoughtfully designed.
- Ask students to reflect on what they thought was the most important material covered and why.
- Keep wording as simple as possible and if you offer choices, make sure that all represent different ways to arrive at the same learning goals.
- Solicit a colleague to review the assessment for feedback.

Let's consider an example from an assessment given in a high-school music theory class.

Question: What is a triad?

This is a constructed-response item because students construct or write their answer. However, this item is lower level because it requires students only to define a term. Furthermore, it does not provide the teacher with a wealth of information to use to inform teaching or his/her understanding of student learning.

Let's consider an alternate example:

Question: Using chord grammar, analyze the piece of music below. Write the following information in the following order below each chord: (1) name each chord or triad (letter name and Roman numeral); (2) label each as a "chord" or "triad"; and (3) identify the inversion of each triad/chord and write the symbol for that inversion. Provide an explanation for your choices (Figure 9.2).

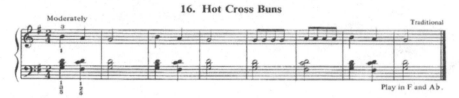

Figure 9.2 Hot Cross Buns.

In contrast, this item elicits student responses that allow the teacher to identify a range of misconceptions in students' thinking that can be used to adjust instruction. Some common misconceptions that this item may uncover are: (a) all chords are triads, (b) triads are not chords, (c) chords cannot include nonharmonic tones, (d) triads include nonharmonic tones, or (e) triads always have to stay in the root position only and cannot be re-voiced (inversions). Asking students to apply their understanding to new problems or to analyze novel situations and then explain their decisions gives the teacher access to students' thinking in ways that can be used to redesign instruction to target and correct misconceptions.

Tips on Writing Good Directions

Regardless of the types of items you include, well-constructed assessments include clear and specific directions. It is easy to take for granted that directions communicate the teacher's intentions, but when directions are unclear and vague, it can result in even the well-constructed items becoming misleading. Let's consider the following example:

• "Directions: Match the following items"

These directions are neither clear nor specific. Instead, let's consider:

• "Directions: Match the words from the column on the left to the phrase in the right hand column. There is only one correct answer. Not all phrases in the right hand column are applicable and options can only be used once."

These directions are both clear and specific and communicate to students exactly what they are supposed to do. Your turn, rewrite the following directions to be clear and specific:

• "List the following in chronological order."

USING TRADITIONAL ASSESSMENTS
TO INFORM TEACHING

Ms. Chung is a fifth grade math teacher at Hillcrest Academy. She is an experienced teacher who is well liked by students and her colleagues. During a typical unit, Ms. Chung assesses her students using a variety of tools. She assigns homework every day of the week. Students receive a check mark for completing the homework. Every Friday students have a mini quiz to assess their understanding of the material covered that week. There are also chapter tests and group projects that Ms. Chung administers monthly. She grades quizzes, tests, and projects and provides students with a numerical grade as feedback on their performance.

Ms. Chung uses a variety of assessments in her classroom. Although these assessments serve to inform students of their progress, Ms. Chung does not use this information to help her make instructional decisions about her teaching. Let's consider an alternate example.

Mr. Pfeffer is a relatively new art teacher at Roosevelt Middle School where students from eight surrounding area elementary schools feed into his sixth grade class. While he is familiar with some of the teachers and curriculum in the elementary schools, he would like to determine more specifically what his students know about impressionist paintings. He decides to use a KWL chart to determine what his student know (K), what they want to know (W), and what they have learned (L) about impressionist works of art. After reviewing students' responses, Mr. Pfeffer learned that some students had a very basic understanding, while others had a much greater level of exposure and knowledge of impressionist techniques. He also found varying levels of interest. As a result, Mr. Pfeffer adjusted his teaching plans on the basis of what he learned from this assessment.

In Mr. Pfeffer's class, assessments are not only a tool to provide students with information about their learning, they are also used by the teacher to track learning and then adjust instructional strategies in ways that *improve* student learning. Teachers who *use* information from assessments are continually engaged in a cycle of collecting student learning data, analyzing student work to understand their strengths and weaknesses, and making instructional adjustments to ensure optimal differentiation among learners.

Airasian (1996) calls this the "sizing up" of students' knowledge and skills at a particular moment in time. For example, if the majority of students have mastered a specific standard, the teacher may choose to use class time to delve into that standard further or explore an applied aspect of it. If, however, assessment data indicates that students need more instruction or more practice, then the teacher may decide to reteach certain elements or assign collaborative exercises targeting a particular skill.

In this way, assessment guides teachers as they establish priorities for teaching and learning and build upon students' strengthens and weaknesses. Rather than viewing assessment as separate from planning or divested from implementing instruction, together they form the cornerstone of effective teaching and learning. They are inextricably linked.

Students differ in their strengths, weaknesses, skills, knowledge, dispositions, attributes, and experiences. As a result, Tomlinson (2001) suggests that *differentiating instruction* is a way for teachers to positively build on student differences when planning lessons, instructional activities, and assessments. Let's return to the example of Mr. Pfeffer, the middle-school art teacher who assessed his students using a K-W-L chart. What did he do with this information?

On the basis of the information he learned from the KWL assessment, Mr. Pfeffer divided his class into collaborative groups on the basis of students' current skill level. Each group received the same task; however, Mr. Pfeffer provided varying levels of scaffolding depending on students' particular learning needs. In groups where students had prior knowledge of impressionist techniques, they completed the task more independently with Mr. Pfeffer checking in periodically. Alternately, in groups where students had little or no prior knowledge of impressionist techniques, Mr. Pfeffer reviewed basic concepts and provided greater scaffolding *as students applied the techniques to the learning activity.*

Differentiating instruction provided Mr. Pfeffer with ample time to work with groups of students as necessary and tailor feedback individually at critical milestones along the way.

Regardless of whether teachers are engaging in whole group, small group, or individual instruction, it is critical to assess what is the realistic amount of time *necessary* versus time *available* to engage in instruction. Quite often teachers discover that students need additional time to adequately complete teacher-planned activities in a meaningful way. It's helpful to remember that pacing is a skill that takes practice to develop over time: as a result, it is important to remember to model flexibility when it becomes clear that adjustments need to be made in organization and planning.

Tips on Determining Appropriate Pacing

- Determine what is the appropriate content of instruction for individual students.
- Ask yourself how much time is *necessary* to complete your planned instruction and then weigh this against a realistic assessment of what time is *available*.

- The "devil is in the details" and being prepared with all materials (including technological needs) can be the critical difference in ensuring that time is not wasted.
- Whatever time you have budgeted, *double it* in the beginning until an instructional cycle is complete, and you can check your notes to compare and adjust.
- Timers are a great way to keep both you and your students on track; so note the time anticipated in your lesson plans and ask a student to be the timekeeper.
- Transitions between activities are often one of the most challenging aspects of teaching for both novice and master teachers; so be clear about expectations and procedures.
- Ensure that you keep your format flexible enough that you can make adjustments along the way.

CONCLUSION

In this chapter, we reviewed how teachers use traditional assessments to inform their teaching practices and student learning, because teachers continue to rely on these types of assessments as a major portion of students' grades. As a novice teacher, you may want to jump right into thinking about how you will use assessments to inform your teaching. But remember garbage in, garbage out. Teachers need to exercise care and caution to ensure that they have planned for an assessment that will yield valid inferences about students' knowledge and skills, and that the assessment items are written to provide information about a range of student thinking processes. Assessments can be powerful tools to inform teaching and learning if they are well designed to yield information that can be trusted. Used in this way, assessments can be used to improve student learning and performance.

APPENDIX 1: SELF-ASSESSMENT QUESTIONS AND CHECKLIST

1. How can I ensure that my assessments result in valid inferences about student learning?
2. How do I know when to use a selected- or constructed-response item on my traditional assessment?
3. How do I know the difference between an assessment item that evaluates lower- and higher-level thinking skills?

4. How do I write a *selected-response assessment* item that measures higher-order thinking skills?
5. How do I write a *constructed-response assessment* item that measures higher-order thinking skills?
6. How do I use information from my assessments to inform my teaching (i.e., content, pace, strategies)?

CHECKLIST FOR SELF-ASSESSMENT

1. Did I use a table of specifications to design my assessment so that the information results in valid inferences about student learning?
   Yes _____ , If yes, provide evidence.
   No _____ , If no, suggest a revision.
2. Do I know how to determine whether to use a selected or constructed response item on my traditional assessment?
   Yes _____ , If yes, provide evidence.
   No _____ , If no, suggest a revision.
3. Can I write a selected-response item that assesses lower level thinking skills?
   Yes _____ , If yes, provide evidence.
   No _____ , If no, suggest a revision.
4. Can I write a selected-response item that assesses higher level thinking skills?
   Yes _____ , If yes, provide evidence.
   No _____ , If no, suggest a revision.
5. Can I write a constructed-response item that assesses lower level thinking skills?
   Yes _____ , If yes, provide evidence.
   No ——, If no, suggest a revision.
6. Can I write a constructed-response item that assesses higher level thinking skills?
   Yes _____ , If yes, provide evidence.
   No _____ , If no, suggest a revision.
7. Can I use information from my assessments to inform my teaching (i.e., content, pace, strategies)?
   Yes _____ , If yes, provide evidence.
   No _____ , If no, suggest a revision.

APPENDIX 2: EXTENSIONS FOR FURTHER EXPLORATION

1. For more information on rubrics, explore the various links on this website: https://www.brown.edu/about/administration/sheridan-center/ teaching-learning/assessing-student-learning/grading-criteria-rubrics.
2. For an in-depth breakdown of constructed-response assessments, visit this link and read about the different kinds of constructed-response assessments and view some of the examples provided. https://www.nagb.org/publications/frameworks/technology/2014-technology-framework/toc/ch_4/descriptions.html.
3. For more examples of selected-response assessments, explore this link. https://www.nagb.org/publications/frameworks/technology/2014-technology-framework/toc/ch_4/descriptions/descriptions1.html.
4. Read about how a middle-school teacher implemented differentiated instruction in her own classroom at: http://www.scholastic.com/teachers/article/8-lessons-learned-differentiating-instruction.
5. View this video for factors that affect validity. http://study.com/academy/lesson/validity-in-assessments-content-construct-predictive-validity.html.

GLOSSARY OF TERMS

Assessment-informed teaching—when teachers use information from assessments to adjust their planning and instruction in informed ways.

Traditional assessments—paper-and-pencil tests that are widely used in K–12 schools.

Selected-response assessment—items in which students choose the correct answer from among the responses listed. Examples include true/false, matching, and multiple choice.

Constructed-response assessment—items in which students construct or write their answer. Examples include short answers and essay items.

Validity—the degree to which evidence and theory support the interpretations of test scores entailed by proposed uses of tests.

Table of Specifications—a two-way chart that aligns instructional objectives, the cognitive level at which each objective was taught, and the amount of class time spent teaching that objective to determine the number and type of assessment items to include on a test.

Scaffolding—the tutelage or support a teacher provides a learner as he or she is engaged in a task.

Sizing up—a term by Airasian (1996) that refers to determining students' knowledge and skills at a particular moment in time.

Differentiating instruction—providing students with different learning activities or assessments on the basis of their readiness levels, interests, or learning preferences.

REFERENCES

Airasian, P.W., (1996). The Impact of the Taxonomy on Testing and Evaluation, Bloom's Taxonomy: A Forty-year retrospective. In Anderson, L.W., Sosniak, L.A. (Eds.), *History of education quarterly, 36*(1), 82–102.

American Educational Research Association, American Psychological Association, & National Council on Measurement in Education. (2014). *Standards for educational and psychological testing*. Washington, DC: American Educational Research Association.

Anderson, L. W., Krathwohl, D. R., Airasian, P. W., Cruikshank, K. A., Mayer, R. E., Pintrich, P. R., Raths, J., & Wittrock, M. C. (Eds.) (2001). *A taxonomy for learning, teaching, and assessing: A revision of Bloom's taxonomy of educational objectives*. New York: Harper Collins Publishers.

Fives, H., & DiDonato-Barnes, N. (2013). Classroom test construction: The power of a table of specifications. *Practical Assessment, Research, and Evaluation, 18*(3), 1–7.

Kastberg, S. (2003). Using Bloom's taxonomy as a framework for classroom assessment. *The Mathematics Teacher, 96*(6), 402–405.

Notar, C. E., Zuelke, D. C., Wilson, J. D., & Yunker, B. D. (2004). The table of specifications: Insuring accountability in teacher made tests. *Journal of Instructional Psychology, 31*(2), 115–129.

Tomlinson, C. (2001). *How to differentiate in mixed-ability classrooms* (2nd Ed.). Alexandria, VA: Association for Supervision & Curriculum Development.

Chapter 10

Authentic Performance Assessments

Charity Dacey and Nicole Barnes

As a new teacher, you may find it challenging to create assessments, but if you take the time to learn how to construct valid assessments on the basis of your learning goals, you can feel confident that your students have mastered what you planned for them to learn. While there are a variety of assessment types, this chapter will focus on how to plan and evaluate authentic performance assessments to monitor and assess students' knowledge, skills, and dispositions. During authentic performance assessments, students use their knowledge and skills to create products or performances on the basis of realistic problems (Barnes & Urbankowski, 2014).

These assessments promote students' academic development and cognitive engagement, which lead to developmental advances and lessen developmental gaps. Take a moment to reflect on the assessments you completed as part of your K–12 education. Then consider what kinds of assessments encouraged collaboration with peers, prompted deeper degrees of self-awareness and self-regulated learning, or challenged you to think outside the box?

WHAT ARE AUTHENTIC PERFORMANCE ASSESSMENTS?

Authentic performance assessments are tasks that assess students' knowledge and skills on problems that mirror real-life (or authentic) situations. On these tasks, students need to *demonstrate* their learning under realistic conditions. Some examples of authentic performance assessments include writing poetry in English class, playing an instrument in music class, or graphing results in a science lab. To help you determine if your assessment is an authentic performance assessment, review the key features presented in Table 10.1.

Table 10.1   Chun's (2010) Features of Authentic Performance Assessments

Feature	Description
1. Real World	Task instructions, prompt, or question describes a real-world problem or scenario to increase and sustain students' engagement by showing students the real-life value in the task that they are completing.
2. Promote Self-Regulation	Students employ self-regulatory processes such as evaluating research, proposing an action plan, and considering alternate ideas/strategies.
3. Require Higher-Order Thinking Skills	Student use higher-order thinking skills as they analyze, evaluate, and synthesize information.
4. Authentic	Students create an authentic product or performance such as a display, song, demonstration, or presentation.
5. Assessed with a Rubric	Teachers use a rubric to assess performance. Typically, the teacher provides students with the rubric ahead of time to encourage self- and peer assessment.

Next, let us consider an example:

Middle-school students in Ms. Horowitz's English class engage in structured debates to meet the following learning objectives: to (a) critically evaluate ideas and draw conclusions, (b) organize ideas effectively, (c) cultivate public speaking abilities, (d) interact with other students, and (e) develop leadership opportunities and group participation. Each team is assigned to argue a position on: Should animals be kept in zoos? To help students brainstorm their arguments and counterarguments they construct Argumentation Vee Diagrams (AVDs) [For more information, see Nussbaum and Schraw (2007)]. Students use AVDs to prepare for their debate. This includes writing an opening statement, rebuttal, a list of anticipated questions, and a summary/concluding statement. Ms. Horowitz evaluates students' performance using a rubric (Table 10.3).

This is an example of an authentic performance task. The assessment is real-world task. Furthermore, to complete the task, students need self-regulatory processes to plan, monitor, and evaluate their progress on preparing for their debate. Students also use higher-order thinking skills such as interpreting, connecting, analyzing, and considering a position from multiple perspectives to complete the task. Finally, Ms. Horowitz uses a clearly designed rubric to grade students' work.

PLANNING AUTHENTIC PERFORMANCE ASSESSMENTS

Planning for authentic performance assessments is like planning for any other type of assessment. First, teachers need to consider their learning goals or objectives to help them decide whether to use an authentic performance assessment and if so, what knowledge and skills the assessment should be used to measure. The inferences teachers draw about student learning are derived from students' progress on learning goals and objectives. A performance assessment is a tool a teacher can use to collect evidence to support the inferences they are making about student learning (Popham, 2013).

Teachers can use a table of specifications to ensure that their performance assessment is aligned with their learning goals/objectives. Second, remember that one of the features of authentic performance tasks is that they elicit and measure students' higher-order thinking skills such as analyzing, evaluating, synthesizing, and creating. Therefore, when designing an authentic performance assessment, teachers should prioritize objectives that require students to use higher-order cognitive processes and minimize using authentic performance tasks to assess lower-order objectives such as remembering or summarizing. For example, in a social studies unit, which of the following objectives would be best assessed using an authentic performance assessment?

Objective 1: Students summarize the causes of the civil war.

Objective 2: Students evaluate the effects of the Battles of Bull Run and Gettysburg on the outcome of the war.

Objective 2 requires students to engage in higher-order thinking processes to answer. It would be appropriate for a teacher to use an authentic performance task to assess students' performance on objective 2. Next, teachers can use authentic performance assessments to address *process-related* learning objectives. Process-related learning objectives focus on the activities, actions, or steps that the student takes to solve the problem or complete a task. Let us consider an example:

Mr. Ramirez is a social studies teacher at Eleanor Roosevelt High School. During a unit on World War I, he assigns the following assessment to his students: How would you go about writing a research paper on the role women played during the war? How would you identify sources? How would you determine if the sources were credible? How would you organize your research? How would you structure your argument?

In this essay, the teacher asks students to reflect on HOW they would identify, sort, prioritize, and use evidence from research to write a research paper. This is an example of a process-oriented task. As students describe the methods and procedures they would use to approach this task, it provides opportunities for the teacher to provide feedback to students on their strategy use and to suggest strategies that may be more effective. Including process-related goals into authentic performance assessments helps ensure that assessments go beyond *what* students know and provide information about *how* students think through a complex problem or task. Finally, teachers can use authentic performance assessments to encourage self- and peer assessment.

Tips for Ensuring Opportunities for Both Peer and Self-Review

- First, make a plan to document student learning progress that is visible, concrete, and accessible to you and to students in the classroom (think of this as a master filing system to ensure that everything has a place).
- Determine from your learning goal the purpose of what you want students to describe:
  - their *thinking* related to concepts and examples (cognitive or metacognitive);
  - their *understanding* of a process, skill, or procedure;
  - their *application* of the concepts or process.
- Ask students to reflect on the areas in which they did, or did not, meet the criteria on the rubric for assignments and how they could improve in the future in clear, measurable ways.
- Remember that students can help you keep track: checklists, charts, and anecdotal records that are collected and filed systematically help you to monitor effectively and assess student progress.
- Consider if students could benefit from evaluating each other's work as part of the learning process.

EVALUATING AN AUTHENTIC PERFORMANCE ASSESSMENT

A *rubric* is a tool teachers employ to assess students' performance using clearly defined criteria to evaluate the quality of student work. Complex learning necessitates the use of complex assessments to evaluate that learning. One challenge is for teachers to learn how to design rubrics that can capture that level of complexity. Gallavan (2009) explains that rubrics that include multiple evaluative criteria and clear descriptors of student learning across proficiency levels (sometimes referred to as *benchmarks*; for example, proficient, satisfactory, and unsatisfactory) are appropriate to assess authentic performance assessments.

There are three kinds of rubrics: *task specific, hypergeneral,* and *skill focused.* Task-specific rubrics measure performance on a particular task. The evaluative criteria and descriptors are particular to the specific elements of that assignment (an example of a task-specific rubric is presented later in the

Table 10.2 Hypergeneral Rubric used in Social Studies

Effective 3	Adequate 2	Unsatisfactory 1
Student can articulate a sequence of events.	Sequence of events is articulated and mostly accurate.	Sequence of events is not articulated or is inaccurate.
Student articulates a complete and cohesive rationale.	Student articulates a rationale, but it is either not complete or cohesive.	Student does not offer a rationale.
Sentences are complete and grammatically correct	Sentences are mostly complete and grammatically correct.	Most sentences are incomplete and are not grammatically correct.

chapter). Hypergeneral rubrics include generic evaluative criteria and descriptors, and so they are general enough to be used to evaluate a range of tasks/assignments. Below is an example of a hypergeneral rubric used in social studies class (Table 10.2).

Lastly, skill-focused rubrics include evaluative criteria that are skill based and descriptors that describe varying levels of performance for those skills. An example of a skill-focused rubric is presented later in this chapter. Selecting which type of rubric to use is a decision made by the teacher depending on her learning goals and objectives. "Tips for Building A Good Rubric," below, was designed for the purpose of helping the novice teacher create a good rubric.

Tips for Building a Good Rubric

- First, check if the purpose matches what you are looking for to assess student learning.
- List the variables to be evaluated and try to avoid having more than four to five. Provide detailed description of criteria.
- Craft-specific descriptions of features to represent each item on the continuum.
- To avoid student misunderstanding, focus on providing clear performance levels and be specific about what constitutes mastery at each particular level.
- Remember to make your rubric developmentally appropriate.
- Some teachers like to use rating labels to distinguish between low and high levels that correspond to description labels.
- Think carefully about how your rubric can provide students with the detailed and valuable feedback they need about their performance to improve.
- Consider following the 3 X 3 X 3 model in the beginning (three levels are first identified, three criteria are identified, and three varieties of evidence are delineated).
- Share your rubric with students and families in advance of using them.

SCORING BIASES IN THE CLASSROOM

One of the challenges of using rubrics is that scoring can be subjective even with the most defined and specific criteria and descriptors. Teachers, like all of us, are susceptible to biases. Some of the common types of biases are discussed next.

Generosity error refers to the tendency to see only the positive in student work. For example, Mrs. Lamos (a math teacher) asks students to calculate the number of rods needed to construct a bridge and to explain how they arrived at their answer. If Mrs. Lamos gave a student full credit for correctly calculating the number of rods needed to construct the bridge even though her explanation for how to solve the problem was incorrect, this would be an instance of generosity error. In contrast, *severity error* refers to the tendency to underrate students' work (Popham, 2013).

If Mrs. Lamos awarded this same student no credit for correctly calculating the number of rods needed to construct the bridge because her explanation for how to solve the problem was incorrect, this would be an instance of severity error. Lastly, the *halo effect* describes a bias in which teachers let their overall impression of a student cloud their assessment of the student's performance. Thus, if Mrs. Lamos graded a student's paper more leniently because she has a positive impression of this student, then this would be an example of the halo effect.

Luckily, there are strategies that teachers can use to reduce their biases. First, grading using a well-designed rubric will help ensure that students' work is evaluated systematically and consistently. Second, the teacher can read a couple of papers first to determine the range in students' answers and to get a sense of the overall quality of the work. Another strategy a teacher can use is to de-identify student work. Instead of writing their names on the top of the paper, students write them on the back or use a number or letter code in place of their name.

AUTHENTIC PERFORMANCE ASSESSMENTS IN THE CONTENT AREAS

Next, we present examples of authentic performance assessments in each of the content areas. As you read the task instructions (assignment) for each performance assessment, think about whether it includes the five features that Chun (2010) proposed (i.e., real world, promotes self-regulation, requires higher-order of thinking skills, authentic, assessed with a rubric). You may also find it useful to use the checklist below while reading the examples. Moreover, this checklist can serve as a tool to help you create your own authentic performance assessments in the future.

CHECKLIST FOR PERFORMANCE ASSESSMENTS IN YOUR UNIT/LESSON

1. Is the assessment appropriately aligned the learning goals and appropriate for your grade level?
   Yes _____ No _____
   Explain _____

2. Does your assessment reflect a real world task?
   Yes _____ No _____
   Explain _____

3. Does your assessment promote students' self-regulation?
   Yes _____ No _____
   Explain _____

4. Does your assessment promote students to engage higher order thinking?
   Yes _____ No_____
   Explain _____

5. Does your assessment have students construct an authentic product or performance?
   Yes _____ No _____
   Explain _____

6. Did you create a rubric to assess student performance on this assessment?
   Yes _____ No _____
   Explain _____

7. Did you take actions to reduce scoring biases?
   Yes _____ No _____
   Explain _____

Example #1: Elementary Physical Education Class

Mr. Phalen is a P-6 health and physical education teacher at Malcolm X Elementary School. He is interested in assessing students' basketball skills. He tells students that NBA players need to practice these skills as part of their weekly training/drill routines. Mr. Phalen sets up his gymnasium to reflect the kinds of tasks that NBA players would likely encounter in practice, which include a dribbling station. Students are evaluated using the following skill-focused rubric to assess their performance.

This is an example of an authentic performance task that specifically breaks down the components of each fundamental skill necessary to learn to dribble

Table 10.3   Skill Focused Rubric

Rubric			
Stance	*Effective* *3*	*Adequate* *2*	*Unsatisfactory* *1*
1. Student flexes at the knees, bends forward, and keeps weight in the forward stride position.	Student always flexes at the knees, bends forward and keeps weight in the forward stride position.	Student flexes at the knees, bends forward and keeps weight in the forward stride position sometimes.	Student does not flex at the knees, bend forward or keep weight in the forward stride position.
2. Student keeps head up; does not look at the ball.	Student is not looking at the ball but scans the court.	Student sometimes looks up to scan.	Student's eyes are on the ball.
Grip			
1. Student keeps wrist limp and dribbles with the finger pads versus palm.	Student is able to push ball down with fingertips.	Student is able to push ball down with fingertips.	Student slaps the ball down.
2. Student uses the nondribbling arm for defense and avoids double dribbling.	Student never commits a double dribble violation.	Student commits double dribble violation once or twice.	Student commits double dribble violation three or more times.
Dribble			
1. Student does not bounce the ball higher than the waist.	Student dribbles the ball at waist level consistently.	Student dribbles the ball at waist level but not consistently.	Student dribbles the ball at multiple levels.
2. Student dribbles the ball through the cone course with control.	Student can dribble through the entire course with control.	Student can dribble through most of the course with control.	Student cannot dribble through the course with control.
3. Student can use both hands equally when dribbling.	Student can use both hands while dribbling with equal measure.	Student can dribble with dominant hand but not as well with nondominant hand.	Student cannot dribble with nondominant hand.

successfully. The scenario is realistic and reflects an authentic task in which students must think about and pay particular attention to their stance, their grip, and the aspects of how everything involved must come together to effectively dribble in a basketball game. While engaged in this activity, students use self-regulated learning strategies such as self-monitoring their movements (e.g., when dribbling, students need to focus on keeping their heads up and avoid looking at the ball). This is an example of a skill-focused rubric that includes both evaluative criteria that are skill based and descriptors that define varying levels of performance for those skills.

Depending on students' performance, Mr. Phalen would then determine if he needs to reteach, provide more practice time to master the aspects of dribbling, or if he could move ahead to the other objectives in the unit. Regardless of the content area being taught, breaking down the components of each skill as illustrated in this example is very important. Likewise, collecting such performance data is only valuable if you take these data, examine it, and then utilize it to make instructional adjustments on the basis of these data. Regardless of what content area you are teaching, this reflective aspect of examining your practice will ensure that you have tackled the most essential piece of ensuring that students have mastered your learning objectives.

Example #2: High-School History

Mrs. DeLorenzo is a high-school history teacher at San Bernardino Regional high school who uses the following authentic performance assessment for her unit on the Civil War: Imagine that it is 1858, and you are an educated citizen living in Illinois. Because you are interested in politics and always keep yourself well informed, you make a special trip to hear Abraham Lincoln and Stephen Douglas debating during their campaigns for the Senate seat representing Illinois. Now imagine it is present day. Write an editorial for the local newspaper in which you identify three issues discussed in the debate that are still affecting our nation today. Be sure to include (1) the general concepts and specific facts (at least two) you know about American history, and especially what you know about the history of the Civil War; and (2) what you learned from the debates you watched (at least one reference to each) that is applicable today. Your performance will be evaluated using a rubric.

This is an example of an authentic performance assessment as evidenced by the ways in which Mrs. DeLorenzo's assignment adheres to Chun's (2010) features of authentic tasks. The prompt describes a scenario that increases students' engagement with a real-word scenario. Likewise, this task promotes students' use of higher-order thinking skills by requiring them to synthesize information. Mrs. DeLorenzo reviews students' responses to this task and uses these data to determine their understanding. In this way, she is able to identify areas where particular students need more scaffolding and assistance as they write their essays.

Example #3: Middle-School Science

Mr. Blake teaches seventh grade science at Forest Hills Middle School. He uses authentic performance assessments to engage students in tasks that have them act as scientists. Consider this example of an authentic performance assessment he used in his class.

You and the other members of your middle-school science club have decided to raise plants as a fundraiser for the class trip at the end of the year. The plants have to be healthy in order to compete with those sold at the local greenhouse. To do so, you need to act like scientists and investigate which substance (water, light, or fertilizer) would have the greatest effect on plant growth. As part of your investigation:

1. Write a question that could be the basis of your investigation.
2. Write the hypothesis for this investigation.
3. Define the independent and dependent variable.
4. Describe at least three essential steps in the procedure needed to conduct your new valid experiment about speeding up plant growth. The procedure must be written so that other scientists could clearly follow your instructions and successfully replicate your experiment.

Mr. Blake's performance assessment meets the features outlined by Chun (2010). First, the task instructions describe a real-world problem or scenario. Further, this task is developmentally appropriate for engaging middle-school students and promotes opportunities for social skill growth. Second, students employ self-regulatory processes by proposing an action plan that describes at least three essential steps in the procedure needed to conduct a valid experiment about speeding up plant growth, and they must consider alternate strategies. In this way, the assessment challenges students to use higher-order thinking skills as they analyze, evaluate, and synthesize information. Fourth, students represent data using tables and multiline graphs that Mr. Blake grades using a rubric.

SELF-REFLECTION QUESTIONS

1. What are the features of an authentic performance assessment?
2. Compare and contrast the three different kinds of rubrics used to assess authentic performance assessments.
3. Describe some techniques you can apply to plan for using an authentic performance assessment in your classroom.

4. Create an authentic performance task in your content area.
5. What are some of the benefits of using authentic performance assessments as part of your overall assessment plan?

CONCLUSION

Performance assessments are effective ways of having students create a product or performance and/or demonstrate a process. While they tend to require extended written and oral responses and encompass complex problems, the time and effort invested in designing them almost always pay off for you and your students. Although it can be daunting to construct performance assessments and clearly defined rubrics, it is important to consider all of the benefits when done effectively, like increased academic and social outcomes.

In this chapter, you learned how to plan and evaluate an authentic performance assessment and how to construct a rubric that captures the complexity of the knowledge and skills that students will demonstrate on that assessment. You also learned about Chun's five features of an authentic performance assessment which are that tasks should be real-world problems, promote self-regulation, require a higher order of thinking, create an authentic product, and assess with a rubric. Now that you have obtained these skills and knowledge, you can incorporate authentic performance assessment into your overall assessment portfolio. Please refer to the self-reflection above to assess your performance.

GLOSSARY OF TERMS

Assessment—a plethora of methods used to identify students' knowledge, skills, and dispositions at any stage of learning (prior, during, or post).

Authentic assessment—when teachers assess students' skills and abilities in real-life situations.

Formative assessment—when teachers monitor student learning during the lesson activities and provide feedback to students to make adjustments that improve student learning or teaching.

Generosity error—during scoring the tendency to see only the positive in student work.

Halo effect—during scoring the tendency to let one's overall impression of a student cloud one's assessment of the student's performance.

Learning goals—aims, objectives, targets, or outcomes.

Performance assessment—any form of assessment teachers use to measure how students perform a demonstration of their learning.

Proficiency level—detailed criteria information provided on a rubric for determining the degree of quality when evaluating performance.

Rubric—a scoring guide that provides detailed information (including proficiency levels) about performance criteria for evaluating student work.

Scoring guide—a tool that articulates the criteria by which student work will be evaluated.

Self-assessment—a process during formative assessment in which students evaluate their own work.

REFERENCES

Airasian, P. W. (2005). *Classroom assessment: Concepts and application.* New York, NY: McGraw-Hill.

Barnes, N. C., & Urbankowski, D. (2014). Planning, implementing, and assessing an authentic performance task in middle grades classrooms. *Middle School Journal, 45*(5), 17–24.

Chun, M. (2010). Taking teaching to (performance) task: Linking pedagogical and assessment practices. *Change: The Magazine of Higher Learning, 42*(2), 22–29.

Gallavan, N. (2009). *Developing performance-based assessments grades 6–12.* Thousand Oaks, CA: Corwin Press.

Green, S. K., & Johnson, R. L. (2010). *Assessment is essential.* New York, NY: McGraw-Hill.

Oosterhof, A. (1999). *Developing and using classroom assessments* (4th ed.). Old Tappan, NJ: Prentice-Hall.

Novak, J. D. (1993). How do we learn our lesson? *The Science Teacher, 60*(3), 51–55.

Nussbaum, E. M., & Schraw, G. (2007). Promoting argument-counterargument integration in students' writing. *Journal of Experimental Education, 76*(1), 59–92.

Popham, W. J. (2013). *Classroom Assessment: What Teachers Need to Know* (7th ed). New York, NY: Pearson.

Witte, R. H. (2012). *Classroom assessment for teachers.* New York, NY: McGraw-Hill.

Chapter 11

Making "IT" Meaningful

Intentional Technology Integration through TPACK

Christopher Luke

The Matrix is everywhere. It is all around us. Even now, in this very room. You can see it when you look out your window or when you turn on your television. You can feel it when you go to work... when you go to church... when you pay your taxes.

—Morpheus, *The Matrix*, 1999

Some fifteen years ago, while reviewing and evaluating the educational landscape in the United States, Prensky (2001) noted,

Today's students have not just changed incrementally from those of the past, nor simply changed their slang, clothes, body adornments, or styles, as has happened between generations previously. A really big discontinuity has taken place. One might even call it a "singularity"—an event which changes things so fundamentally that there is absolutely no going back. This so-called "singularity" is the arrival and rapid dissemination of digital technology in the last decades of the 20th century. (p. 1)

That explosive and nearly exponential growth of technology and computing power over the last few decades has increased, resulting in a technologically infused and technologically dependent society. In the twenty-first century, technology impacts nearly every aspect of life: work, leisure, entertainment, relationships, politics, religion, culture, and education. Millennial students have never known a time without videogames, iPads, computers, the Internet, and social media. Prensky refers to these students who have grown up with computers and Internet as "digital natives." For a majority of today's students in the United States, technology is the common denominator, and it is ubiquitous.

Of course, education systems and teaching professionals have attempted to keep pace and increase *technology infusion* (the extent to which technology permeates an organization, system, or framework) in schools by leveraging various technologies for pedagogical purposes and adapting teacher education processes. Nearly all preservice teacher candidates are required to complete coursework that emphasizes instructional technology. Additionally, advanced degree programs (e.g., educational technology; learning, design, and technology; instructional technology, etc.) are readily available at most universities either online or face-to-face.

Furthermore, state and national technology standards (e.g., ISTE) outline what students, teachers, and administrators should know and be able to do with technology. Many schools across the country have adopted *1:1 technology*, providing each student with a laptop or tablet in order to individualize learning, increase independence, and extend learning opportunities outside of the school setting. Technology is clearly and deeply embedded within teaching more now than ever before.

The speed of innovation and the proliferation of new technologies, however, make the successful integration of technology with teaching a daunting task, especially when theory and practice collide in actual classroom settings. A simple Google search for "how to teach with technology" yields a staggering seventy-one million results, illustrating the breadth of resources available for novice practitioners while simultaneously drowning them in data. The intent of this chapter is to focus novice teachers and mentors on critical concepts related to instructional technology that will make technology integration meaningful and manageable.

THE AFFORDANCES OF INSTRUCTIONAL TECHNOLOGY

Perhaps the first question that needs to be addressed is, "Why should novice teachers incorporate technology into their teaching?" In its simplest form, *instructional technology* is combining education and technology to enhance instruction and improve student learning outcomes. Access to technology alone, however, does not necessarily lead to better-quality teaching.

Vignette #1—Rise of the Machines

Mike is a twenty-four-year old eighth grade social studies teacher in his second year of teaching. Classroom management is a constant concern for Mike, and he struggles with keeping students engaged and on-task. Much of his time is spent monitoring and addressing misbehavior and discipline issues in the classroom. Since it is already difficult to maintain order in the classroom,

Mike is concerned that 1:1 iPads will simply be another way for students to be off-task. To minimize distractions, students are required to put their iPads on a shelf at the back of the room each day as they enter. Mike has discovered, though, that many of the students want to use the iPads more, and he has developed a system that allows students to earn "free time" on the iPads for good behavior or when their in-class work is done. During "free time" students are rarely involved with anything related to social studies; instead, they spend their time playing mobile video games, checking email, listening to music, and browsing popular topics.

This vignette illustrates a number of unfortunate yet common occurrences related to instructional technology. In some classrooms, teachers avoid incorporating technology because it has the potential to distract students. As with other tools, activities, and approaches, teachers can avoid many difficulties by outlining consistent expectations for technology use, clearly explaining appropriate and inappropriate technology use, implementing equitable policies and procedures, and providing modeling and scaffolding for students, especially during their initial attempts with instructional technology.

It is also disconcerting that Mike uses access to the iPads either as a reward or as a punishment for student behavior. Ideally, and whenever possible, access to learning opportunities and learning resources should be available to all students. This particular reward system, though, may actually be part of a larger issue—that the instructor does not have a clear understanding of the myriad ways that technology can be successfully utilized in his classroom to support and promote learning.

Tips for Teachers

In order to have a better understanding of your own technology skills,

- locate and complete a self-assessment of technology skills online and
- meet with your school's technology specialist and complete an evaluation.

To expand your technology skills,

- identify and evaluate (ten) online resources for teaching with technology in your content area. Focus on sites that allow connections and interactions with other teaching professionals both face-to-face and online.
- form a cohort at your school with other teachers who are interested in exploring ways to teach with technology and
- identify (three) unfamiliar technologies or applications and complete a K-W-L chart for each one. Specific content areas may want to consider the following as a starting point:

Language Arts—sites that promote collaboration, dialogue, and critique; venues for digital storytelling; venues for sharing student work with larger audiences

Math—online math tutors; games and tablet applications that emphasize mathematics in action; sites that showcase math in the real world

Science—sites that show scientific experiments in action; resources for technological or scientific inventions

Social Studies—resources for community outreach and community involvement; collaborative blogs and wikis or e-pals

Art—access to a wide variety of artists and genres available through online galleries; videos demonstrating techniques and principles of art

Physical Education—technologies that focus on demonstrations and simulations of various exercises and sports; visual representations and 3-D models.

Two decades ago, during the infancy of the Internet and before the proliferation of computers, Bush (1997) outlined four fundamental uses for instructional technology for language learning (which also apply to other disciplines), including: (a) a means to deliver or support the delivery of instruction, (b) a tool to enhance the educational process, (c) a medium to access information, and (d) a medium to facilitate communication. More recently, Lynch (2015) listed collaboration, information gathering, remote learning, and teacher preparation as ways that digital technology has changed the K–12 environment.

Using those fundamentals as a reference point, and considering more current technological advances, the following "affordances of technology" list highlights additional possibilities for instructional technology across all content areas and disciplines.

Affordances of Technology

1. A means to deliver or support the delivery of instruction
   a. creating online, hybrid, and remote courses (i.e., *e-learning* that focuses on web-based environments that allow students and teachers to interact through computer and Internet technologies outside the school setting and without time constraints);
   b. using multimedia and social media platforms;
   c. exploring virtual reality and advanced simulations;
   d. allowing students to generate and construct knowledge;
   e. increasing students' autonomy;
   f. addressing multiple intelligences and different learning styles and preferences

2. A tool to enhance the educational process
   a. *Gamification* (using theories and principles of game design to increase student motivation);
   b. individualizing and differentiating instruction;
   c. addressing student diversity;
   d. working with students with special needs;
   e. engaging and motivating students;
   f. assessing learning efficiently;
   g. engaging students, parents, administrators, and other stakeholders
3. A medium to access information
   a. broadening the classroom to a global perspective;
   b. accessing information instantly;
   c. incorporating educational applications;
   d. facilitating mobile and on-demand access to information;
4. A medium to facilitate communication
   a. improving student-teacher engagement;
   b. enhancing student-student interaction;
   c. supporting student-community relationships;
   d. establishing student-expert connections;
   e. fostering a community of learners.

It is important to remember that technology is not intended to replace teachers; rather, it is to enhance teaching and learning processes. In their work, Pitler, Hubbell, and Kuhn (2012) provide specific technology applications to guide teachers in three main areas: (a) creating the environment for learning, (b) helping students develop understanding, and (c) helping students extend and apply knowledge. While the context and resources of the specific classroom will to some degree determine the potential technology applications, the only real limitations are the knowledge and skill of the instructor.

Tips for Teachers

- Identify one specific technology (e.g., hardware, equipment, application, program, website, etc.) that can be matched with each of the affordances on the technology list. As an example, a blog could be used to enhance student-student interaction.
- Review your own current technology use. Categorize each use of technology within the framework of the "affordances of technology" list.
- Identify (five) apps designed for educational purposes in your content area. Evaluate which of the "affordances of technology" could be addressed with each app. Assess the overall quality and utility of the apps.

Intentional Technology Integration

With all the demands, responsibilities, and stresses placed on novice teachers, how can they become more versed in and adept at teaching with technology? In order to successfully teach with technology, educators must have content knowledge, pedagogical knowledge, and technological knowledge.

Vignette #2—The Force Awakens

Brittney is a twenty-two-year-old high-school art teacher in her first year of teaching. She has a solid foundation in instructional technology and is adept at social media. When she designs lessons, she is intentional about aligning learning outcomes and activities with appropriate technologies. Brittney attempts to use technology to broaden her students' understanding of art and to engage them in creative learning experiences. Her students are currently working on a digital art project to be showcased at a local community library. Students have explored a variety of online digital art galleries individually, in small groups, and as a whole class and held discussions and critiques on a class blog. Brittney also arranged for a prominent artist to speak with the class and to demonstrate her painting techniques in real time to the students via a videoconference. The students are now creating their own surrealist paintings. When the paintings are finished, the students will use their smart phones to take pictures of their art and create short narrative videos explaining each piece. They will then pull everything together on their laptops using presentation software. The final art showcase is scheduled to run at the local library on a large screen television for two weeks. Brittney has noticed that the students are very excited about and invested in this project, particularly the opportunities to speak with an art expert and to share their work with an authentic audience at the library.

As teachers plan to integrate technology, they must be careful to not focus too heavily on the innovativeness or novelty of the technology itself and lose sight of the pedagogical value it may afford. Additionally, for many novice teachers who have grown up with technology, there may be a sense of familiarity or comfort that could lead to overconfidence. Knowing about technology and knowing how to use it are not the same as knowing how to effectively teach with technology. In this vignette, Brittney provides a solid example of leveraging technology appropriately and aligning specific technologies with learning goals and activities.

The technologies she incorporates directly facilitate learning, but they are not the focus of the project and they do not dominate the curriculum. Internet technology has allowed Brittany's students access to a wide range of art resources and a venue to share their thoughts and opinions with others. It also enabled them to connect with an expert artist in the real world. Finally, the authenticity of the project, coupled with an authentic venue and an authentic audience for their own work, has resulted in greater student motivation and engagement. In this case, technology has supported a successful learning experience.

The *Technological Pedagogical Content Knowledge* (TPACK) framework illustrates how the aforementioned knowledge bases intersect and overlap, with the most successful teaching and learning episodes occurring at the center, in the area designated as technological pedagogical content knowledge (Figure 11.1). Koehler and Mishra (2009) explain TPACK as follows:

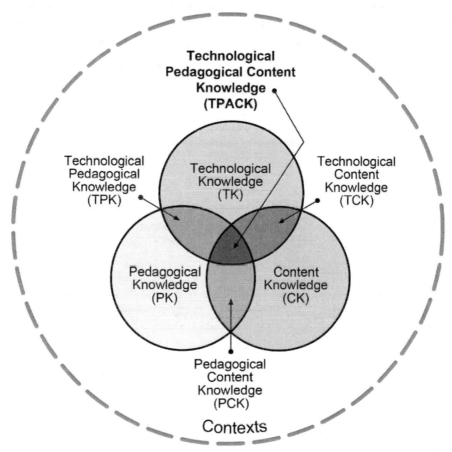

Figure 11.1   TPACK Framework. *Source:* From http://tpack.org. Reproduced by permission of the publisher, © 2012 by tpack.org.

Underlying truly meaningful and deeply skilled teaching with technology, TPACK is different from knowledge of all three concepts individually. Instead, TPACK is the basis of effective teaching with technology, requiring an understanding of the representation of concepts using technologies; pedagogical techniques that use technologies in constructive ways to teach content; knowledge of what makes concepts difficult or easy to learn and how technology can help redress some of the problems that students face; knowledge of students' prior knowledge and theories of epistemology; and knowledge of how technologies can be used to build on existing knowledge to develop new epistemologies or strengthen old ones. (p. 66)

In essence, to successfully teach with technology, teachers must know *when* to use the technology, *how* to use the technology, and *why* to use the technology. Critically, this technological knowledge must be coupled with pedagogical knowledge (how to teach) and content knowledge (what to teach). Everything in the lesson plan and teaching episode must be well thought out and *intentional*, including the technology. Intentionality, or doing things in a way that is planned, intended, and designed, is sometimes left out when it comes to incorporating technology into teaching. One way for novice teachers to increase intentionality, though, is to utilize the process of backward design in their planning.

Backward design (Wiggins & McTighe, 1998, 2005) is a framework for lesson, unit, and course design that starts with what students should know and be able to do (learning outcomes) and works backward from those end goals to the instructional activities and accompanying standards. There are three phases involved in the process: (a) identify desired results, (b) determine acceptable evidence, and (c) plan learning experiences and instruction. In the first phase, the teacher considers what students should know and be able to do at the end of instruction. Generally, there is an emphasis on key principles, theories, concepts, and themes.

Next, during the second planning phase, the teacher determines the acceptable evidence of learning (both processes and products). This might include a variety and range of formal and informal assessment measures that allow students to demonstrate their learning. Finally, in the third phase, the teacher selects appropriate teaching methods, develops specific instructional sequences and activities, and gathers necessary resources. During this last phase, the teacher engages in a reflective process that takes into account the knowledge, skills, styles, and preferences of the students that will impact the success of the lesson or unit.

Instructional technology most often enters the backward design process in the third phase. Once the desired results have been established and the acceptable evidence identified, it makes sense for the teacher to consider utilizing technology to enhance instruction and meet learning outcomes. It should be noted, though, that technology (in most instances) is not the focus of the lesson and that many lessons are successful without any technology.

Vignette #3—The Fast and the Furious

Carmen is a forty-two-year-old divorced mother of two. She is a native Spanish speaker in her first year of teaching. The high school has a 1:1 technology initiative and all students have laptop computers. Carmen had an instructional technology course in college, but she has shied away from using much technology in her own classes. On Thursday, the principal is coming to conduct a teaching evaluation. Although she has done very little with the laptops, Carmen decides to create a lesson that is heavily based on technology since she knows that is what the principal is expecting. She creates a PowerPoint presentation that contains all her lecture notes and grammar drills. She also finds two YouTube videos that cover the same information and a website with vocabulary flashcards and grammar exercises. Thursday arrives and the lesson does not go well. During the PowerPoint presentation the students are not really engaged in the learning process, and they do not pay attention to the videos either. The last few moments of class are fast and furious as Carmen darts around the room getting students to the website, helping them find the correct activities, explaining how to do the activities online, attempting to troubleshoot multiple technology issues, and keeping students on-task. The bell interrupts the chaos and the students hurriedly pack up their laptops and books. As the students leave the room, Carmen wonders silently to herself if they learned anything from the lesson that day.

Merely using technology for the sake of using technology is a pitfall that will often lead to ineffective and inefficient instruction. Although Carmen identified various technologies and incorporated them into the lesson, the planning and preparation were lacking. The technology was not connected with learning outcomes and not blended logically into activities. In this vignette, nothing that Carmen did was inherently wrong or bad, but much of it was ineffective and could be improved. For example, she could have incorporated authentic cultural materials into the PowerPoint presentation and the capabilities of PowerPoint could also have been used to highlight relationships and connections for the grammar points.

With some preparation and forethought, the time on the website could have met individual needs if Carmen had previously identified students' weaknesses and then directed them to specific resources and activities online to address those needs. Additionally, the teacher could have modeled how to navigate and use the website with the whole class before having students work independently. For the YouTube videos, previewing activities (e.g., hypothesizing, predicting, discussing), while-viewing activities (e.g., skimming and scanning), and post-viewing activities (e.g., synthesis, application, extension) could have strengthened instruction.

When considering the use of technology, teachers are encouraged to be intentional in their review, selection, and implementation. Consider the following Guidelines for Technology Integration.

Guidelines for Technology Integration

1. Develop learning goals before selecting a technology (backward design).
2. Determine possible technologies for the lesson or unit.
3. Identify and understand the benefits, strengths, and limitations of each technology.
4. Assess teacher familiarity and skill with the technology.
5. Assess student familiarity and skill with the technology.
6. Ensure that necessary resources are available and functioning properly.
7. Make logical and intentional connections among the technology, pedagogy, and content.
8. Select technology that contributes to and advances learning outcomes.
9. Integrate technology to support learning.
10. Evaluate the technology use during and after teaching.

As novice teachers apply these guidelines they will find that technology integration can be more manageable for them and more meaningful for their students.

Tips for Teachers

• Conduct a survey that gauges and assesses your students' interest in, skill with, and knowledge of various technologies. This survey could be an instrument from your school or district, an online instrument, or something made specifically for your students.
• Design a unit of instruction (preferably three to five days) on the basis of backward design principles, the affordances of technology list, and the guidelines for technology integration. Incorporate multiple technologies every day to enhance instruction and improve student learning outcomes. Share your unit with a colleague and have her observe you teaching the unit to provide feedback.
• Create a professional development plan for the next three to five years that deals specifically with instructional technology integration. Identify key resources, plan activities for growth and development, and set specific, attainable goals with concrete deadlines and accountability procedures.

CHECKLIST FOR TEACHING WITH TECHNOLOGY

When considering ways to integrate technology with teaching, the following checklist can aid in determining if a particular technology should be used for instruction or not.

1. Does the technology connect with learning outcomes?
   Yes _____ No _____
   Provide some concrete evidence _____

2. Will the technology help students learn the material?
   Yes _____ No _____
   Provide some concrete evidence _____

3. Will the technology detract from the learning experience in any way?
   Yes _____ No _____
   Provide some concrete evidence _____

4. Is the technology in the lesson integral to gaining new knowledge?
   Yes _____ No _____
   Provide some concrete evidence _____

5. Is technology used merely for the sake of using technology?
   Yes _____ No _____
   Provide some concrete evidence _____

6. Is there a logical and intentional match between the technology and instructional activities?
   Yes _____ No _____
   Provide some concrete evidence _____

7. Are students familiar with the technology used in the lesson/activity?
   Yes _____ No _____
   Provide some concrete evidence _____

8. Do students have the necessary skills to use the technology effectively?
   Yes _____ No _____
   Provide some concrete evidence _____

9. Do I, as the teacher, have the necessary knowledge and skills to use the technology effectively?
   Yes _____ No _____
   Provide some concrete evidence _____

Continued

10. Are the necessary resources available and functioning properly?
    Yes _____ No _____
    Provide some concrete evidence _____
11. Are there back-up plans in case the technology fails?
    Yes _____ No _____
    Provide some concrete evidence _____
12. Is this the best use of classroom instructional time?
    Yes _____ No _____
    Provide some concrete evidence _____

Questions for Self-Reflection and Self-Evaluation

A key element in the reflective process is *self-efficacy*, or the belief of the teacher (coupled with skill and confidence) in her own ability to successfully integrate technology to positively enhance teaching and learning. Teachers, particularly novice teachers, must regularly and conscientiously engage in a self-reflection process. Not only do teachers need to evaluate their self-efficacy as it relates to teaching with technology, but they need to evaluate and reflect holistically as well.

The reflective process should lead teachers to the very core of their philosophy and methodology as they attempt to incorporate "best practices" instruction into their own repertoire. Effective self-reflection helps teachers make commitments. It leads to concrete professional development and personal growth. The following self-reflection questions may be useful in examining appropriate technology usage.

1. When it comes to instructional technology, how do I become a more effective *risk-taker* (i.e., someone who is willing to experiment, take calculated risks, analyze successes, and learn from failures)?
2. What can I do to expand my knowledge and ability to use technology for meaningful learning?
3. What is my confidence level (and skill level) in utilizing technology effectively as a teaching tool? What is holding me back from learning and adapting new technologies in my classroom? How can I become more proficient at self-directing and self-teaching as new technologies emerge?
4. How is my TPACK informing my current teaching approaches? What evidence is there of positive effects on student learning?
5. What are my areas of strength in teaching with technology? What are areas that need improvement?
6. What specific plans to I have in place to improve the way I teach with technology?

CONCLUSION

There are three overarching and connected themes that run through this chapter. First, millennial students comprise an incredibly diverse student population that is constantly changing and evolving. Today's students are more connected, more wired, and more tech savvy than ever before in history. Our students need and deserve teachers who can address their interests, learning styles, learning preferences, and educational and life goals. Second, the pace of technology development continues to increase, and technology will continue to influence nearly every facet of daily living, including education

It is imperative that our larger education systems find ways to embrace, harness, and adapt technology to benefit all instructors and learners. Third, individual teachers must take control of and responsibility for their learning in order to improve their instructional technology skills. At the local level, more teachers who can effectively and meaningfully teach with technology are needed in every school and across every discipline.

The promises and potential for utilizing technology to enhance education are nearly limitless. For novice teachers, the options available, coupled with ongoing innovations, may seem daunting, but successful integration of technology into teaching is both feasible and desirable. Teachers can start with an honest and thorough self-evaluation of their current teaching abilities and their current technology skills. As part of this reflective process teachers should identify barriers to their own growth and development. They can then formulate and implement a professional development plan with measurable and manageable goals that will enable them to become more technologically proficient.

By utilizing the vignettes, frameworks, guidelines, evaluations, and models in this chapter, teachers will be better able to make informed, intentional, and pedagogically sound decisions about how, when, and why to incorporate instructional technology into their own methods, classrooms, and curricula. As teachers review the affordances of technology, expand their technological pedagogical content knowledge, and implement the processes of backward design, they will become more adept at successfully integrating technology into their teaching. These teachers can make "IT" meaningful for themselves and for their students. This infusion of technology will help to invigorate teachers, students, and classrooms and will ultimately lead to greater student motivation and improved learning outcomes.

APPENDIX 1: EXTENSION MATERIALS

Nearly limitless resources are available online and in print that deal with the topic of teaching with technology. A few examples are included below, but

novice teachers and mentors are encouraged to conduct their own searches to
locate additional materials that align with their teaching styles, philosophies,
and classroom contexts. The vision and mission statements included here
provide context and come directly from the official websites for each organization. Other excellent sources for teaching with technology include the
state department of education and national and state organizations for specific
content areas and disciplines.

1. George Lucas Educational Foundation—www.edutopia.org

   Our vision is of a new world of learning based on the compelling truth that
   improving education is the key to the survival of the human race. It's a world
   of creativity, inspiration and ambition informed by real-world evidence and
   experience. It's a world where students become lifelong learners and develop
   21st-century skills. It's a world where innovation is the rule, not the exception.
   It's a world where schools provide rigorous project-based learning, social-
   emotional learning, and access to new technology. It's a world where students
   and parents, teachers and administrators, policy makers and the people they
   serve are all empowered with a shared vision to change education for the better.

2. 4Teachers.org Teach with Technology—www.4teachers.org

   4Teachers.org works to help you integrate technology into your classroom
   by offering online tools and resources. This site helps teachers locate online
   resources such as ready-to-use Web lessons, quizzes, rubrics and classroom
   calendars. There are also tools for student use. Discover valuable professional
   development resources addressing issues such as equity, ELL, technology
   planning, and at-risk or special-needs students.

3. International Society for Technology in Education (ISTE)—www.iste.org

   The vision of ISTE is a world where all learners thrive, achieve and contribute.
   As the creator and steward of the definitive education technology standards,
   our mission is to empower learners to flourish in a connected world by cultivating a passionate professional learning community, linking educators and
   partners, leveraging knowledge and expertise, advocating for strategic policies,
   and continually improving learning and teaching.

4. Office of Educational Technology (OET)—tech.ed.gov

   The mission of the Office of Educational Technology (OET) is to provide
   leadership for transforming education through the power of technology. OET
   develops national educational technology policy and establishes the vision for
   how technology can be used to support learning. OET supports the President's
   and Secretary's priorities by:
   • Promoting equity of access by ensuring all learners are connected to broad-
     band Internet.

- Supporting Future Ready educators and a robust ecosystem of entrepreneurs and innovators.
- Leading cutting-edge research in learning analytics and data to provide new types of evidence and customize and improve learning.

5. Technological Pedagogical Content Knowledge (TPACK)—tpack.org

Technological Pedagogical Content Knowledge (TPACK) attempts to identify the nature of knowledge required by teachers for technology integration in their teaching, while addressing the complex, multifaceted and situated nature of teacher knowledge.

6. Association for Supervision & Curriculum Development—ascd.org

ASCD is a global community dedicated to excellence in learning, teaching, and leading. ASCD's innovative solutions promote the success of each child.

GLOSSARY OF TERMS

1:1 technology—providing every student with a laptop or tablet in order to (a) individualize learning, (b) increase student independence and self-motivation, and (c) extend learning opportunities beyond the physical classroom and school.

Backward design—a framework for lesson, unit, and course design that starts with what students should know and be able to do (learning outcomes) and works backward from those end goals to the instructional activities and accompanying standards. Three phases are involved in the process: (a) identify desired results, (b) determine acceptable evidence, and (c) plan learning experiences and instruction.

Digital native—a person born or raised during a time period when there is significant digital technology and rapid technological advancement which often results in familiarity with computers and Internet from a young age.

E-learning—a web-based environment that enables students and teachers to interact through computer and Internet technologies outside the physical and temporal restrictions of a regular classroom.

Gamification—using theories and principles of game design to increase student motivation and enhance engagement in learning processes and activities.

Instructional technology—combining education and technology to enhance instruction and improve student learning outcomes.

Intentional technology integration—knowing when to use the technology, how to use the technology, and why to use the technology for educational purposes; using instructional technology with intention and purpose.

Risk-taker—a teacher who is willing to experiment with technology, take calculated risks, analyze successes, and learn from failures.

Self-efficacy—the belief of the teacher (coupled with skill and confidence) in her or his own ability to successfully integrate technology into teaching to positively enhance teaching and learning.

Technological pedagogical content knowledge—the basis of effective teaching with technology, requiring an understanding of the representation of concepts using technologies; pedagogical techniques that use technologies in constructive ways to teach content; knowledge of what makes concepts difficult or easy to learn and how technology can help redress some of the problems that students face; awareness of students' prior knowledge and theories of epistemology; and knowledge of how technologies can be used to build on existing knowledge to develop new epistemologies or strengthen old ones.

Technology infusion—the extent to which technology permeates an organization, system, or framework. In the context of this chapter, technology infusion could refer to something as broad as the U.S. educational system or as narrow as a school district or an individual teacher's methodology.

REFERENCES

Abrams, J. J., Burk, B., Kennedy, K. (Producers), & Abrams, J. J. (Director). (2015). *Star wars: Episode VII—The force awakens* [Motion picture]. United States: Lucasfilm.

Bush, M. D. (1997). Implementing technology for language learning. In M. D. Bush and R. M. Terry (Eds.), *Technology-enhanced language learning* (pp. 287–349). Lincolnwood, IL: National Textbook Company.

Deyle, M., Kassar, M., Lieberman, H., Michaels, J. B., Vajna, A. G., Wilson, C. (Producers), & Mostow, J. (Director). (2003). *Terminator 3: Rise of the machines* [Motion picture]. United States: C-2 Pictures.

Koehler, M. J., & Mishra, P. (2009). What is technological pedagogical content knowledge? *Contemporary Issues in Technology and Teacher Education, 9*(1), 60–70.

Lynch, M. (2015, May 20). 4 ways digital tech has changed K-12 learning. *The Journal: Transforming Education through Technology*. Retrieved February 26, 2016, from https://thejournal.com/articles/2015/05/20/4-ways-digital-tech-has-changed-k12-learning.aspx.

Moritz, N. H. (Producer), & Cohen, R. (Director). (2001). *The fast and the furious* [Motion picture]. United States: Universal Pictures.

Pitler, H., Hubbell, E. R., & Kuhn, M. (2012). *Using technology with classroom instruction that works* (2nd Ed.). Alexandria, VA: Association for Supervision and Curriculum.

Prensky, M. (2001). Digital natives, digital immigrants. *On the Horizon, 9*(5), 1–6.

Silver, J. (Producer), Wachowski, A., & Wachowski, L. (Directors). (1999). *The matrix* [Motion picture]. United States: Warner Bros.

TPACK.org (2011, May 13). What is TPACK? *TPACK.org*. Retrieved February 26, 2016, from tpack.org.

Wiggins, G., & McTighe, J. (1998). *Understanding by design*. Alexandria, VA: Association for Supervision and Curriculum Development.

Wiggins, G., & McTighe, J. (2005). *Understanding by design* (Expanded 2nd Ed.). Alexandria, VA: Association for Supervision and Curriculum Development.

Section III

PEDAGOGICAL DECISIONS

Chapter 12

No One Left Behind

Grouping Students with Intention, Skill, and Responsiveness

David Lee Keiser and Anne Lockwood

It really boils down to this: that all life is interrelated. We are all caught in an inescapable network of mutuality, tied into a single garment of destiny. Whatever affects one destiny, affects all indirectly.

—Martin Luther King, Jr. (1967)

The purpose of this chapter is to provide novice teachers with *strategies for student grouping*. The strategies we offer will help teachers face the challenge of student-group work and will help provide perspective on the purposes and particularities of the art and science of student grouping. To *scaffold*, we offer the template of intention, skill, and responsiveness. Simply said, novice teachers need to be clear in their intentions for group work, skillful in their execution of said group work, and responsive to the cognitive and social and emotional needs of their class.

This chapter addresses the challenge and necessity of effective student grouping to develop caring and compassionate classroom communities. It introduces novice teachers to various forms of student groupings, focusing on the particular challenges of grouping with diverse student populations. The chapter contributes to a toolkit for novice teachers, particularly for those dealing with the subjects of English, social studies, and physical education.

Teachers make many pedagogical decisions every day, and most days some of these decisions involve grouping students, both in their own classes and even at times during school duties and other activities requiring teachers to supervise many students. There exist unlimited possibilities for student grouping given the nature of human difference and school organization. From the proverbial morning school bus until after-school activities, students are by design purposefully grouped as a matter of practice. For example, an educator

215

might ask oneself whether a *homogeneous grouping* arrangement or one in which groups are made up of students with similar ability levels best meets the learning needs of one's students, or if perhaps the activity might be more effective with a *heterogeneous grouping* arrangement, in which students of varying ability levels work collaboratively. When giving specific examples of grouping strategies, the chapter will focus upon or highlight the broad content areas of English/language arts, social studies, and physical education.

GROUPING STUDENTS WITH INTENTION, SKILL, AND RESPONSIVENESS

When novice teachers face their students, sometimes the basic exchange of information, often conveyed from a stance in the front of the room, is challenging enough. Despite recent renewed attention to the lecture method, most twenty-first-century educators rely, or should rely, on a variety of pedagogical methods. And yet, the essentials of good teaching, including the ability to group students when needed, often stem from this basic stance—the ability to convey information. To use a martial arts analogy, in the African Brazilian dance of Capoeira, the basic movement is called the ginga (jin-ga). Basically, it is a rocking of the body to a broad strutting in place. All movements emanate from it, but you rarely see it in a game between two players; it is simply the basic stance.

In teaching, you should rarely see a teacher standing and lecturing to a group of silent students, but in some ways it is the basic stance—conveying information to students receptive to learning and to being taught. And again, even in this basic stance, the purpose of the activity, the skill brought to it, and the ability to assess its effectiveness are required. Just as the martial artist knows that he or she practices in order to be able to perform and to learn from his or her performance, the teacher knows that he or she purposefully chose a particular activity and will reflect upon its effectiveness after its completion.

Our contribution transcends the basic stance and reorients novice teachers to the work of student grouping. This chapter addresses the importance of intention in the broad sense of mindful teaching and particularly as it applies to student grouping and includes salient suggestions for grouping strategies.

Being responsive to student needs, including during group work, requires novice teachers to prepare, document, reflect, and revise their assumptions and practices inherent in how and why they group students.

The chapter begins with a brief overview of student grouping, intended not as a comprehensive historical review, but rather as a grounding invitation. We move from a conceptual discussion to practical implications and suggestions for practice and offer scaffolding for novice teachers to implement ideas in the classroom. It includes a short glossary of terms, questions, and prompts for self-reflection. The chapter will be anchored in several places with notes from the field to illustrate salient concepts addressed herein. We will conclude with a challenge to novice teachers to embrace the complexity that arises from human interactions within schools and classrooms.

Remember *ISR: Intention, Skill, and Responsiveness*; keeping all three concepts at the forefront of student-group work will increase possibilities of success and minimize the beautiful confusion that can result. Below are sample questions intended to highlight this framework, as well as written descriptions of each:

Intention: Be sure you are clear in your intention for the grouping. What would make the activity successful? Are there identifiable goals for the activity? What is its purpose? How does it fit into a lesson plan, an instructional unit, and/or the course curriculum?

Skill: How did you go about planning the group work activity? Did you keep in mind your students' cognitive, behavioral, and social-emotional needs and competencies? Did you prepare for multiple reactions and responses? Did your activity reflect appropriate learning goals for the students? Were your goals aligned with state or other standards?

Responsiveness: During and after the activity, were you able to assess and perhaps amend the activity to make it more responsive? Were you able to assess what worked, what didn't, and how you would do it differently the next time? Was there an appropriate conclusion to the activity? Was there an evaluative component?

The idea of formally setting an *intention* for a given activity, or sitting, is a practice associated with mindful teaching, or *contemplative pedagogy*. An intention is gentler than a learning aim or goal and may be empowering for students and constructive for groups if positive intentions are shared or made public. For example, the concept is important for teachers before group work; that is, "I intend to engage my students in a synopsis/enactment/simulation/ role play of the shooting of the Kent State Four." Or, "I intend to introduce the game of volleyball so that all students participate." Or, "I intend to cover the first half of Romeo and Juliet, and prepare students to see the stylized cinematic version by Baz Luhrmann."

By *skill* we mean the facility and suasion through which the teacher uses group work in the classroom. This includes attention to various forms of diversities in the classroom, content knowledge, pedagogical content knowledge, and the ability to create a safe and engaging classroom community. Much skill is accrued through years in classrooms and planning and executing activities, including trials and errors.

We appreciate that at the end of the day all teaching strategies need to have evaluative components or at least mechanisms to assess whether or not the strategy met its purposes. We also understand that group work, by its nature, elicits various forms of *responsiveness*; the mindful teacher foretells the need to be responsive to student needs and includes a reflective and evaluative component to learning activities like group work.

CONCEPTUAL FRAMEWORK

We concur with Starko (2010) that at least four points undergird the rationale behind student groupings: it can increase student autonomy, provide opportunities for developing intrinsic motivation, increase student motivation, and provide *cooperative learning* opportunities, which is to say, teachers should group with intention, rather than as a default pedagogical strategy. When done skillfully, student-group work can increase participation, commitment, and comprehensive as students learn to learn from one another as well as from the teacher.

Several distinctions must be made between simple group work and the more complex but desirable process of cooperative learning. Cooperative learning, according to Parkay and Stanford (2007), is marked by the following characteristics: students work in small groups of four to six students; projects require that students help one another; groups may compete against one another; and finally group members' talents, interests, and abilities are utilized to meet common group goals. The practice of grouping students is more than that of crowd control or classroom management. When implemented with intention, skill, and responsiveness, student-grouping practices can result in meaningful and fruitful engagement in the classroom.

Cooperative learning may be understood through the lens of developmental psychologist Lev Vygotsky's (1978) Zone of Proximal Development, or "the distance between the actual developmental level as determined by independent problem solving and the level of potential development as determined through problem solving under adult guidance or in collaboration with more knowledgeable others" (p. 86). In other words, it is the space in which higher cognitive functions can be developed in learners through collaboration or cooperative learning with others.

For many students, group work can lead to deeper engagement, to increased socialization, and perhaps most importantly, to meaningful learning that is relatable to the world beyond the classroom. The mindful teacher who adopts cooperative learning practices should take care to promote and maintain authentic learning tasks that are meaningful to the students and are aligned with their goals as well as those of the teacher.

In short, students must understand the "why" of what they are being asked to do (Parkay and Stanford, 2007) and how those tasks have meaning outside the four walls of their classroom. Such an understanding can enable students to perceive schooling not as an obstacle but rather as a foundation from which they can participate fully in a democratic society. Group work also presents an opportunity for the mindful teacher to engage in *culturally responsive teaching* that draws upon the students' beliefs and prior experiences and knowledge. In addition, some of the benefits listed above, such as deeper engagement and increased socialization, serve social and emotional learning goals as well.

In the increasingly diverse classrooms of the twenty-first century, the term "cooperative learning" can overlap with the concept of *differentiated instruction*. This refers to the practice of individualizing instruction to meet each student's unique learning needs to maximize his or her potential for success: in simpler terms, treating a class of learners not as one whole to be taught in one way (i.e., the aforementioned whole-class instruction), but as a composite with many distinct parts, each with distinct learning needs. Similarly, teachers must recognize that within the differentiated classroom, there exist various learning styles and multiple intelligences, and that students both learn and demonstrate their learning in different ways. Tomlinson (1999) describes differentiated instruction as a type of complex instruction that allows for equity of learning for all students within a culturally, linguistically, and academically heterogeneous classroom. Thus, with the adoption of thoughtful and intentional cooperative learning practices, the teacher can ensure that no child gets left behind.

The collaboration inherent in cooperative learning, at least in the United States, may be examined as a microcosm of the democratic society in which learners must (ideally) one day take part. For most students in public schools, the need to get along with others is essential, and teachers are uniquely positioned to both create and maintain learning environments that nurture compassionate connections. Intentional, skillful, and responsive student grouping can scaffold students' development of social-emotional learning and intelligence, and, in doing so, prepare them for diversity and engagement outside the classroom as well.

What's a Teacher to Do?

Recent developments in U.S. educational practice have produced a marked shift from the ideal of teacher-centered instruction to one of student-centered learning. This shift is reflected in the increasing salience of cooperative learning research and cooperative learning practices in the classroom, and subsequently, a shift from *whole group (or class) instruction*, in which the teacher presents the same material in the same way to an entire group or class, to *small group or individualized instruction*, in which learning activities are tailored to meet each student's learning needs. Though cooperative learning is, by definition, student centered, the teacher's fundamental role in ensuring the success of cooperative learning cannot be overstated.

Said another way, "An effective cooperative group is not a collection of kids thrown together for a brief activity" (Slavin, 2014). That is, unless mindful consideration of the learning activity and the learning goal(s) leads the teacher to adopt such a random grouping arrangement, in which students are grouped by chance, perhaps by their physical placement in the classroom (proximal grouping), or by calling off numbers. But, as Slavin suggests, the teacher's role in student-centered cooperative learning does not end with the decision to adopt it. Even the best-intentioned teachers need strategies to use, to fall back upon, and to share with others. Here are some strategies to help prepare for, implement, and reflect upon student-group work. Regardless of strategy, some guiding questions include:

Visualizing: Try to imagine what a successful activity would look and feel like. What will need to be covered? How will students interact with one another? What does the flow of the activity look like? How will it end?

Planning: Write or type the steps for your given activity and the sequence of events; that is, "Students will read a poem alone, discuss it with the peer sitting next to them, and be prepared to share their insights with the larger group." If materials such as chart paper or markers are needed, be sure to have them in ample supply.

Facilitating: How is the activity directed? Are you the facilitator or do students share the role? Within each group of students, are roles delineated? Is there a reporter or discussion leader?

Evaluating: How will you know if the activity is effective in what you intended? Is there a formative assessment within the unit? Will you ask students directly for feedback, in writing or verbally?

Specific forms of groupings are now described, with a chart to follow.

By Ability with Attention to Differentiated Learning and/or Multiple Intelligences

Building on the work of Gardner (1999) and the acceptance of *multiple intelligences theory*, mindful teachers look for ways to elucidate and demonstrate the variegated forms of intelligence in any given classroom. How can one teacher meet the needs of heterogeneous classrooms in which multiple intelligences and ability levels necessitate differentiated instruction? With the intention to cultivate students' individual strengths and intelligences, a teacher might facilitate a group activity in which students of varying abilities, talents, etc. work together on a project that requires creativity and multiple points of view to meet the desired objective.

A 2004 study illustrates the concept of grouping students according to varying levels of ability. In it, the researchers observed a fifteen-year-old student (Ed) playing basketball with a group of eight- to ten-year-old students. Ed did not shoot the basketball himself, but rather constantly dribbled the ball to prevent the group of younger students from stealing it. He then passed the ball to his single teammate (Daryl, an eight-year-old), so Daryl could shoot the basketball. During this activity, Ed exercised his dribbling skills, while his younger counterparts exercised their speed and agility, as well as their shooting skills. The physical gains to be made by the children in learning environments in which they are allowed to cultivate physical skills with more capable "others" are evident, but as the researchers suggest, the gains to be made by the adolescents are just as meaningful; included among them are nurturance, creativity, and leadership (Gray and Feldman, 2004).

By Proximity or Random with All in Mind

Students are grouped according to chance alone. Students might work with those positioned closest to them within the classroom or call off numbers. Teachers utilize this strategy commonly during shorter group work activities such as think-pair-share or shared free writing and when it is less important for students to move about the room for the given activity.

With English Language Learners in Mind

Grouping students with ELLs in mind requires the teacher to be mindful of the ratio of non-native to native speakers within one group. Pairing or grouping non-native with native speakers is a strategy that might be utilized to the mutual benefit of both: native speakers might provide scaffolding for the non-native speakers, and in doing so, further strengthen their own learning, while non-native speakers benefit from the language experiences of the native speakers. Unless there are specific linguistic goals to having all ELLs together, as a rule it is better not to segregate ELLs, but rather include and incorporate them throughout the student groups.

With Students with Exceptional Learning Needs in Mind

Due to the variegated nature of exceptionality, our comments here will be general and a bit brief. In the inclusive classroom, in which students labeled as having special needs work with students who are not, every attempt should be made to include students irrespective of label, level of cognitive function, or behavior. That being written, teachers will need to make judgments on the basis of particular situations, that is, the ability of other students to fully interact, the match of the activity and the particular child, and the numerous social-emotional variables always present, but often elevated in inclusive classrooms. In physical education, adaptive physical education is a strong field and many teachers are prepared explicitly to plan for, include, and reflect upon students with exceptionalities seen and unseen. The physical and often emotional needs of students may preclude full participation, but not full inclusion.

Jigsaw

According to Aronson and Patnoe (1997), a jigsaw construction allows the role of the expert in the classroom to shift from teacher to students. Students work in groups of five to six and become resources for each other. A jigsaw grouping arrangement requires that each group, ideally one of four to six groups in an average-sized class (Aronson & Patnoe, 1997), is set a task that contributes to the overall goals of a lesson. As its name suggests, each individual piece is necessary to complete the whole. In pairs or groups, students work together on a particular task; then, all pairs/groups come together as a class to piece together, as it were, their respective components.

In one jigsaw model, each small-group member becomes an "expert" on his or her group task/material and then shares his or her expertise with the "experts" of other groups (i.e., during this second stage, each new group contains within it different "experts" so that all content is covered for each student within the new group). Roberts and Van Deusen-MacLeod (2015) offer a "Source-Focused Jigsaw" strategy to analyze source documents related to Paul Revere. In small groups, students analyze a particular source and use a chart to fill in information obtained from the source (Interesting Facts, Family Life, Type of Source, etc.). After this stage, students separate into other groups, with each student in the new group having previously analyzed a different source. The now "expert" students share their information with all members of the group, allowing each of them to fill in his or her chart comparing the sources.

Station Teaching or Learning Centers

Students work in small groups, each of which is set a particular task, or provided with a learning activity, that is focused on a particular part of the lesson. Students rotate through each of the stations so that upon completion, their exposure to the lesson is comprehensive. The particularities depend on the subject and grade level, with attention to variables such as mobility and sequencing.

Often, elementary classrooms have stations that become part of the room, easy to access if not permanently displayed. Secondary classrooms, often used for many different classes of students, can also use station teaching, albeit at times more temporarily, that is, stations set up to prep a debate for government class might be then repurposed for the next, economics class, or the like. In any case, learning stations or centers need to be well organized with needed materials and seats, and ample space should come between them, so that students are reminded that each center or station has a distinct purpose (Table 12.1).

Table 12.1   Selected Groupings (for English/Language Arts, Social Studies, and Health/PE)

Grouping	English/Language Arts	Social Studies	Physical Education
By Ability with Attention to Differentiated Learning and/or Multiple Intelligences	Media usage, performance, publication Students work together to create a film, which would require them to contribute in varying ways.	Debates, reenactments, simulation Students of varying abilities, talents, etc. can stage debates, reenactments, or simulations relating to current or historical events by rotating roles throughout.	Structured and unstructured activities Scrimmages, less competitive games, group and individual instruction.
By Proximity or Random with All in Mind	Think-pair-share Students begin by brainstorming ideas on their own and then share thoughts and ideas with a partner. Finally, each pair shares with the class as a whole. In an ELA class, this strategy might be used to initiate discussion of a text.	Think-pair-share Students begin by brainstorming ideas on their own and then share thoughts and ideas with a partner. Finally, each pair shares with the class as a whole. In a social studies class, this strategy might be used to initiate discussion of figures, source documents, critical events, etc.	Equity rules Students use rules that ensure participation by all; that is, three passes before shooting in basketball, or hitting it over the net in volleyball, or hitting around the order, rather than after three outs, etc.
With English Language Learners in Mind	Scaffolding Non-native-speaking students are paired with native-speaking students to learn new vocabulary words before practicing integrating new vocabulary independently.	Scaffolding Strong active readers are paired with less active readers to read closely and analyze primary source documents.	Scaffolding Teacher demonstrates activities as well as discusses them; vocabulary cards and lists as needed.

(Continued)

Table 12.1 Selected Groupings (for English/Language Arts, Social Studies, and Health/PE)—*Continued*

Grouping	English/Language Arts	Social Studies	Physical Education
With Students with Exceptional Learning Needs in Mind	Scaffolding Resources such as SPARK Notes, age-appropriate videos, connections to students' lives, graphic novels, additional materials.	Scaffolding In addition, concepts are both described and demonstrated. Wherever possible, enactments and simulations help.	Scaffolding In addition, teacher breaks down activities into task analysis, with direct instruction. Adaptive PE activities and prompts.
Jigsaw	Jigsaw A complex text can be broken down to smaller, more manageable parts; each group summarizes one part of the text and then the class comes together and discusses the text as a whole.	Primary sources Each group has a task that contributes to the overall goals of a lesson. In a social studies class, small groups might discuss and/or analyze different primary source texts relating to the same content.	Project adventure Students need to collaborate to achieve a shared goal, such as scaling a wall, walking a rope course, or other team-building activities.
Station Teaching or Learning Centers	Stations For example, in an ELA class, students may be asked to recreate or update a text on film. For this project, each group could take on a different responsibility (i.e., scriptwriting, props, operating equipment, acting, etc.).	Stations Students work in small groups, each of which is set a particular task that contributes to the final product. In a social studies class, students might be asked to create a documentary film about a particular figure or event. For this project, each group could take on a different responsibility (i.e., scriptwriting, props, operating equipment, acting).	Stations In a PE class, students might engage in relays or obstacle courses, in which each component is focused on a particular type of physical activity.

Using the Structure: Intention, Skill, and Responsiveness

For any cooperative learning activity you choose for your classroom, be sure to address the three overarching prompts of intention, skill, and responsiveness as offered by the chapter.

For example, if you were to use the above example of a jigsaw activity, were you clear in the intention or purpose for using it (keeping in mind student interest, competencies, personalities, and academic levels)? Did you prepare the activity and run it skillfully, attending to student engagement and performance? After the jigsaw, did your lesson achieve its ends? That is, was the jigsaw successful in breaking down the text, allowing students to go deeper in shorter passages, and then in groups reassemble the given work?

SUGGESTIONS FOR SELF-ASSESSMENT

With any learning activity, the mindful teacher must continually assess and reflect on the value and efficacy of his or her actions in the service of meaningful and authentic learning. Below find a sample grid for planning and self-assessment for learning goals, activities, and groupings, as well as sample questions for self-assessment.

Self-Reflection Questions

- What type of grouping construction are you using?
- Why is this grouping arrangement the most appropriate?
- How does it support your learning goals?
- If the arrangement is appropriate for this activity, can it be used for others as well?
- What changes did you make to the group learning activity while it was being carried out?
- How did those changes affect the efficacy of the learning activity?
- How did you assess the students during and after the group learning activity?

CONCLUSION

This chapter addressed the challenge and necessity of effective student grouping for achievement and equity in order to develop caring and compassionate classroom communities. In introducing novice teachers to various forms of student groupings, we focused on the particular challenges of grouping for excellence and equity with diverse student populations. We encourage novice teachers to use templates to help them in the creation, maintenance, and evaluation of student-group work.

If our schools represent the "single garment of destiny," cited by Dr. King in the opening epigraph, we want both students and teachers to create and benefit from this "inescapable network of mutuality." Novice teachers can do

CHECKLIST FOR GROUPING

I. Intention

1. Are learning goals established prior to implementation of group construction?
   Yes _____ No _____
   Provide Evidence _____
2. Are group learning activities aligned with the learning goals?
   Yes _____ No _____
   Provide Evidence _____
3. Are group learning activities carried out with an appropriate group construction?
   Yes _____ No _____
   Provide Evidence _____

II. Skill

4. Was sufficient time used to plan the group work activity?
   Yes _____ No _____
   Provide Evidence _____
5. Was planning carried out with students' cognitive, behavioral, and socioemotional needs in mind?
   Yes _____ No _____
   Provide Evidence _____
6. Were multiple/varied responses and reactions to the group learning activity anticipated and planned for?
   Yes _____ No _____
   Provide Evidence _____

III. Responsiveness

7. Did you assess efficacy of the group learning activity both during and after its implementation?
   Yes _____ No _____
   Provide Evidence _____
8. Did you amend the activity or shift student roles in response to the assessment?
   Yes _____ No _____
   Provide Evidence _____
9. Were group learning activities concluded appropriately?
   Yes _____ No _____
   Provide Evidence _____

so successfully, in part by approaching their students with affirmation, compassion, and a bit of faith. Thoughtful student grouping can not only benefit students' social, emotional, and cognitive development, but also increase opportunities to engage in meaningful learning and dialogue both inside school and in the greater democratic society.

GLOSSARY OF TERMS

Contemplative pedagogy—AKA Mindful Teaching, methods and practices that support student attention, empathetic connection, compassion, and altruistic behavior, while simultaneously supporting student creativity and learning of content (Zajonc, 2013).

Cooperative learning—classroom practices in which students work together in groups to help each other learn (Slavin, 2014).

Culturally responsive teaching—pedagogy that focuses on and draws upon students' cultural knowledge, prior experiences, frames of reference, and performance styles to enhance learning experiences (Ford et al., 2014).

Differentiated instruction—method of teaching and learning that acknowledges and honors each student's individual learning needs and maximizes each student's potential for learning (Tomlinson, 1999).

Heterogeneous grouping—an arrangement in which students of varying levels of ability are grouped together for a learning activity.

Homogeneous grouping—an arrangement in which students of similar levels of ability are grouped together for a learning activity.

Multiple intelligences theory—theory put forth by Howard Gardner (1999) that there exist multiple intelligences or "a biopsychological potential to process information that can be activated in a cultural setting to solve problems or create products that are of value in a culture" (pp. 33–34). Howard's nine types of intelligence are linguistic, logical-mathematical, musical, spatial, bodily kinesthetic, naturalistic, interpersonal, intrapersonal, and existential (Moran, Kornhaber & Gardner, 2006).

Scaffolding—a support mechanism, provided by a more competent individual, that helps a learner successfully perform a task within his or her zone of proximal development (Ormrod, 2003).

Small-group instruction—method of instruction in which material is presented to smaller groups of students, which allows for more tailored instruction.

Whole group or class instruction—method of instruction in which material is presented in the same manner to an entire group or class.

Zone of Proximal Development—the range of tasks between one's actual developmental level and one's level of potential development. In other words, the range of tasks that one cannot yet perform independently but can do so with the help and guidance of others (Ormrod, 2003).

REFERENCES

Aronson, E., & Patnoe, S. (1997). The Jigsaw Classroom: Building Cooperation in the Classroom (2nd ed.). New York: Addison Wesley Longman.

Ford, B. A., Stuart, D. H., & Vakil, S. (2014). Culturally responsive teaching in the 21st century inclusive classroom. *Journal of the International Association of Special Education, 15*(2), 56–62.

Gardner, H. (1999). *Intelligence reframed: Multiple intelligences for the 21st century.* New York: Basic Books.

Gray, P., & Feldman, J. (2004). Playing in the zone of proximal development: Qualities of self-directed age mixing between adolescents and young children at a democratic school. *American Journal of Education*, (2), 108.

King, M. L. (1967). *A Christmas sermon.* Atlanta: The Martin Luther King, Jr. Center for Social Change.

Moran, S., Kornhaber, M., & Gardner, H. (2006). Orchestrating multiple intelligences. *Educational Leadership, 64*(1), 22–27.

Ormrod, J. (2003). *Educational psychology: Developing learners.* Upper Saddle River, NJ: Pearson Education, Inc.

Parkay, F., & Stanford, B. (2007). *Becoming a teacher.* Boston: Pearson Education, Inc.

Roberts, S. L., & Van Deusen-MacLeod, B. (2015). The jigsaw revisited: Common core social studies and English language arts integration. *Social Studies Research & Practice, 10*(2), 56–66.

Slavin, R. E. (2014). Making cooperative learning powerful. *Educational Leadership, 72*(2), 22–26.

Starko, A. J. (2010). *Creativity in the classroom: Schools of curious delight* (4th Ed.). New York: Routledge.

Tomlinson, C. A. (1999). *The differentiated classroom: Responding to the needs of all learners.* Alexandria, VA: Association for Supervision and Curriculum Development.

Vygotsky, L. S. (1978). *Mind in society* (Edited by M. Cole, V. John-Steiner, S. Scribner, & and E. Souberman). Cambridge, MA: Harvard University Press.

Zajonc, A. (2013). Contemplative pedagogy: A quiet revolution in higher education. *New Directions for Teaching & Learning, 2013*(134), 83–94.

Chapter 13

Developing, Implementing, and Assessing Problem-Based Learning

Stephanie Curtis, Joseph DiGiacomo, and Vincent Walencik

The purpose of this chapter is to educate teachers on *what* Problem-Based Learning (PBL) is, *why* it is instructionally useful in today's classrooms, and *how* it can be developed, implemented, and assessed across all subject areas and grade levels. We will first work to clarify and define *what* PBL is and give you a choice of how to define it for yourself. Next, we will discuss *why* PBL should be used in today's classrooms, with a focus on what the research discusses. Finally, we will move on to *how* PBL can be implemented in the classroom and broken down into development, implementation, and assessment stages with the inclusion of a seven-step problem-solving process and sample rubric for your reference.

Problem-Based Learning provides teachers with a way to present meaningful and multifaceted instructional practices to their students relevant to their lives, while embedding the required grade-level content standards. Through the use of research-based evidence and provided examples, this chapter will cover the *what*, *why*, and *how* of PBL and ways in which it can be utilized in the classroom and adapted to individual teaching styles.

WHAT IS PBL?

In this chapter, the term "PBL" represents both *Project-Based Learning* and *Problem-Based Learning* because often they are used interchangeably. The table below provides definitions and characteristics of each PBL. After reading and assessing these characteristics, it is up to you to do one of the following:

1. Define PBL using one of the provided definitions.

2. Define PBL by combining parts of the provided definitions.
3. Create your own definition of PBL.

In order to be able to write a definition relevant to your instructional practices, let us first compare and contrast characteristics of both Problem-Based Learning and Project-Based Learning:

Defining Problem-Based Learning

- Aimee Hosler (Education World, Problem-Based Learning: Tips and Project Ideas) states that in Problem-Based Learning students work together to solve real-world problems in their schools and communities. This requires students to draw from several disciplines and apply those subjects in a practical way.
- Characteristics of Problem-Based Learning (SFSU, 2015) include:
  ○ Learning takes place in the contexts of authentic tasks, issues, and problems that are aligned with real-world concerns.
  ○ Students take responsibility for their own learning.
  ○ Stresses problem-solving skills, effective reasoning, and self-directed learning.
  ○ Begins with an open-ended problem on which all learning is centered.

Defining Project-Based Learning

- "Project Based Learning is the act of learning through identifying a real-world problem and developing its solution. Kids show what they learn as they journey through the unit, not just the end" (Wolpert-Gawron, 2015).
- "Project Based Learning is the ongoing act of learning about different subjects simultaneously. This is achieved by guiding students to identify, through research, a real-world problem (local and global) developing its solutions using evidence to support the claim, and presenting the solution through a multimedia approach based in a set of 21st-century tools" (Wolpert-Gawron, 2015).

Now it's your turn to compare and contrast Problem-Based Learning and Project-Based Learning

Write two similarities:

1.

2.

Write two differences:

1.

2.

If you Google either Problem-Based Learning or Project-Based Learning, links to both terms will emerge. As you may have noticed, the difference between the two is a matter of semantics (Morgan, 2013). Trying to discern one from the other may be an exercise in futility, though it is possible that the final product/solution produced by the students may separate Problem-Based Learning from Project-Based Learning.

Now it is time to write you definition of PBL:

_____

_____

_____

Refer to *your* definition throughout this chapter as we discuss the *development, implementation,* and *assessment* of PBL.

WHY USE PBL?

Like your students, you may be thinking, "When am I ever going to use this?" This section will focus on the *why* of PBL and its application to twenty-first-century learning. Future classrooms must become less segregated by subject matter and more centered around students' abilities to solve real-world problems while applying content knowledge from several subjects. Although the concept of PBL has been around since Piaget, there are still some concerns surrounding PBL from both teachers and students.

That being said, three major educational reports have agreed upon a list of competencies and foundations that schools need to provide their students if they are to be successful in a rapidly and continually integrated workplace and global environment (SCANS, 2000; Hersh, 2009; Partnership, 2015). In accordance with these reports, by developing and implementing PBLs, students will engage in cooperative learning, acquiring and evaluating information, and thinking creatively. These skills, plus many others, are critical for today's students' success in increasingly global workplaces.

It is imperative that we create new kinds of schools, freed from an educational system deeply rooted in the distant past and the kinds of schools so many of us attended decades ago. Creating schools for the 21st century requires less time looking in the rear view mirror and more vision anticipating the road ahead. (George Lucas, 2013)

How does George Lucas's quotation relate to why we should use PBL for our students?

In the next section, you will see how through PBLs, students will actively learn these twenty-first-century skills.

HOW TO USE PBL

While there are many different formats of PBL, the general components remain consistent. We will focus on *how* to use PBL through developing, implementing, and assessing. Each of these sections will further be broken down to account for their different steps when working to develop, implement, and assess PBLs. The format used in this chapter is designed for multidisciplinary uses and incorporates cross-content curricular standards. Additionally, in each section of the PBL process, we will discuss the roles of both the teacher and students.

Developing PBL

When developing PBLs, there are four important aspects to keep in mind: situation statement, solution statement, testing statement, and content standards. This development process is teacher driven and built off of relevant and meaningful application to the students' everyday lives. While the students are not active developers of PBLs, they are the main participants and therefore must be kept in mind throughout the creation process. Each of the four main aspects when developing PBLs will be explained below and further highlighted through the use of a vignette from a high-school social studies classroom.

Situation Statement

Creating a *situation statement* for a PBL is the most important aspect of the entire development process. It is important to remember that the world is filled with problems waiting to be solved. This is vital to keep in mind when referring back to the definition of PBL from earlier, which likely included some variation of "real-world problems" and/or "authentic issues." When formulating your situation statement, you should focus on identifying problems in your students' local and global communities because a well-constructed PBL situation statement will expand beyond the four walls of the classroom environment.

The situation statement is made up of two main parts: *condition* and *consequences*. A condition is a brief description of an event that has occurred or is occurring. An example condition would be a student's backpack breaking. Consequences are the results that will take place due to the stated condition or description. The consequence for your backpack breaking would be your books falling out.

Solution Statement

As educators, it is not our job to simply give students all the answers to a problem. The second part of the development process, the *solution statement*, works to describe what the student should do to rectify the stated problem in ambiguous terms. "Ambiguity" is a word that teachers rarely embrace, but it is a vital aspect of the inquiry-based process as we work to encourage students to think for themselves. For example, if the goal is to have something float across a tub of water without sinking, educators shouldn't say build a boat. This will cut out any creativity from the students as they will instantly be in a mind-set to build a boat, when in actuality they can build countless things that will float across a tub of water.

Testing Statement

When developing PBLs, guiding measures must be created to help align the students' possible solutions to the stated problem. This is called the *testing statement*, which works to provide criteria for evaluating solutions the student devises throughout the PBL. In typical assessments, students are taught the information first and then are provided with a list of information that they will be tested on later.

In PBLs, however, the testing statement is provided to the students and informs them on how their results will be tested *before* they start developing possible solutions. While the testing statement may sometimes sound vague, a PBL rubric, similar to the one provided later in this chapter, is used to further assist the teacher in assessing students' implementation of the PBL.

Content Standards

The PBL is developed with specific subject content in mind so that students will be able to APPLY this information to the problem. Therefore, teachers must identify specific content standards appropriate for the grade and ability level of the students and relevant to the problem. In addition, a means to assess the application of the stated standards must be provided in the PBL. Students should work to complete benchmarks that relate to the application of the stated content standards to the problem.

These benchmarks determine the degree to which the students apply the subject content. Without these, the final product becomes an arbitrary project, not grounded in content standards. These benchmarks work to demonstrate that the PBL is a method of teaching and learning that is used to reinforce content knowledge and standards for the students.

Developing in Action

The following vignette focuses on the development stage of a PBL, highlighting each main component of situation statement, solution statement, testing statement, and content standard:

> *Students of an eighth grade classroom were learning about major early explorers (Columbus, Vespucci, Magellan, Hudson, etc.) in their social studies lesson. They worked to track the voyages of these explorers using real maps to help visualize the routes the explorers took when discovering new lands. One of the students in the class was new to the school, having moved to the area of Honduras, and he was having difficulty grasping the English language. Together, the students became "explorers" in a new land as they worked to map out and plot the school building itself. Similar to these early explorers, the student from Honduras was navigating a new land that did not speak his language, and he aimed to work on mapping the building and finding the rooms he would need to locate throughout the day (classrooms, lavatories, main offices, guidance offices, etc.). With the creation of this map, the students would be able to identify the routes that could be used to get around the school in order to locate various rooms during the day.*

Now it's your turn to figure out the condition and consequence(s) in the vignette above:

The Condition:

The Consequence(s):

The teacher in this class saw an opportunity to implement PBL that was relevant and meaningful to her students. While focusing the situation statement on their local school community, the students were tasked to explore their school as if they were in a strange land. This was a real-world problem for her newest student as he really was exploring a new land. In order to do this, the students were given the solution statement to focus on mapping and plotting the building in any way they saw fit.

This is purposely left ambiguous so that the students can develop unique solutions when working on the PBL. The testing statement given to the students in order to align their work to the stated problem focuses on creating a map that could be used by the students, especially the newer one who may be unfamiliar with the school, to more easily move around the building and find different rooms. It is important to keep in mind that the testing statement is given to the students before they begin the PBL in order to guide them toward the end goal. In this problem, the testing statement is: The students will be able to "navigate" around the school to find the rooms they need. Finally, the content standards covered in this PBL focus mostly on social studies–related topics such as immigration and exploration.

For an expanded PBL that would include cross-curricular content, mathematics standards on two- and three-dimensional representations could be incorporated into the map-making process as well. Overall, this PBL would be deemed a success if the students, especially the new one from Honduras, are able to "navigate" their way around the school with the use of their map.

Implementing PBL

After the development stage has been completed, the PBL is implemented in the classroom. Here, student's and teacher's roles are shifted. During the development process, teachers have a majority of the control while accounting for student influences. In the implementation stage of the PBL process, however, students engage in a seven-step problem-solving model, and the teachers strictly monitor their advancement. The teacher's role is to keep the students on an appropriate pace within each step of the model. Teachers monitor students' progress throughout, using a checklist and a summative rubric during the assessment.

Seven-Step Problem-Solving Process

Below is the seven-step process that the students engage in during PBLs. In this chapter we will explain each step in more detail (Figure 13.1).

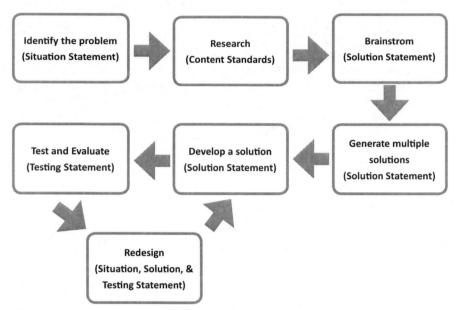

Figure 13.1 Seven Step Problem Solving Process.

Identifying the Problem

The first step of the model is identifying the problem. In this stage, students are given the situation statement and they must identify the problem that needs to be solved. All students are provided the same situation statement, but as individuals they may deem certain information more problematic than others. This lends itself to uniquely generated solutions. Before students move on to the next stage, the teacher should check for student understanding of the problem.

Research

After the problem has been identified, students begin the research portion of the model. This is where students engage in the bulk of the content standards identified. Teachers may provide multiple resources such as technology, textbooks, experts in the field, and many more to assist student's efforts. In the implementation process, this is the stage where the teacher has the most involvement with student learning. Depending on the content, some preteaching or reteaching may need to take place. Benchmarks and forms of formative assessments should be monitored throughout this stage by the teacher to ensure student understanding of the material.

Brainstorming

Once students gain background knowledge of the problem, they begin the *brainstorming* process. This is where students apply their research to the solution statement. The solution statement, in the development process, is a guideline set by the teacher and is intentionally open for interpretation by the student. During the brainstorming process it is important that students understand that their ideas do not have to work. This means that no idea is a bad idea. The brainstorming process does not have to be based solely on logic, but more so on creativity and thinking outside the box.

Always remember to color outside the line. (Fran Greb)

- *How does this quotation contradict how we teach our students to think in the typical classroom?*
- *How does this quotation align itself with the PBL process?*

Generate Multiple Solutions

Through the brainstorming process, students should have come up with a plethora of ideas. As discussed, student ideas do not have to be realistic in the brainstorming stage. In this stage of *generating multiple solutions*, the ideas should be honed to a degree of feasibility. If students are working individually, they can design (sketch out, create a layout, etc.) two or three of their best ideas.

If students are working in groups (recommended), have each student sketch out their best idea. Having students work individually and then combine forces with their group can lead to unique and innovative final designs. During this stage, the teacher should be monitoring all student engagements and be assessing the process, not the designs themselves.

Develop a Solution

Once all possible solutions have been presented, it is time for students to execute their design. All previous steps have led up to the development of the sketched-out solution. Teachers should leave plenty of time for this stage because although there has been prior planning, executing the design will be the most time-consuming. To expedite this process, teachers (and students) should provide all the materials necessary before reaching this stage.

This way, there are no surprises or missing pieces as they begin working on their solution. It is expected that students will stray from their sketched design, but it is important that they record all edits because a major element of the implementation stage is revising throughout the process.

Test and Evaluate

After students have completed their design (or time allotted is up) it is time to test and evaluate their solution. The way their product will be tested should have already been made clear through the testing statement. Depending on the PBL, students may all test their solutions at the same time or groups may have to test one at a time. In either case, the teacher should plan for whole-class involvement during the evaluation phase. When students are testing their solution, the teacher should be assessing the process, and evaluating its relevance to the original development statements, rather than if the solution worked or not.

Redesign

The "final" stage of the seven-step process is probably the most important. Unlike typical summative assessments, PBLs teach students that the solution is never truly finished. The purpose of the *redesign* stage is that even if a student's design worked, there are always ways of improving and making it better. Think about the iPhone, for example. Just when you think it can't get any more advanced, they come out with a new model, and then further versions within that model. That is because there are always opportunities to go back and redesign. If a student's solution did not work, this is the time to circle back to the "develop a solution" stage or even further back in the model if necessary.

Roger Lewin said, "Too often we give children answers to remember rather than problems to solve." As teachers, it is hard to relinquish control of your students' learning, especially if your job depends on their successes. Through this seven-step model, students are engaging in twenty-first-century life skills and the ability to actively take control of their learning.

Implementation in Action

Implementing PBL is not easy. The hardest part is trying to separate each step, because they often naturally blend together throughout the process. The following problem was given to a group of middle-school students to solve in their eighth grade math class. This assignment, presented in the form of a PBL, had the students count the rise and run on a coordinate plane to calculate the slope of a line:

> *Wheelchair ramps are a judicial requirement in all building constructions. The Americans with Disabilities Act of 1990 (ADA) gives Wheelchair Ramp Specifications that include codes and guidelines on required ramp slopes and lengths. This ensures that disabled persons and patients are able to move in and out of buildings without undue difficulties. A student in our school has recently lost the ability to use his legs and now requires the use of a wheelchair to get around school. His parents have added ramps to their house to make*

access easier, but it is very difficult for your peer to get to all of his classes with ease. Create a system that can assist your peer in getting around to all of his classrooms.

The following vignette is a conversation between classmates during the brainstorming stage of the PBL described above:

Annie suggested to her partner during brainstorming that they should design a pulley system around the school that can lift the student with disabilities from room to room. Quickly, Annie's partner shot down her idea saying that was impossible! Overhearing this, the teacher stepped in to remind all the students that during this stage of the PBL model, there are no bad ideas! Annie realized that her classmate may have been right and that maybe another one of their design ideas, like building a ramp, may be a more feasible solution.

The students in the classroom were given a situation statement that related directly to one of their peer's life as they identified the problem. Background information was also provided to the students as part of their research about the specific handicap from the Americans with Disabilities Act of 1990. The wording of the solution statement is strategically chosen to not force students into just creating a ramp. The teacher chose to use ambiguous terminology to increase the chances of unique student solutions.

During the implementation stage, two students were working together to brainstorm possible solutions. One student made the suggestion of an apparatus that can airlift the peer. Her partner was quick to deny this idea because it was not realistic. The teacher, however, saw this as a teachable moment to differentiate between the steps in the problem-solving model as they worked to generate multiple solutions.

After this stage, the two students would continue through the problem-solving model to finish the testing and redesign phases with their final solution. Depending on the time constraints set by the teacher, there may be a hybrid redesign phase as well. This would be more of a student reflection than an actual rebuild.

Assessing PBL

A concern of educators is: How can I be sure that subject standards are being met via PBL? In many cases the product of a PBL is what others actually see. What may not readily be seen is the application of content as applied to the PBL. Teachers are responsible for making sure they teach to the standards, as previously discussed during the development stage. Assessments are vital in

Table 13.1   Summative PBL Rubric

Problem-Solving Step	1	2	3
Identify the problem	Does not demonstrate understanding of the problem. Answers are illogical or incomplete.	Demonstrates understanding of the problem. Answers are logical and accurate.	Demonstrates advanced understanding of the problem. Answers are logical and accurate and extend thinking beyond the scope of the lesson(s).
Research and brainstorm	Limited/no application of lesson content, comparison of solutions, nor rationale for solution choice.	Applies lesson content, makes comparison of solutions, and provides a logical rationale for solution choice.	Extends application of lesson content, makes extensive comparison of solutions, and has advanced ability to examine criteria and explain rationale for solution choice.
Design and build	Orthographic sketches are missing or incomplete. Limited/no logical plan for prototype development. Prototype is not testable or built according to criteria and constraints.	Orthographic sketches are drawn to scale and labeled. Logical plan for prototype development. Testable prototype built according to criteria and constraints.	Multiple orthographic sketches are drawn to scale and extensively labeled. Elaborate plan for prototype development. Testable prototype built according to criteria and constraints with added features.
Test and redesign	Design was partially tested and results were not fully recorded and contain many inaccuracies. Design was not evaluated for improvement. No redesign.	Design was tested twice and results accurately recorded. Design was evaluated for improvement. Redesign included a sketch and identification of improvements.	Design was tested more than twice and results accurately recorded. Design was extensively evaluated for improvement. Redesign included multiple sketches and identification of improvements. A new prototype was developed.

determining the degree to which the students are proficient in applying those standards, and how they engage in the problem-solving process.

To determine student understanding of the standards, both the teacher and students can monitor progress using various assessment methods. These

CHECKLIST FOR PBL APPROPRIATENESS

1. Does the problem have real-world relevance to the student?
   Yes _____ No _____
   Provide Evidence_____

2. Does the problem focus on the students' own experiences and interests?
   Yes _____ No _____
   Provide Evidence_____

3. Are local resources and experts available to assist?
   Yes _____ No _____
   Provide Evidence_____

4. Does the problem have potential for students to present investigation to others in a variety of forms (role playing; demonstrations; construction; oral presentations; visual media; computer generated presentations using PowerPoint, etc)?
   Yes _____ No _____
   Provide Evidence_____

5. Does the problem include opportunities for students to demonstrate what they have learned to persons beyond the classroom?
   Yes _____ No _____
   Provide Evidence_____

6. Does the problem require students to apply a structured process for problem solving?
   Yes _____ No _____
   Provide Evidence_____

7. Is the problem sensitive to local culture, as well as culturally appropriate?
   Yes _____ No _____
   Provide Evidence_____

8. Does the problem apply and assess grade appropriate local and state content standard?
   Yes _____ No _____
   Provide Evidence_____

9. Is the problem rich enough to allow for grade appropriate extended and in-depth investigation over a period of time?
   Yes _____ No _____
   Provide Evidence_____

10. Is there sufficient time and materials to undertake the problem?
    Yes _____ No _____
    Provide Evidence_____

assessments can be altered on the basis of each PBL; however, some criteria remain consistent. Students should be assessed on how their final product relates back to the development components of situation statement, solution statement, testing statement, and content standards, and how students engage in each of the seven problem-solving steps during implementation. The rubric below is one method that can be used as a culminating summative assessment for a PBL as it engages with each of the seven steps in the problem-solving process (Table 13.1).

An alternative to the above rubric would be a formative assessment. Many educators are familiar with the K-W-L process:

K = What do I *k*now about the problem?
W= *W*hat don't I know about the problem?
L= What did I *l*earn?

In a PBL, the main focus is on student learning and not on teaching content. The PBL works to assess students on HOW they apply knowledge when solving a problem and their ability to self-assess throughout the process. In this case, an added "H" in K-W-H-L becomes extremely important:

H= *H*ow will I learn what I need to know?

Using the formative assessment, K-W-H-L, teachers can monitor student's level of understanding throughout the PBL in addition to the summative assessment rubric.

Both of these assessments can be used together, separately, and/or individualized on the basis of your classroom's needs. The goal of the assessment is to provide choice when assessing students throughout the PBL process.

SELF-REFLECTION QUESTIONS

1. How is the PBL relevant to the students and how can it be applied to their real problems in their lives and/or community?
2. In what ways will the PBL involve the students in cooperative learning, acquiring and evaluating information, and thinking creatively?
3. How did you work to ensure students moved through the seven-step process at an appropriate pace during PBL implementation? How did you monitor their progress throughout?
4. In what ways does the PBL relate back to the subject and content standards you are trying to cover?

5. How did your assessment rubric cover each of the seven steps from the implementation stage?

CONCLUSION

This chapter worked to dissect the *what, why,* and *how* of PBL in the classroom. We began with *what* Problem-Based Learning is, but we invite the reader to draft a meaningful definition that is relevant to their own teaching practices. Teachers' understanding will help in their classroom as they work to develop and implement PBLs to assist with student learning. We next looked into *why* PBLs are important, with a focus on their instructional importance as they work to engage students in cooperative learning, acquiring and evaluating of information, and thinking creatively. Research-based practices confirm how critical these skills are for student success and vital for twenty-first-century learning.

A major part of this chapter focused on *how* to use PBL to enhance student learning through a process consisting of developing, implementing, and assessing. Each of these stages is then further broken down to show the process that must take place throughout a PBL. Particular attention is paid to the situation statement, solution statement, testing statement, and content standards during the development stage. This is the foundation for the rest of the PBL process. Here, teachers have high levels of control, though the students remain the instructional focus.

The shift between teacher and student ownership takes place during implementation. Based off of all the work the teacher did during development, students are able to engage in the seven-step problem-solving model with limited teacher facilitation. Finally, both the teacher and students can assess the successfulness of the PBL using both formative and summative assessments, including with the use of the sample assessment rubric.

Through this PBL process, students and teachers engage in a cooperative and educational experience that is grounded in real-life experiences and content standards. "Why do I have to learn this?" "When am I ever going to use this stuff?" Through the integration of PBL into the curriculum as a method of teaching and learning, teachers may never have to answer these questions from their students again.

Tips for Assessment of Content Standards

- To test the effectiveness of Problem/Project-Based Learning, administer a pretest to students in a standardized format to test for understanding of content. After PBL, administer a similar posttest to reassess students' understanding and compare.

- Content assessment in a PBL requires identification of the standards (as stated in local and state standards) and activity questions that assess the student's ability to apply the stated content standard to the PBL situation statement (the problem).

Tips for Timeline

- Determine an appropriate timeline for PBL, ensuring that it aligns with the curricular unit that is being addressed. Provide students with pacing guide/schedule for PBL. Determine check-in times with students to monitor progress.

Tips for Materials

- Identify materials that will be provided by you and what materials will be provided by students (e.g., bag of junk, technology, experts). Preteach how to use more advanced tools (scroll-saw, computer programs, etc.) prior to starting PBL.

Tips for Grouping

- When designing the PBL identify how students will be grouped.
- Options include individual grouping, grouping by partners, homogeneous grouping by ability, heterogeneous grouping by ability.

Tips for Presentation of Solutions

- Determine how students will demonstrate their use of the problem-solving process when solving the PBL (e.g., PowerPoint presentation, portfolio, invention notebook, etc.).

APPENDIX 1: EXTENSION MATERIALS

1. http://www.edutopia.org/project-based-learning
   This site has many videos, blogs, discussion boards, and research relating to Project-Based Learning that is a great supplement for any teacher looking for extra assistance and information.
2. http://bie.org/
   Bucks Institute for Education (BIE) helps teachers prepare students for successful lives through the use of Project-Based Learning across all grade levels and subject areas. BIE maintains this site where they create, gather, and share PBL instructional practices and products for teachers.
3. http://inclusive-istem.com/inclusive-istem-resources/mentor-teacher-resources/design-challenges/.

This is the official website of the "Restructuring Preservice Preparation for Innovative Special Education" (RePPrISE) Project at Montclair State University, which prepares middle and secondary educators in STEM education. This link provides downloadable examples to authentic teacher-created design challenges that have been implemented in their classrooms.

GLOSSARY OF TERMS

Situation statement—problem statement given to the students, identifying problems in their local and global communities. The situation statement is made up of two main parts: *condition* and *consequences.*

Condition—a brief description of an event that has occurred or is occurring.

Consequence—the results that will take place due to the stated condition or description.

Solution statement—a statement that describes what the student should do to rectify the stated problem in the situation statement, in ambiguous terms.

Testing statement—criteria provided to students in order to align their work to the stated problem and let them know how their solution will be tested.

Seven-step problem-solving model—process inspired by the engineering design process that the students engage in during the implementation stage.

Brainstorming process—stage during implementation where students apply their research to the solution statement. Ideas during this stage do not need to be logical or have to work. This is the stage where creativity and thinking outside the box is encouraged.

Generating multiple solutions—stage during implementation where student ideas from the brainstorming process are worked out to a degree of feasibility. This can be represented by sketches and blueprints.

Redesign—stage during implementation where students can evaluate how their solutions were tested and improve on their designs, whether they were successful or not.

K-W-L—a formative assessment that focuses on students and what they *K*now about a problem, *W*hat they don't know about the problem, and what they *L*earn.

K-W-H-L—this is similar to the K-W-L, with the addition of students understanding *H*ow they will learn what they need to know.

We would like to thank the following people for their support and help on this chapter: Ola Alghalayeni, Zack Arenstein, Victoria Bennett, Victoria Biseglia, Christina Bridges, Abraham Gelb, Kelsey Matkowski, Suzanne Nagourney, Charmee Park, Pamela Ramierz, and Brooke Schwartzman.

RESOURCES

BIE. (2015). Essential project design elements checklist | Project Based Learning. Retrieved from http://www.bie.org.

BIE. (2015, September). What is Project Based Learning (PBL)? Retrieved from http://bie.org/about/what_pbl.

BIE. (2015, September). Why Project Based Learning (PBL)? Retrieved from http://bie.org/about/why_pbl.

George Lucas. (2003). Edutopia. Retrieved from http://www.edutopia.org/foreword-george-lucas.

Hersh, R. (2009, April 20). Out 21st-century "risk"—teaching for content and skills. Retrieved from http://www.edweek.org.

Hidden curriculum (2014, August 26). In S. Abbott (Ed.), *The glossary of education reform*. Retrieved from http://edglossary.org/hidden-curriculum.

Hosler, A. (2013). Problem-Based Learning: Tips and project ideas. Retrieved from http://www.educationworld.com.

Katz. L. (1989). Engaging children's minds: The project approach. Retrieved from eric.edu.gov.

Larmer, J. (2015, July 13). Project-Based Learning vs. Problem-Based Learning vs. X-BL. Retrieved from http://www.edutopia.org.

Morgan, K. (2013). Project and Problem-Based Learning—just semantics or real difference? Retrieved from http://kellymorganscience.com.

NCREL. (2015, August 31). Skills and competencies needed to succeed in today's workplace. Retrieved from http://www.ncrel.org.

Partnership for 21st Century Learning. (2015, May). Framework for 21st century learning. Retrieved from www.P21.org.

Roger Lewin. (2016). Today in Science History. Retrieved from http://todayinsci.com/L/Lewin_Roger/LewinRoger-Quotations.htm.

SFSU. (2015, September). Problem-Based Learning. Retrieved from http://online.sfsu.edu\.

U.S. Department of Labor. (2000). Skills and tasks for jobs: A scans report for America. Retrieved from http://wdr.doleta.gov/opr/FULLTEXT/1999_35.pdf.

Victoria University. (2014). Problem-Based Learning (PBL). Retrieved from http://learningandteaching.vu.edu.

Weimer, M. (2009, November 12). Problem-Based Learning: Benefits and risks. Retrieved from http://www.facultyfocus.com.

Wolpert-Gawron, H. (2015, August 13). What the heck is Project-Based Learning? Retrieved from http://www.edutopia.org.

Chapter 14

Creating a Dialogical Learning Community to Promote Dialogical Teaching and Learning

Jaime Grinberg, David Schwarzer,
and Michael Molino

The purpose of this chapter is to define *dialogical teaching and learning* and to equip you with the tools you need to create a *dialogical learning community* (DLC) in your own classroom. The practice of dialogical teaching is one of several pedagogical decisions that teachers must consider on a regular basis in their practice. Some teachers believe that they are implementing dialogical teaching practices by the simple act of asking students to talk to each other or by asking questions to the entire class.

This chapter will explain the distinction between using *dialogue* and being dialogical. This distinction is paramount, particularly in the case of *scripted curricula*, oftentimes written as dialogue in which both the questions and expected answers are provided to the teacher. This chapter will help you create a DLC by using five dimensions essential to its implementation. Moreover, it will provide you with concrete activities for lesson planning that will promote intentional dialogical experiences for your students.

WHAT IS DIALOGICAL TEACHING AND LEARNING?

There are multiple ways of conceptualizing dialogue, from a Socratic tradition (Laverty, Demarzio & Grinberg, 2006) to the more contemporary critical dialogical pedagogy of Paulo Freire (Kincheloe, 2008). In this chapter, "dialogical" refers to purposeful conversations and exchanges of ideas facilitated and guided by the teacher. Through these conversations, students explore, present, ponder, interrogate, and challenge perspectives.

Such dialogical conversations are not only verbal (spoken language) and nonverbal (body language), but could also take place across multimodal forms of communication (writing, music, art, etc.) and could certainly be supported or enhanced with the use of technology. Developing dialogical habits of mind—in which students express their own thoughts and perspectives and also learn to question facts and ideas—contributes to students' content-area growth as well as their understanding of themselves while learning to function in a democratic environment (Brookfield & Preskill, 2005).

Dialogical teaching necessitates attentively listening to—and not just hearing—the students. It means actively engaging in a dialogical mode: looking at the student's point of view, attending to his or her social, emotional, and intellectual needs. Even controversial utterances presented by students are legitimate and valid to them; however, one of the roles of the teacher is to discuss and challenge them, and to incite them to consider opposite points of view. It also means that other students in the classroom understand that articulating your own viewpoint, even if controversial, is a democratic practice that is essential to dialogical teaching.

What Is a Dialogical Learning Community?

Dialogical teaching and learning can occur in different teaching contexts; however, research suggests that fostering a dialogical approach within learning communities is highly effective (Brookfield & Preskill, 2005; Grinberg, 2002; Kincheloe, 2008). Not all learning communities are inherently dialogical in nature. On the basis of a literature review of research on dialogical teaching and learning, we will highlight five dimensions that are crucial to the creation of a DLC.

Creating a Symmetrical Classroom Environment in Which Everyone (Including the Teacher) is a Member

In a DLC there are symmetric power relations between the teacher(s) and the students. The construction of knowledge is part of the responsibility of the whole community under the guidance of the teacher as a more experienced peer (Vygotsky, 1978). Each classroom setting has unique defining characteristics. The purpose of this section is to help you reflect on the challenges and opportunities within your own classroom setting to promote a DLC. You may ponder why the classroom setting might be so important for dialogue. The following vignette from a novice second grade teacher demonstrates an environment in which there is a clear power imbalance between students and teacher that actually inhibits the creation of a DLC.

> *Jim is a second grade novice teacher in an elementary school. He was sitting in a rocking chair reading to the class, showing the students a large book with plenty of pictures and large letters which he was reading upside down.*

The students were attentively sitting on the carpet. Jim was asking questions such as, "What do you think will happen?" or pointing out to the characters in the pictures. He seemed to be using dialogue. They were answering the questions and were asking a few questions themselves while the teacher was "correcting" how they expressed themselves. However, not all students were participating in this reading activity. A group of five children was sitting in the row located next to the "cubbies" on the eastern wall of the classroom. These five students were assigned to work on their art project. It seemed interesting that while the teacher was reading and conducting a discussion that seemingly fostered dialogue, some children were not actually participating. They were located outside of the "dialogical" space.

Jim designed his classroom as a space to encourage dialogue. When his department mentor asked him about his decision to have a "dialogical" space for some of the students and a different space for five others, he was not sure how to answer. He talked about the importance of centers and choice as a central part of the curriculum and the complete avoidance of whole group activities. Moreover, he said that the amount of students that could be seated comfortably on the carpet needs to be reduced.

The mentor probed and said that such use of the physical environment could also produce a de facto *asymmetrical relationship* which sends a message: those students on the carpet or the couch are part of the learning community and are learning to dialogue, while the others are not participating. Jim, however, believed that he was providing his students with a sense of agency by choosing to work on their own activities. That choice could be interpreted as a form of segregation, at least from the dialogical space. Paying close attention to the environment is relevant when analyzing what type of learning occurs or does not occur in a particular activity.

Since this conversation, Jim is much more aware of the decisions that he makes about the classroom environment and their implications for dialogical teaching. He has decided to either have a whole-class discussion as part of dialogical teaching or create two rotating subgroups to develop a DLC.

Tips

- Consider, like in Jim's case, that you may have a "chair situation" (asymmetrical relationship) in your classroom.
- Where is your desk situated in the classroom? Make sure it is in a spot so that you are not hiding from the students and that you are facing them.
- Who posts comments, artwork, quotations, and classroom documents on the classroom wall? Make sure that you and your students are involved in creating the environmental print for the classroom community.

Learning the Cultures of the Local Community, School, Classroom, and the Students

Each classroom has its own cultural milieu that is crucial to understand in order to create a DLC. By researching, experiencing, and participating in the local community, novice teachers become better equipped to connect classroom experiences and learning activities with students' funds of knowledge. At one of the universities at which one of the authors worked, there was a very powerful assignment that all student teachers were encouraged to participate in.

Understanding the learner as a whole individual and knowing his or her preferences in areas such as literature, music, art, dance, sports, and media are critical in being able to establish a trusting bond. Knowing your students not only as learners, but also as people is also important. Through the discovery of commonalities and differences among students' experiences, you can create meaningful dialogical experiences in your content area that are core values for your discipline. When students are validated for who they are, they start developing a sense of trust and feel more open to accept others and to engage in dialogue. Trust and comfort are building blocks to real dialogue.

Following is a list of sequential activities that students needed to complete:

1. Student teachers were asked to "hang out" in areas near the school community. Purposefully, no clear guidelines were provided.
2. They were encouraged to conduct ethnographic observations of the community. Copious notes were recorded.
3. Student teachers interviewed several informants from both the community at large.
4. They analyzed their findings and to make connections to their content areas.
5. Once the student teachers felt comfortable enough about their understanding of the larger community, they moved into a more in-depth look at the school culture by observing and interviewing informants from the school.
6. They conducted a "child study" which involved shadowing a child in school for 2 or 3 days from class to class and all other school areas (such as the playground or library).
7. Plan and deliver a community-centered curriculum.

(Grinberg & Goldfarb, 1998, pp. 134–135)

This project enabled one of the student teachers, whose content area was ESL, to understand the background and context of the local neighborhood and the institutional and human resources available. It also provided a better understanding of who the students are and where they come from (i.e., socioeconomic and cultural factors).

Moreover, the student-teacher felt that documenting the cultures of the school and the classroom gave her much insight into the organization of a DLC. She kept entry logs every day when in school in which she documented the routines, the rules, and the level of student participation. The analysis of the data gathered proved to be very valuable when meeting with her cooperating teacher. She could ask concrete questions and share insights about the community/school. It also prepared her better for planning instruction to this particular community and school. She developed a dialogical unit plan for her ELL students in which they

- collected oral histories of their families,
- traced their genealogical roots,
- analyzed their findings,
- created a multimodal visual representation of their research, and
- presented their projects to their peers (in English and/or their native tongue).

Tips

- Spend some time in the local community. Start observing the broad community (i.e., a local grocery store, barber shop, church, café, or restaurant) and interviewing some of the members.
- Find out if any teacher in the school is using dialogical teaching. Then, interview the teacher. Here are some potential questions you might use:
  - What challenges have you faced implementing this approach in your class?
  - How do students in this community react to this method?
  - What materials do you use in your class that might be useful to me?
- Observe and interview students within your class. Here are some potential questions you might use:
  - What activities do you participate in within the community (i.e., sports, recreational activities, church gatherings, etc.)?
  - What school activities do you enjoy that encourage you to actively participate? Tell me about them and why you enjoy them.
  - Tell me about a teacher who really valued your opinions. What do you think he or she did to make you feel like your point of view mattered?

Fostering Discipline-Specific Dialogue

Creating a DLC in which students become "young geographers," "young artists," or "young biologists" is one way to promote disciplinary inquiry. Students will develop discipline-specific language and *funds of knowledge*. Doing so gives students the opportunity to explore new ideas, speculate with answers, ask more questions, articulate alternate perspectives, and learn to listen to others and to express themselves with clarity. Let's consider the following vignette of Maria, a tenth grade student-teacher in a culturally, racially, linguistically, and socioeconomically heterogeneous school:

Maria is an animated student teacher who shares her passion for algebra with her students. She insists that many of the math problems she provides can be solved in several ways and that there is no one specific solution that is better than all of the others. Maria provides her students every day with a culturally and linguistically appropriate challenging problem to solve online (as homework)—different groups have different problems. Utilizing a platform that the district provides (edmodo), teacher and students can "chat" online and brainstorm ideas, as well as search for possible solutions. As part of this assignment, students are also encouraged to explore the web and bring their findings to their peers for discussion. The teacher is interested in dialogue not only as a means to solving problems, but also as a way of stimulating critical thinking, inquiry skills, and as a process. By analyzing students' attempts at solving the problems, she can also understand what the students are think-ing, how they are thinking, and what misconceptions may emerge from these dialogues as a way to inform her instructional planning. Students are develop-ing mathematical language and the disciplinary discourse through the use of meaningful dialogue.

Maria knows the subject she teaches, knows her students' funds of knowl-edge, and knows how to scaffold instruction through an online dialogical homework assignment that was culturally and linguistically responsive. She used food items that are readily and widely used in the students' families (Maracucha, elotes, halal meat, etc.), and she encouraged students to find resources on the web in all the languages they spoke. She even presented some of these resources in class. Creating a dialogical assignment as a routine for your class can be a challenge where technology can be very helpful.

Tips

- Create a "word wall" for terms and expressions that will contribute to dia-logue in your content area.
  - *Language Arts*: Where is the textual evidence to support your claim?
  - *Math*: What theorem can you apply to this concept?
  - *Science*: What experiments might one conduct to support your hypothesis?
  - *Social Studies*: What documents might you consult to support your claim?
- Utilize technology available within your school district to promote dialogi-cal teaching.
  - *World Languages*: On Twitter, create a hashtag in the target language so that students can express opinion statements. In French, the hashtag would be #JePense. Students would respond with their own opinion state-ments (i.e., #JePense que la vie est belle.).
  - *Art*: Create a website where students will upload their work. They will comment using statements to compare and contrast their own art project to those of their classmates.

○ *Physical Education*: Create a blog for your class that encourages dialogue about challenges and successes of a physical education goal. Students will write a blog post answering the following questions and then respond to their peers' responses:

What is your fitness goal? What do you plan on doing to meet your goal? What are some challenges that you are facing? How do you plan on addressing them?

Creating a Democratic DLC

John Dewey, a highly influential educator and philosopher, argued that an important aspect of the purposes of schooling is to learn to live in a democracy. Such learning must happen by building the right environments and providing for experiential learning that would be democratic (Grinberg & Lewis, 2009). A democratic learning environment could be nourished by a DLC by making such experience a subject matter of study. For a DLC to be a true DLC, it must be democratic: on the one hand significant learning of subject matter and on the other hand significant learning on how to live in a community where rights and duties are practiced (Grinberg et al., 2005).

There is a need to create an inclusive climate of: comfort and trust; respect and engagement; and finally, tolerance and acceptance in order for teachers to promote a DLC (Grinberg, 2009). Learning to live in a community, to be a member of a community, is not an easy task and requires much effort, not only from the participants but also fundamentally from the teacher. The expectation is that students will gain ownership over their own experiences, individually and collectively. Procedures for discussion, the right expressions, the language and tone, and the body language and silences have to be moderated in such a way that students feel at ease with others while maintaining their own individuality without imposing on each other.

Tips

• Create a Bill of Rights for your class. (See Sun-Joo's Bill of Rights in Appendix 1.)
• Use democratic practices such as voting, polling, and debating different controversial ideas and points of view.
  ○ When having students debate each other, prearrange groups in a randomized way.
• With the physical education teachers, create "trust" exercises with your students such as guiding a blindfolded peer, trust fall exercise (i.e., falling and letting a classmate catch their partner before they fall on the mats), and so on.

Learning How to Navigate Conflict

Conflict emerges from time to time as an inevitable consequence of dialogic teaching. Thus, in a process of dialogue where there has to be argumentation, demonstration, and defense of a proposition, conflict should be expected. The teacher's job is not one of a spectator of the dialogue; rather, he or she must

1. establish ground rules for interactions;
2. monitor the types of conversations taking place;
3. guarantee that all students feel safe and that their opinions are validated;
4. ensure that there are plenty of opportunities for all students to share equally (without forcing participation);
5. ensure that no one student is dominating the conversation.

Tips

- Create a list of statements with your students about the following situations:
  A. How do we in this class challenge each other's opinions in a constructive way?
  B. How do we reject each other's alternate perspectives in a constructive way?
  C. How do we contemplate the merits of these arguments (not only within the norms of the subject matter but also in terms of personal styles and emotions)?
- Create a "pass card" for students to promote participation. When students do not want to publicly participate, they will use their pass card to exempt themselves from participating (only once).
- Create a manual for handling conflict within a DLC (these are separate or an extension to classroom rules).

SELF-REFLECTION QUESTIONS

Consider videotaping a classroom dialogical teaching situation that you have planned. After listening and/or viewing it reflect on the following questions:

a. Are you using dialogue, dialogical teaching or are you creating a dialogical learning community? How do you know? Provide some evidence.
b. What are the three strengths that you observed while watching the video?
c. What are three challenges that you observed while watching the video?
d. What indications are there that you are creating a safe environment for students to dialogue even on controversial issues?
e. What content-area-specific language did you see used by students during the videotaped session?

CHECKLIST TO IMPLEMENT DLC

1. Do you create a symmetrical classroom environment in which everyone is a member?
   Yes _____ No _____
   Provide some concrete evidence _____

2. Do you know the culture(s) of your local community?
   Yes _____ No _____
   Provide some concrete evidence _____

3. Do you know the culture(s) of your school?
   Yes _____ No _____
   Provide some concrete evidence _____

4. Do you know the culture(s) of your classroom?
   Yes _____ No _____
   Provide some concrete evidence _____

5. Do you know the culture(s) of your students?
   Yes _____ No _____
   Provide some concrete evidence _____

6. Do you foster discipline-specific dialogue?
   Yes _____ No _____
   Provide some concrete evidence _____

7. Have you created a democratic DLC?
   Yes _____ No _____
   Provide some concrete evidence _____

8. Is each of your students participating in the discussions?
   Yes _____ No _____
   Provide some concrete evidence _____

9. Are you ensuring that no single student is dominating the discussion?
   Yes _____ No _____
   Provide some concrete evidence _____

10. Do you know how to navigate conflict?
    Yes _____ No _____
    Provide some concrete evidence _____

CONCLUSION

The purpose of this chapter was to distinguish between dialogue, dialogical teaching, and creating a DLC. We are all aware of the push for scripted curricula that makes dialogical learning communities even more unnatural. Within this chapter, we presented you with five dimensions that you should consider while developing this type of pedagogical decision. We provided you with some vignettes to illustrate some examples of novice teachers navigating the complexities of the DLC. We also provided you with tips, concrete applications, and self-reflection activities to intentionally center and focus your classroom practice.

This is not a recipe to be followed blindly. It is intended as a reference for you to use and modify to the context of your own classroom and your own professional experiences.

Creating a successful DLC, like any other pedagogical choice, is a journey: it will take time and effort. But, it needs to start with a FIRST step. We are looking forward to seeing you navigate the implementation of dialogical teaching and learning in general, and the creation of your own DLC in particular.

APPENDIX 1: EXTENSION MATERIALS

Socratic Dialogue versus Critical Pedagogy: Self-Reflection

Socratic dialogue and critical pedagogy dialogue are two of the best known. If you are interested in creating a DLC, following are two self-reflection activities created to encourage you to define what kind of dialogue you are currently using in your classroom. We have provided two recognized versions: socrative and critical pedagogy dialogue.

Socratic dialogue is a question-and-answer dialogue named after the famous Greek philosopher who initiated its practice as a pedagogical tool centuries ago. In this type of dialogue, the teacher guides the students by questioning them on a regular basis.

Following are some questions you can ask yourself to see if you are utilizing this approach in your pedagogy:

- Are you treating all thoughts as process, not final products? How?
- Are you responding with questions that might elicit more thought?
- Do you treat all thoughts as part of a larger system? Thus, do they serve as connections in a network? How?
- Do you lead with questions in order to search for the connections? Give an example of one instance in which you did this.
- Do you unpack the ideas presented in class by students in order to promote student learning?

- Look for the assumptions from where the ideas as well as the questions come (prior knowledge).

Critical pedagogy dialogue is designed to problematize by asking questions that are sometimes not as obvious as the "traditional" ones.

To problematize implies that we ought to consider multiple possible alternatives; it invites us to play with what counts as facts, truth or false, and to consider possible multiple coexisting realities. For instance, looking at the same cell through a microscope, different students in the same learning community might ask very different questions, or they might be interested in different issues regarding the cell.

Following is a list of questions you may consider using if interested in creating a DLC that is critical pedagogy oriented.

- How are facts and information used and how are facts judged?
- Whose facts and whose information are presented?
- What facts and information are not considered and why?
- Who can and who cannot benefit from these facts and information?
- What facts and information need to be investigated?

AUTOBIOGRAPHICAL POEM

Have students create their own autobiographical poem and share with the class:

First line: your first name
Second line: three words that describe you
Third line: something you love
Fourth line: something you hate
Fifth line: something you fear
Sixth line: something you wish
Seventh line is your last name

APPENDIX 1: SUN-JOO'S BILL OF RIGHTS

Sun-Joo, an experienced middle-school teacher in Ann Arbor, Michigan, shared with other teachers in the district an approach that she has developed to establish ground rules in her own classroom with the purpose of fostering an environment that is conducive to a dialogical approach. She clearly understands that creating an environment in which all ideas, attempts, and even mistakes are valued is crucial to promoting an effective DLC.

A Student's Bill of Rights

I have a right to be happy and to be treated with compassion in this room:
This means no one will laugh at me or hurt my feelings.
I have a right to be myself in this room:
This means no one will treat me unfairly because I am black or white, fat or thin, tall or short, boy or girl.
I have a right to be safe in this room:
This means no one will hit me, kick me, push me, pinch me, or hurt me.
I have a right to hear and be heard in this room:
This means no one will yell, scream, shout, or make loud noises.
I have a right to learn about myself in this room:
This means that I will be free to express my feelings and opinions without being interrupted or punished.

ARTICLE ON CLASSROOM ENVIRONMENTS

For more information on the importance of the classroom environment in establishing a safe, productive, and effective DLC, take a look at the following article from Edutopia.com:

http://www.edutopia.org/blog/classroom-environments-make-difference-andrew-marcinek.

VIDEO ON THE THEORETICAL FOUNDATIONS OF DIALOGICAL TEACHING

For more information on the theoretical foundations of dialogical teaching, take a look at the following YouTube video: https://www.youtube.com/watch?v=Imgk-og7D0w.

GLOSSARY OF TERMS

Dialogue—purposeful conversations and exchanges of ideas facilitated and guided by the teacher. Such exchanges serve to explore ideas, present different points of view, speculate with possible explanations, share doubts, challenge established perspectives or positions, provoke critical thinking, contemplate new ideas and discuss their merits, listen to how a student or group of students think and feel about a particular issue, topic, dilemma, or problem, and to motivate debate, stimulate curiosity and engagement as that knowledge is not transmitted as discrete units of information, but that becomes part of the process in which the student owns that knowledge and becomes part of her or his own repertoire in order to be able to deepen understanding. Dialogue also serves as a way of unveiling how power functions, challenging detrimental conditions, and knowing how power could generate possibilities for betterment and for justice.

Dialogical teaching—is the teaching approach fostered by a teacher in which dialogue serves as the main element to cultivate inquiry and understanding, including developing habits of behavior and habits of mind that can be transferred to multiple environments and situations. Such teaching incorporates certain aspects of uncertainty because there is no expectation of absolute control over where the dialogue might lead; thus, planning for it does not necessarily warrant outcomes within certain time or by the type of questions drafted a priori or problems presented for discussion. This teaching has been labeled "adventurous" and demands from the teacher further planning and seizing the "teaching moment" which might not have been predicted, but that enables meaningful learning.

Dialogical learning—is the learning that occurs when a student participates in a dialogical environment. Such learning involves knowledge that is processed, owned, and understood by the student after having been engaged in a conversation, asking questions, inquiring, awakening curiosity, and challenging and being challenged. Through talking and exploring, the student elaborates conjectures, solves problems, and transfers scripts, thus building new knowledge which expands prior psychological schemata stimulated by the dialogue. This could be both symbolic (dialogue with the subject matter or the problem at hand) and verbal (probing ideas, listening, asking, speculating, rejecting, accepting, affirming).

Dialogical learning communities—These function as an educational environment where dialogical teaching and learning takes place for the whole classroom or through a variety of group activities such as projects, debates, experiments, discussions, and cooperative activities. These involve and include the individual student within the classroom context by emphasizing some levels of cooperation, exchange, support, dependency, and collective explorations. In these DLCs students develop habits of communication, behavior, and mind—they learn how to participate in a dialogue, how to express themselves, how to listen to others, and how to respond or question each other as members of a group where respect and trust occur. In addition they also learn about each other and what different students bring to the conversation as a way of learning to live as a participant in a community. Dialogue, in all its possibilities, also implies that a set of relationships in which the teacher and students engage are opportunities to learn and to explore, to dream and to inquire.

Teachers have the responsibility of creating the right environment to nurture, sustain, and develop a dialogical approach and create an inclusive climate of comfort and trust, respect and engagement, tolerance and acceptance, caring and listening, with the ambitious expectation that students will gain ownership over their own experiences, individually and collectively. Procedures for discussion, the right expressions, the language and tone, and the body language and silences have to be moderated in such a way that students feel at ease with others while maintaining their own individuality without imposing on each other. *In DLCs students also have the power to initiate, suggest, facilitate, and lead.*

Scripted curricula—is a curriculum that incorporates units, lesson plans, and assessment tools designed a priori regardless of who the students are and who the teacher is, the school location, or the resources available. A scripted curriculum provides directives and functions as a recipe to be followed. While there is a contribution in curricular terms as the material and content tends to be scaffolded successfully, it limits the teacher's intellectual power to adapt and design his or her own lessons. Oftentimes a problem also emerges when a teacher is evaluated on the basis of the implementation of such scripted curriculum. Research has shown that historically such scripted curriculum has failed to advance meaningful improvement of teaching and that of curricular reform (Ball & Cohen, 1996). With a scripted curriculum it is very difficult to develop dialogue because it is so controlled that it takes away the learning potential of a student's curiosity and spontaneity.

Asymmetrical relationship—in a DLC power is shared among its members and it includes both the students and teachers. When such power is utilized arbitrarily, capriciously, and unreasonably to establish preferences or practices that enable some to learn, but others not, then it can be said that the teacher has created unproductive and unfair learning conditions because relationships are asymmetrical. As such, the DLC fails to function. Power does not come in quantities, but it is always in a state of relationship so that teachers could use it to enable successful DLCs. Thus, the teacher is the authority and cannot and should not relinquish such responsibility, for the teacher has experience and expertise in addition to the trust that is inherent in the role. The authority is not only that of the role but also that which emerges from the relationships and environment created to support the dialogical learning community. When designing activities and facilitating dialogue, a teacher asks how that authority to exercise power would be used, for what purposes, and under which circumstances in order to enable meaningful learning and students' voices to be heard in a fair, stimulating, and comfortable environment fostered by and also fostering equitable relationships.

Funds of knowledge—it refers to the knowledge that students have and bring with them to school, which is based on the cultural environments of their own families and communities (Moll et al., 1992). These include ways of communicating, language, and skills needed to sustain their own social, cultural, and economic environments, as well different manifestations of culture in terms of music, folklore, food, art, literature and literacy, land conflict resolution, among other forms of becoming and being a part of their own sociocultural context (Grinberg, Goldfarb & Saavedra, 2005). Many times students find that schools do not recognize or do not value what they bring with themselves as important sources of knowledge (Grinberg, Goldfarb & Saavedra, 2005). We argue that recognizing and valuing these funds of knowledge are extremely important to build the environment that sustains a dialogical learning community.

REFERENCES

Ball, D. L., & Cohen, D. K. (1996). Reform by the book: What is—or might be—the role of curriculum materials in teacher learning and instructional reform? *Educational Researcher, 25*(6–8), 14.

Brookfield, S., & Preskill, S. (2005). *Discussion as a way of teaching*. San Francisco, CA: Jossey-Bass.

Grinberg, J. (2002). "I had never been exposed to teaching like that": Progressive teacher education at Bank Street during the 1930's. *Teachers College Record, 104*(7), 1422–1460.

Grinberg, J. (2009). Playing with ideas: Some notes about learning communities and connected teaching elements. In Tyson Lewis, Jaime Grinberg, and Megan Laverty (Eds.), *Philosophy of education: Modern and contemporary ideas at play* (pp. 807–817). Dubuque, IA: Kendall & Hunt.

Grinberg, J., & Goldfarb, K. (1998). Moving teacher education in/to the community. *Theory into Practice, 37*(2), 131–139.

Grinberg, J., Goldfarb, K., & Saavedra, E. (2005). Con coraje y con pasion: The schooling of Latinas/os and their teachers' education. In Pedro Pedraza and Melissa Rivera (Eds.), *Latino education: An agenda for community action research, a volume of the National Latino/a Education Research and Policy Projects* (pp. 227–254). Mahwah, NJ: Lawrence Erlbaum Associates.

Grinberg, J., & Lewis, T. (2009). John Dewey: Introduction. In Tyson Lewis, Jaime Grinberg, and Megan Laverty (Eds.), *Philosophy of education: Modern and contemporary ideas at play* (pp. 95–97). Dubuque, IA: Kendall & Hunt.

Kincheloe, J. (2008). *Critical pedagogy*. New York: Peter Lang.

Laverty, M., Demarzio, D., & Grinberg, J. (Eds.) (2006). *Common questions and disparate voices: A philosophical conversation on education.* Boston: Allyn & Bacon/Longman.

Moll, L., Amanti, C., Neff, D., & Gonzalez, N. (1992). Funds of knowledge for teaching: Using a qualitative approach to connect homes and classrooms. *Theory into Practice, 31*(2), 132–141.

Vygotsky, L. (1978). *Mind in society: The development of higher psychological processes.* Cambridge, MA: Harvard.

Chapter 15

Fostering a Scientific Approach to Teaching and Learning

Deductive and Inductive Teaching

Helenrose Fives and Melissa Susnosky

The purpose of this chapter is to explain the goals of concept learning and how teachers can use inductive and deductive approaches to facilitate this kind of learning in students. "Concepts" refer to organized and meaningful representations of the world (Klausmeier, 1992). For example, imagine walking through a park and seeing several trees. On your walk you do not need to differentiate the flowering cherry tree from the maple next it. Each does not need to be looked at and understood independently—they are all trees and fit into a single conceptual understanding or concept of "tree." The ability to engage in this kind of grouping allows learners to think in more complex and adaptive ways. Concept learning, then, is the process by which concepts are developed. In this chapter we will offer a variety of strategies to help you help your students develop conceptual understandings.

THE FOUR ESSENTIAL ELEMENTS OF CONCEPT TEACHING

When teaching with the goal of conceptual understanding, there are four essential lesson elements that must be addressed during instruction, though not necessarily in a fixed order.

1. *Explicate the concept name*: Learning the label or name for a concept is a necessary part of understanding what the concept is. Typically, learners have prior experience or knowledge of the concepts you plan to teach. In these instances, you should help them develop a clearer understanding of how a name is used. The following vignette shows a new teacher, engaged in a complex, activity-focused science lesson, where the nature of the concept to be learned was lost in the action of the classroom.

Tina's fifth grade class spent thirty minutes with pieces of wire, D-batteries, and flashlight light bulbs. Students were told to "make the light bulb light." By the end of the class session everyone had a lit bulb, some had put multiple batteries and bulbs together in a series, and some had fried their light bulbs. Tina never helped students to make the connection to the concept that was the focus of that activity—electrical circuits. Worse yet, the students were assigned homework on different kinds of circuits, and Tina started her next lesson by saying, "Since we learned about circuits yesterday we can move on today." While these students indeed explored the nature of circuits, they had no way of knowing that "circuits" were what they created.

Naming the concept and explaining the use of that label to learners seems an obvious aspect of any lesson; however many new teachers fail to make this clear to their learners.

2. *Engage schematic knowledge*: "Schematic knowledge" is a specific kind of prior knowledge; it is our knowledge of a concept *in relation* to other concepts and ideas (Alexander, Schallert & Hare, 1991). In order to experience meaningful conceptual learning, learners must integrate new conceptual information into their existing understandings (i.e., schematic knowledge). In the example below, Kimberly, a physical education teacher, tries to make explicit students' schematic knowledge.

Kimberly introduced a kickball unit to her first grade class. Students engaged in the activity for a couple of weeks as they made meaning of the positions in the field, what constituted an "out," and other game-related concepts. Transcending to the next topic, t-ball, Kimberly broke the class up into two teams. Giving instructions to the students, she stated, "T-ball has many of the same rules as kickball. Can we think of all the ways that these games are similar?" She then facilitated a small discussion to help students make clear connections between the two games and the ways that they are connected.

Above, Kimberly used her students' schematic knowledge of kick ball to make connections to the new topic of t-ball. Engaging students in finding similarities and differences among related concepts facilitates concept learning. Making connections to prior content often seems obvious to teachers in their own content area, but since students rarely make these connections on their own, teachers need to systematically and explicitly connect this knowledge for students. Activation, assessment, and integration of schematic knowledge is necessary for effective teaching practice.

3. *Examine concept attributes (defining and irrelevant)*: In the study of concept learning, researchers have described the common features that are

shared by members of a category as "attributes." Attributes are things that are typical of many members of the same category (Bruning, Schraw, Norby & Ronning, 2004). It is critical that teachers identify a new concept's *defining attributes*. These are relevant attributes that are *required* for concept membership.

Using our tree example, defining attributes would include that trees are plants, have a central trunk, bark, leaves, branches, roots, and are made of special tissue that the average person refers to as "wood." To be a tree a plant *must* have all of these things; if even one is missing, then the plant is no longer a tree. For instance, palm trees, banana trees, and bamboo all have bark, roots, and leaves. But they do not have that special tissue—wood—and are therefore not considered to be trees by arborists.

One way to help learners develop conceptual understandings is to facilitate the examination of concept attributes for those features that are defining of the concept and those that are irrelevant, but possibly quite common. For instance, a common attribute of trees may be that they are tall. However, this is an *irrelevant attribute*, because not all trees are tall—tallness may be common to the concept of a tree, but it is not required for a tree to be a tree (consider the bonsai). When teaching about a concept it is important to help learners distinguish from those attributes that are *defining* (i.e., required for concept membership) and those that are *irrelevant* (i.e., typical of members within a category/concept but not necessary; Klausmeier, 1992).

4. *Explore examples and nonexamples*: Examples refer to positive instances of a concept, that is, instances where the concept is present. Nonexamples are negative instances or instances where the concept is not present. The more complicated the concept, the more is the need for examples and nonexamples. Both examples and nonexamples are needed for learners to fully understand the boundaries of a concept (Tennyson & Park, 1980). Below we see Carl, a first-year high-school English teacher, not only embracing the use of examples and nonexamples, but also bringing concept label, schematic knowledge, and attributes to his lesson.

> *Carl taught a unit on the concept of "tragedy" in Shakespeare's dramas to his English literature class. In his first lesson on tragedy, he started by asking the class, "What is a tragedy?" and listed the students' responses on the board. The following comments were recorded:*
>
> *When a little kid gets cancer Death An Accident My mom's cooking*
> *Wearing socks with sandals 9-11 My English grade A bad thing*
> *After recording the students' comments, Carl asked students to turn to a partner and evaluate each example to determine which were "real" tragedies and which were exaggerations.*

Carl introduced the topic of "tragedy" by relying on students' schematic knowledge *and* through the generation of examples and nonexamples. Learners can often get a deeper understanding of a concept when they can compare examples and nonexamples. For instance, the idea of "Wearing socks with sandals" as tragic was put into perspective when considering actual tragedies such as the events of September 11 or a child diagnosed with cancer. To decide what a "real tragedy" was, students began to identify the defining attributes of tragedy. Thus, this example illustrates how all four essential elements of a concept learning lesson can come together.

Tips for Implementing the Four Essential Elements of Concept Teaching

- Explicate the concept name: Learners are new to the content and need help navigating the sea of curriculum and vocabulary with clear landmarks of essential concept terminology.
- Engage schematic knowledge: Learners need help understanding how new concepts fit into their existing schematic knowledge. This means that teachers must activate this knowledge, assess it, and explicitly help students make connections between new concepts and existing schemata.
- Examine concept attributes: Learners need to distinguish between defining and irrelevant attributes in order to develop conceptual understandings. Designing instructional activities that focus on these facilitates deep learning.
- Explore examples and nonexamples: Learners need to distinguish between examples and nonexamples when learning concepts. Teaching concepts in such a way that students can differentiate between the two is an important step towards understanding.

TWO THEORETICAL APPROACHES TO TEACHING ABOUT CONCEPTS

Cognitive theorists have differed in their interpretation of how people best come to know and understand concepts. Some, like Ausubel (1963), emphasized a *Rule-e.g.* (example) method of concept attainment that relies on deductive reasoning. In the Rule-e.g. method teachers provide direct instruction on the defining attributes (the rule) followed by the application of those attributes to specific examples. On the basis of this perspective, Ausubel developed a theory of learning called "meaningful verbal learning," which is facilitated through a teaching strategy called *expository teaching*.

In contrast, Bruner (1960) argued that humans learn using inductive reasoning, and he advocated the E.g.-rule method. In this approach concept learning occurs through repeated experiences with specific examples until the learner can generate the rule(s) on the basis of those experiences. The initial emphasis in learning is on experiencing examples and nonexamples and using schematic knowledge to make sense of what is observed. Bruner argued that this type of learning was best achieved through the teaching strategy of *discovery learning*.

Ausubel's Expository Teaching

The goal for any teaching experience, according to Ausubel (1963), is for the learner to experience meaningful verbal learning. Unlike in rote learning, where learners memorize facts verbatim, in meaningful verbal learning, learners must connect any new information or concepts to their existing schematic knowledge in meaningful ways. This helps learners develop deep, personal connections to the new concept. Ausubel appreciated concept learning through language and argued that individuals did not need to directly experience every concept in order to develop an understanding of it. Rather, through language, we can come to know things in connection with our existing schematic knowledge.

Toward this goal of meaningful verbal learning, Ausubel suggested expository teaching, which relies on deductive reasoning, as a viable method for classroom teachers to implement in their teaching practice. *Deductive reasoning* is employed when learners develop, or deduce, conclusions through the application of rules, definitions, or principles. It is facilitated when teachers first provide students with the rule or definition of the concept, including its defining attributes, and then move students to applying that rule to specific examples. An expository lesson on "what is a tree" would likely begin with a definition of tree and asking students to apply that definition to a series of examples and nonexamples.

Tips for Using Deductive Reasoning to Teach Concepts

Features of Deductive Reasoning:

Processing Type: Top-down, where one moves from principle or rule to specific examples

Quality of Conclusion: Leads to a certain conclusion when premises are accurate

Teaching Strategy: Used in expository teaching

Tips for Deductive Reasoning

- Establish when deductive reasoning can be used (i.e., when initial premises are known and accurate).

- Explicitly teach the processes of deductive reasoning.
- Make clear to learners that for deductive reasoning to work the initial claim must be accurate.
- Help students see that when the initial premise is accurate deductive reasoning leads to certain conclusions.

A key contribution that Ausubel made to instructional activities was the concept of an *advance organizer*. An advance organizer is an instructional tool that teachers use, typically at the beginning of a lesson, to orient the students to the concept to be learned. Two types of advance organizers may be used: comparative and expository. A *comparative advance organizer* is used to activate schematic knowledge and help students start considering what they already know about the concept under investigation (Mayer & Bromage, 1980).

In our lesson on trees, we might begin by asking students to draw a tree, define a tree, or simply picture a tree in their minds. In contrast, an *expository advance organizer* provides the learner with new information they will need to use to understand the concepts about to be learned (Mayer & Bromage, 1980). Our tree lesson could start with a clear definition of "tree" with the defining attributes listed as an advance organizer. Appendix 1 provides an expository advance organizer for the beginning of this chapter. Because the organizer is complete, it is expository in nature.

An expository lesson should follow a basic structure that emphasizes the use of deductive reasoning. First, the lesson begins with an advance organizer. Second, content (the concept) is presented from the broadest understanding to specific examples, defining and irrelevant attributes are identified, and experiences with examples and nonexamples are offered. Connections to schematic knowledge should be emphasized by helping students to see similarities and differences between the new concept and their existing schema. Third, the lesson closes with a reference back to the advance organizer and emphasizing the rule associated with the concept.

Tips for Expository Teaching

- Ask the students to share any prior experiences they have had with the concept. Track ideas in a comparative advance organizer.
- Use different modes of communication: lecture, videos, textbooks—concepts do not need to be explained via a one-way communicator.
- Advance organizers are not limited to graphic organizers (e.g., Venn diagram). Branch out and try different advance organizers such as skimming a text book, story narratives, drawings, or video clips.

Bruner's Discovery Learning

Bruner's (1960) perspective on cognitive growth argued that through cognitive disequilibrium learners would engage in problem-solving to come to a deeper understanding. On the basis of this premise, learners need to be given opportunities to make discoveries of concept rules depending on their experiences with specific examples. Thus, *discovery learning* relies on an inductive approach to reasoning. *Inductive reasoning* requires learners to develop the rules or principles of the concept on the basis of direct experience with many examples and specific details. In a discovery lesson on trees, we might begin with several examples of trees and ask the students to identify what all trees have in common. In this way we move from specific examples to the defining attributes or rule.

Inductive reasoning requires instances in which the learner must rely on intuitive thinking. *Intuitive thinking* requires learners to make connections across ideas with insufficient information; these connections then become the basis for hypotheses that can be evaluated. Whereas deductive reasoning is based on applying a rule to examples, inductive reasoning requires *creating* the rules, which often involves guesswork—or intuitive thinking. In our tree lesson, students may come up with any number of criteria for defining a "tree" that may or may not lead to the "correct" rule.

Tips for Using Inductive Reasoning to Teach Concepts

Features of Inductive Reasoning:

- Processing Type: Bottom-up, where one moves from specific examples to generate a rule or principle
- Quality of Conclusion: Leads to a likely conclusion based on varied premises; recognizes that information available may be incomplete
- Teaching Strategy: Used in guided discovery learning

Tips for Inductive Reasoning

- Establish when inductive reasoning can be used (i.e., when initial premises are unknown and conclusions must be drawn).
- Explicitly teach the processes of inductive reasoning.
- Learners need to understand that inductive reasoning leads to a *likely* conclusion.
- Help students see that while conclusions may be likely they are tentative based on the limited information used to draw them.

The problem with intuitive thinking for many educators is that students often fail to make the "correct" imaginative leap, and with discovery learning, the educator needs to let that happen until *the learner* determines the flaw in his or her solution. The second challenge of this approach for many is the openness of the strategy. Letting students figure out the solutions on their own seems to be inefficient and time-consuming. Therefore, a more conservative approach, referred to as *guided discovery*, has been developed. Guided discovery allows for the teacher to take a more active role in designing and directing the lesson. Research comparing pure discovery versus guided discovery learning has overwhelmingly favored a guided approach when looking at outcomes of student achievement and concept attainment (Mayer, 2004).

Like pure discovery lessons, guided discovery lessons begin with a problem for the students to solve. Next, the teacher provides guidance in the problem-solving by directing students toward relevant attributes of the concept and encouraging intuitive guesses. Rather than providing direct responses to student questions or problems, the teacher offers hints, suggestions, or simply asks questions to better direct the learners.

The lesson should conclude with students developing a rule or statement of the conceptual understanding they have constructed, a list of defining attributes, and a description of the four elements of the concept. One could possibly demonstrate this understanding by completing a blank version of the organizer found in Appendix 1. Students would be expected to fill in the center box with the concept, list the defining attributes and relevant schematic knowledge, and provide examples and nonexamples.

Tips for Guided Discovery Learning

- Redirect students by asking probing questions. Answering a question with another question often allows students to rethink their difficulty.
- Gather the students together at the end of the lesson to identify the concept name and review how the students came to their conclusions. Be careful of turning this into an expository lesson in the last ten minutes of class—the goal of guided discovery is for students to come to their own understanding.
- Be creative when constructing a guided discovery learning lesson: use a variety of techniques such as experiments, simulations, and case studies.

REFLECTION FOR PRACTICE

Preteaching: Before designing a lesson or unit of study, consider the following questions to guide your planning activities:
- Consider your subject area. What are the essential concepts that learners need to understand to be successful in your subject area? Brainstorm a list of these concepts.
- Where in your curriculum do you introduce and use these concepts with students?

- What would be the best ways to help students develop conceptual understandings for the specific concepts you have identified? Are some of these concepts more suited to expository or guided discovery lessons?

Postteaching: Following a lesson on concepts or where conceptual understanding was your goal, consider the following questions to help you evaluate your practice:

- How well were the four essential elements of concept teaching addressed in your lesson? How do you know this?
- What were the most challenging ideas that your students struggled with in the lesson? Why do you think this was?
- What would the lesson have looked like if you used a different approach? For instance, if you used expository teaching, how might the lesson have been different had you used guided discovery?
- What can you use from this lesson to inform your instruction in the future?

CONCLUSION

Learning and understanding concepts allows humans to navigate the world in which we reside. Concept learning emphasizes the importance of recognizing the relations among ideas and how they influence each other, as opposed to understanding the world, and more specifically academic material, as a series of independent and discrete tasks to master and then forget.

When teaching for conceptual understanding, teachers must help students establish conceptual meaning by addressing the four essential elements of concept teaching: name the concept, establish defining attributes, connect to relevant schematic knowledge, and identify examples and nonexamples. Two instructional approaches are recommended for facilitating concept learning: expository teaching (Rule-e.g. method) and discovery learning (E.g.-rule method).

Expository teaching emphasizes a top-down approach to reasoning where the concept is introduced via an advance organizer and learners are expected to apply the defining attributes (rules) to examples. In contrast, discovery learning uses bottom-up reasoning that requires learners to generate the defining attributes (the rules) on the basis of a series of specific examples. Each teaching approach has potential to help students develop conceptual understandings. The effectiveness of either will be determined by the artistry of the teacher who must select the method, match it with the curriculum, and align these with identified learning goals. Teachers should use the Four Essential Elements of Concept Teaching (see Appendix 1) as a guide in their work to facilitate student learning.

CHECKLIST FOR IMPLEMENTATION
OF CONCEPT TEACHING

1. Explicate the Concept Name
   a. Did you probe students by asking questions about the concept to activate prior knowledge?
   Yes _____ No_____
   Provide some concrete evidence _____
   b. Was the concept clearly labeled (named) during the lesson?
   Yes _____ No_____
   Provide some concrete evidence _____
2. Engage Schematic Knowledge
   a. Did you engage students in discussions about prior experiences related to the current concept?
   Yes _____ No_____
   Provide some concrete evidence _____
3. Examine Concept Attributes (Defining and Irrelevant)
   a. Did you incorporate defining and irrelevant attributes of the concept in the lesson?
   Yes _____ No_____
   Provide evidence _____
   b. Can students successfully identify or give examples of a defining and irrelevant attribute of the concept?
   Yes _____ No_____
   Provide evidence _____
4. Explore Examples and Non-example
   a. Did you incorporate specific examples and non-examples of the concept in the lesson?
   Yes _____ No_____
   Provide evidence _____
   b. Can students successfully identify examples and non-examples of the concept?
   Yes _____ No_____
   Provide evidence
5. For the Inductive Approach of Expository Teaching
   a. Did you start the lesson with an advanced organizer?
   Yes _____ No_____
   Provide evidence _____
   b. Which type of advanced organizer did you use?
   Comparative _____ Expository
   Provide Evidence _____

   c. Did you refer back to the advance organizer at the end of the lesson?

     Yes _____ No_____

     Provide evidence _____

6. For the Deductive Approach of Discovery Learning

   a. Did you pose a problem at the beginning of the lesson?

     Yes _____ No_____

     Provide evidence _____

   b. Were the students actively engaged in identifying defining attributes from examples

     Yes _____ No_____

     Provide evidence _____

   c. Did you guide the students when necessary in the process?

     Yes _____ No_____

     Provide evidence _____

   d. Did the students generate the concept rule?

     Yes _____ No_____

     Provide evidence _____

APPENDIX 1: THE FOUR ESSENTIAL ELEMENTS OF CONCEPT TEACHING

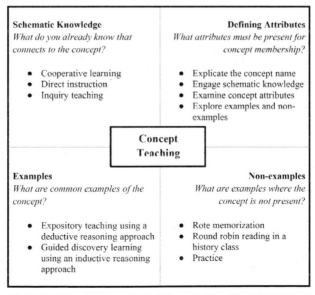

Schematic Knowledge *What do you already know that connects to the concept?*	**Defining Attributes** *What attributes must be present for concept membership?*
• Cooperative learning • Direct instruction • Inquiry teaching	• Explicate the concept name • Engage schematic knowledge • Examine concept attributes • Explore examples and non-examples

Concept Teaching

Examples *What are common examples of the concept?*	**Non-examples** *What are examples where the concept is not present?*
• Expository teaching using a deductive reasoning approach • Guided discovery learning using an inductive reasoning approach	• Rote memorization • Round robin reading in a history class • Practice

Figure 15.1   The Four Essential Elements of Concept Teaching.

APPENDIX 2: EXTENSIONS FOR FURTHER EXPLORATION

1. Evaluate your understanding of concept learning by reviewing "How the strategic teacher plans for concept attainment," an excerpt from *The Strategic Teacher: Selecting the Right Research-Based Strategy for Every Lesson* (Silver, Strong & Perini, 2007). The piece opens with a teaching vignette that will allow you to identify the 4 Es of concept teaching. http://www.ascd.org/ascd-express/vol4/420-silver.aspx.
2. If you need more clarification on what a concept is (and is not), the article titled "Concept learning: How to make it happen in the classroom" by Ehrenberg (1981) is a great source as she distinguishes between facts, concepts, principles, attitudes, and skills. The article was published in *Educational Leadership* but is available at the following website: http://www.ascd.org/ASCD/pdf/journals/ed_lead/el_198110_ehrenberg.pdf.
3. For specific ideas on how to design and develop the examples and nonexamples part of a concept lesson, see this blog by Connie Malamed titled "6 proven ways to use examples and nonexamples." http://theelearningcoach.com/elearning_design/examples-and-nonexamples/.
4. For more information about the pitfalls of discovery learning and alternate perspective, refer to the article by Marzano (2011) titled "Art and science of teaching/the perils and promises of discovery learning," published in *Promoting Respectful Schools* and posted on the ASCD website: http://www.ascd.org/publications/educational-leadership/sept11/vol69/num01/The-Perils-and-Promises-of-Discovery-Learning.aspx.
5. The following video demonstrates several practical examples of advance organizers you can use in your classroom to capture students' background knowledge and introduce a new concept. https://www.youtube.com/watch?v=ARFKDv8aUik.
6. For a practical example of discovery learning in action, refer to the following video as a science teacher explains the incorporation of inquiry instruction to her classroom. https://www.youtube.com/watch?v=VQSiQ63GRrQ.

GLOSSARY OF TERMS

Attributes—the common features shared by members of a particular category.

Concepts—organized, meaningful representations of the world.

Defining attributes—relevant attributes that must be present for a given instance or example to achieve concept membership.

Irrelevant attributes—typical, but not required, features of members within a category.

Schematic knowledge—knowledge of a concept in relation to other concepts and ideas already existing from prior experiences.

Expository teaching—teaching using a deductive reasoning approach where a rule is first presented and then applied to examples.

Deductive reasoning—a top-down reasoning approach where one moves from a rule or principle to applications of the rule to examples.

Advance organizer (expository advance organizer and comparative advance organizer)—an instructional tool used at the beginning of a lesson to introduce a concept. A *comparative advance organizer* activates prior knowledge and helps students start considering what they already know about the introduced concept. An *expository advance organizer* provides new information that students will need in order to understand the concepts to be learned.

Guided discovery learning—a teaching approach where the teacher actively guides the students through inductive reasoning to construct or identify the defining attributes of the concept learned.

Inductive reasoning—a bottom-up reasoning approach where one moves from specific examples of the concept to defining attributes or rules of the concept.

Intuitive thinking—the process by which learners generate hypotheses for solving problems based on their imagination and experience.

REFERENCES

Alexander, P. A., Schallert, D. L., & Hare, V. C. (1991). Coming to terms: How researchers in learning and literacy talk about knowledge. *Review of Educational Research, 61*(3), 315–343.

Ausubel, D. P. (1963). *The psychology of meaningful verbal learning.* New York: Grune & Stratton.

Bruner, J. S. (1960). *The process of education.* New York: Vintage Books.

Bruning, R. H., Schraw, G. J., Norby, J. M., & Ronning, R. R. (2004). *Cognitive psychology and instruction* (4th Ed.). Upper Saddle River, NJ: Pearson Merrill Prentice Hall.

Klausmeier, H. J. (1992). Concept learning and concept teaching. *Educational Psychologist, 27*(3), 267–286.

Mayer, R. E. (2004). Should there be a three-strikes rule against pure discovery learning? *American Psychologist, 59*, 14–19.

Mayer, R. E., & Bromage, B. (1980). Different recall protocols for technical text due to advance organizers. *Journal of Educational Psychology, 72*, 209–225.

Tennyson, R. D., & Park, O. C. (1980). The teaching of concepts: A review of instructional design research literature. *Review of Educational Research, 50*(1), 55–70.

Chapter 16

Collaboration in the Inclusive Classroom

Jennifer L. Goeke, Pohun Chen, and Niobel Torres

Collaboration enhances the effectiveness of instruction in general, particularly in an inclusive classroom. Hence, the purpose of this chapter is to discuss the conceptual framework for collaborative teaching under the umbrella of social constructivism. Furthermore, we will address two central aspects of teaching practice that require collaboration with other personnel to advance the achievement of students with disabilities in inclusive classrooms: coteaching and working with paraprofessionals.

Although collaboration also happens in other forms within the school and classroom environment, these types of collaboration are specifically focused on meeting diverse learning needs within a single classroom. As inclusive educators, it is critically important to collaborate effectively with other professionals so that the needs of all students can be met. The following will start with conceptual framework before moving into critical features of coteaching—co-planning, co-instructing, and co-assessing.

BACKGROUND AND CONCEPTUAL FRAMEWORK

As students with disabilities continue to gain access to general education classrooms, the work of all educators necessarily becomes increasingly collaborative. Teaching and learning are both collaborative processes. Collaboration enhances teaching and learning when it occurs on multiple levels, such as when (a) students, teachers, families, and community members work collectively to prioritize education and support schools, educators, and students; (b) educators collaborate with their colleagues to plan, deliver, and assess innovative teaching and set high expectations for themselves and their students; and (c) students work together toward learning goals that support academic and social-emotional growth and development. This type of teaching and learning environment is based on the conceptual framework of social constructivism.

Social constructivist theorists such as Dewey (2009), Vygotsky (1980), and Bloom (1956) focused on how students learn. Vygotsky, in particular, posited that learning is a social act that must not be done in isolation. This principle forms the foundation for collaborative teaching and learning. Collaborative learning environments are a necessity for learning; students and teachers learn more, are more engaged, and feel more value in learning when they have opportunities to work collaboratively (Bruner, 1985; Vygotsky, 1980; Slavin, 1989).

CO-TEACHING

The Idea in Brief

There are many ways in which new teachers might find themselves collaborating with other professionals in the classroom. Perhaps the best-known form of collaborative teaching is co-teaching, a model of instruction that utilizes two educators (e.g., one special educator and one general educator) in one classroom to deliver special education to learners identified with disabilities. In this chapter, we provide a detailed overview of co-teaching as well as an in-depth look at alternative teaching, a co-teaching model that allows teachers to individualize instruction within the general education classroom.

The Idea in Practice

Mr. Green and Ms. Wang taught a unit on electricity to their tenth grade physics class. They did so through the integration of a design challenge on building a hands-free light. On Day 1, the teachers presented the design brief, problem statement, background information, and instruction on key skills needed to design an electrical circuit. Since the first portion of the lesson was devoted to presenting background content, Mr. Green and Ms. Wang decided that Team Teaching *a short lecture was appropriate for their students. During this portion of the lesson, the teachers alternated roles; one teacher color-coded key note-taking points for the students on the board while the other lectured, and vice versa. Because the second portion of the lesson concentrated on targeted skills within the design challenge, Ms. Wang delivered explicit instruction in Ohm's Law calculations, while Mr. Green circulated, observed, and recorded how well students were following along with the process. They concluded the lesson with an exit slip in which students were required to complete an Ohm's Law calculation question.*

During their collaborative planning time at the end of Day 1, Mr. Green shared with Ms. Wang the results of his observation notes, and they also reviewed the exit slip data. Because there were several students who struggled with both the guided and independent practice portion of the calculation lesson, the teachers agreed that they would start the second day's lesson with an Alternative Teaching *structure. As a result, Mr. Green led a small group consisting of the struggling students, to whom he explicitly taught a strategy for remembering and self-monitoring the steps for Ohm's Law calculations. He oversaw continued guided practice for ten minutes, during which the students completed a brief assessment probe on calculating Ohm's Law. Ms. Wang spent the time with the rest of the class, guiding them through research resources for the design challenge. After fifteen minutes, the students in Mr. Green's group reintegrated with their team members for the brainstorming session. Mr. Green then reviewed choosing design parameters with a morph chart, while Ms. Wang circulated and assisted group members with choosing elements sufficient for three prospective designs. The teachers collected each student's design portfolio at the end of the day to review progress.*

At the end of Day 2, the teachers discussed how they would implement the Design and Build days of the design challenge unit. They agreed that since the teams were at different progress points in their designs, they would implement Station Teaching *for the next two days. Mr. Green chose to lead a station on practical wiring skills such as cutting, stripping, crimping, and connecting. Ms. Wang led a station on evaluating circuit design for short circuits and overloads. Students worked at independent stations to complete sketching and then building their chosen design.*

To test, redesign, and present, Mr. Green and Ms. Wang decided to use a Parallel Teaching *structure to maximize the attention and feedback to each student team. Following the presentations, they told the class that they would be collecting portfolios in two days. When the portfolios were submitted, they discussed how they would divide the grading and then graded three portfolios together to ensure that they were both using the rubric consistently.*

What Is Co-teaching?

Co-teaching is a model of instruction that utilizes two educators (one special educator and one general educator) in an inclusive classroom. Although primarily known and established in the literature as a model for *special education service delivery* within the general education classroom, co-teaching has also begun to be practiced and studied as a method for mentoring novice teachers. Currently, the literature related to novice mentoring is emergent and inconclusive; what is important to remember is that the term "co-teaching" can be used to describe a variety of collaborative teaching formats. In this section, co-teaching is discussed as illustrated in "The Idea in Action" above: as a model in which two educators (usually a general and a special educator) both *deliver substantive instruction* to a diverse or blended group of students (including students with disabilities) in a single physical setting (Bauwens, Hourcade & Friend, 1989; Cook & Friend, 1995).

Co-taught instruction may be delivered in several formats or models, each of which varies the roles of the co-teachers and the group sizes of students. There are six approaches to co-teaching, each with specific strengths and weaknesses. Co-teachers should select among these models strategically depending on the learning goals and instructional needs of their students. These models are described in Table 16.1.

As noted by Friend, Cook, Hurley-Chamberlain, and Shamberger (2010), the co-teaching model with the most potential for overuse and abuse is one teach/one assist. As defined below, this model involves one teacher (typically the general educator) having primary instructional responsibility while the other (typically the special educator) managing behavior or assisting individual students as needed. Critiques of this model conclude that it fails to fully exploit the specialized knowledge and skills of the special educator, who is relegated to the role of an assistant.

As a result, one teach/one assist lacks the instructional potency to advance the achievement of students with disabilities or other diverse learners. The presumption that the "assistance" of the special educator (e.g., redirecting attention or behavior, pointing to the correct page number, providing brief explanations) is enough to ensure that students with disabilities "keep up" with the general education curriculum is not well documented. A working knowledge of co-teaching models beyond one teach/one assist is essential for ensuring that the instructional needs of students with disabilities are met within an inclusive classroom.

Co-teaching can benefit inclusive classrooms in many ways. Because of the collaboration required for this type of teaching, teachers more effectively exchange instructional strategies, gain an increased understanding of all students' needs, increase the level of content taught to students with disabilities, create an environment where students with disabilities are more accepted by their peers, and reduce teacher burnout (Scruggs, Mastropieri & McDuffie, 2007). The highly collaborative nature of co-teaching means that much of its success depends on the relationship between the two co-teachers. Many writers have compared it to a marriage, and as such, time must be invested to make it work. Dieker and Murawski (2003) identified productive planning time as a critical element of co-teaching success.

During this time, co-teachers discuss what content will be taught and how it will be delivered, how their roles and responsibilities vary and will be assigned for the coming lesson(s), or how a particular assessment will be administered and graded. For beginning co-teachers, a recommended role for the general educator is as the leader of *content* instruction, while the special educator is the leader of *strategy* instruction (Conderman, Hedin & Brenahan,

Table 16.1   Models of Co-teaching

Co-teaching Model	Description/Recommended Usage	Strengths	Weaknesses
One teach, One observe	One teacher has primary instructional responsibility, while the other collects observational data; Recommended usage = seldom	Useful for collecting student data	Doesn't exploit full expertise of both educators
One teach, One assist	One teacher has primary instructional responsibility, while the other redirects behavior or assists individual students as needed; Recommended usage = seldom	Easily implemented with no common planning time	Doesn't exploit full expertise of both educators; relegates one educator to assistant role
Station Teaching	Content is divided into stations and students are divided into groups. Each group spends a specific amount of time at each station; Recommended usage = frequent	Useful for teaching or reviewing a large amount of content in a short time; frees teachers to work with small groups	Requires extensive planning and orchestration; requires students to be self-directed
Parallel Teaching	The class is divided in half; each teacher delivers the same instruction to half the class; Recommended usage = frequent	Reduced student-teacher ratio; increased interaction/active participation	Increased noise level in the classroom can be distracting to some students
Alternative Teaching	Each teacher instructs a group of students (typically one larger group and one small group); content taught by each teacher differs depending on the instructional needs of the group; Recommended usage = frequent	Instructional needs of diverse groups of learners can be met appropriately and effectively	Increased noise level in the classroom can be distracting to some students; static groupings replicate separation for some students
Team Teaching	Both teachers share lesson instruction; typically one teacher presents content while the other presents strategy; Recommended usage = frequent	Both teachers deliver meaningful instruction	Can be distracting for some students to divide attention between two presenters

2014) within the large group. As the relationship develops, co-teachers may become more comfortable sharing and varying these roles.

Murawski and Dieker (2004) suggested specific ways with which co-teachers can utilize their roles effectively. For example, if one teacher is lecturing, the other can be modeling a note-taking strategy on the SmartBoard or implementing "brain breaks" to help students process lecture content. While one teacher is passing out papers, the other can review directions or model the first problem on an assignment. Notice that these recommendations do not say, "If the general educator is doing this," then "the special educator can be doing this." When necessary, co-teaching pairs should, of course, delegate responsibilities according to their individual areas of expertise. However, many teaching tasks require no specific expertise and thus should be allocated equitably between co-teachers. The intention behind these suggestions is that both co-teachers are actively involved in the classroom and each teacher delivers substantive instruction *at all times*.

Critical Features of Co-teaching

Although successful co-teaching is often determined by the quality of the relationship between co-teachers, *effective* co-teaching must be about more than the relationship; it must be about the learning and behavioral outcomes for diverse learners in an inclusive classroom, especially those with disabilities. Effective co-teaching involves *parity*, meaning both teachers feel respected and valued for their contributions and students perceive each teacher as equally invested and involved in their learning. Parity involves sharing all of the key roles in a co-taught classroom, including:

- **Co-planning**: Dedicated time to determine the content that will be taught, to identify and strategically apply co-teaching models and assign roles, and to plan assessment methods.
- **Co-instructing**: Classroom leadership and behavior management should be distributed and both co-teachers should work with all students while using a variety of co-teaching strategies to address instructional needs.
- **Co-assessing**: Jointly discuss diagnostic, formative, and summative assessments of all students. Determine grades jointly and share the grading workload. Discuss and determine how assessment will impact future instruction.

Perhaps the most important thing to remember is that *instructional delivery in a co-taught classroom should be significantly different than what a single teacher could provide on her/his own*, so that both professionals are actively applying their specific expertise to address individual student needs. If instruction is delivered only by the general educator and the special educator is relegated to the role of paraprofessional, it is unlikely that the achievement of students with disabilities will be satisfactory or *accelerated*. For this reason, Friend and Burrello (2005) recommended that the co-teaching model one teach/one assist be used *sparingly*; despite this recommendation, it continues to be the model with the most potential for overuse and abuse.

GUIDELINES FOR CO-PLANNING, CO-INSTRUCTING, CO-ASSESSING IMPLEMENTATION

In order to co-plan, you need to remember that exemplary co-teaching is seen in classrooms where teachers co-plan collaboratively to benefit both the class as a whole *and* the needs of individual students. For these reasons, the role of the special educator should not be diminished. Both teachers should co-plan and be seen by their students as equals and should participate *fully and actively* in whichever co-teaching model they are implementing at the time. This can only happen if co-teachers establish an open dialogue and speak honestly with each other about their goals and objectives for collaboration on an ongoing basis, for example:

- Set up a schedule that delineates co-planning time and discuss how this time will be used.
- Discuss how instructional responsibilities will be shared (e.g., grading, discipline, etc.) and how parity between both teachers will be established and communicated to students and parents.
- Discuss which co-teaching models are likely to work best, each teacher's active role within the models, and how adaptations will be made for students with disabilities.
- Determine how to evaluate the effectiveness of the co-teaching models that are being implemented.

In order to implement effective co-instruction, the field of special education has begun to consider ways in which we can move beyond one teach/one assist as the default co-teaching model. As discussed above, this model has become widespread due to its relative ease of implementation. For example, when co-planning time is in short supply or nonexistent, the special education co-teacher can float in each day and give the illusion of "support" for students with disabilities by redirecting attention, providing individual assistance on an "as needed" basis (i.e., when the student is already struggling or confused), and/or adapting tests and homework assignments.

Though convenient for many teachers and administrators trying to manage complex teaching schedules, this arrangement fails to consider whether or not students with disabilities may need more intensive co-instruction to be successful. In order for co-instructing to impact the achievement of students with disabilities in co-taught classrooms, more intensive instructional models that reduce the teacher–student ratio and provide consistent bursts of explicit, targeted teaching may be required. A co-teaching model particularly suited for this type of co-instructing arrangement is Alternative Teaching.

Alternative Teaching has the following characteristics:

- One co-teacher instructs a large group while the other works with a smaller group on different content, skills, or strategies.
- Co-teachers work together to determine alternative teaching groups, objectives, and anticipated outcomes, activities, and assessments for the content they are teaching to their individual groups.
- Alternative Teaching is appropriate for enriching or remediating instruction for a small group and is commonly used to differentiate instruction in co-taught classrooms.

A few key reminders about Alternative Teaching:

- This model allows both co-teachers to actively address the learning needs of students at risk for failure in a particular area of the core curriculum, especially if they are both skilled in the subject area and in delivering interventions.
- Alternative Teaching intensifies the role of the special educator in a co-taught classroom by utilizing his/her specialized skills in identifying students' learning needs; assessment/progress monitoring; designing systematic, intensive, and explicit instruction; and collaborative, data-based decision-making.
- Students are not allowed to fail consistently over time without targeted attempts to fill in gaps in their basic skills; facilitate understanding, conceptual development, and deeper learning; and accelerate their achievement in the core curriculum.
- Alternative Teaching is *never* defined as "the special educator works with the students with disabilities at a separate location within the classroom." It should never be used as a default co-teaching model that divides students into predetermined, fixed groupings. This defies the philosophy and goals of collaboration and inclusion.

When co-assessing, one of the obvious benefits is being able to distribute the workload of grading between two teachers in a classroom. Indeed, recommendations for co-assessing practice usually include sharing the grading burden. Co-assessment should involve more, however, than simply dividing a stack of papers, each teacher completing his or her fair share, and an "even" workload for professional parity. If, for example, the class is using co-instruction, but the general educator does all of the grading, how will the special educator know what differentiation strategies might be effective or how students with disabilities are performing in relation to their peers? Therefore, we believe that co-assessing is an important aspect of an effective and efficient co-teaching model.

Although co-teachers may interpret graded work differently—the general educator may view it in terms of students' mastery of the content, while the special educator sees areas in need of further modification—each of these viewpoints is essential to helping all students in a co-taught classroom to progress. In a classroom where co-instruction is effectively conducted, both teachers are consistently and intimately aware of *all* students' progress, and they connect this awareness to ongoing, detailed co-planning and co-instructing.

The Idea in Summary

Keeping in mind these recommendations for co-teaching implementation, the Co-Planning Worksheet (Table 16.2) can be used to co-plan effectively. This guide can be completed at the start of an instructional unit, during regular co-planning sessions, or anytime co-teachers need to focus their collaboration on the key aspects of planning and implementing instruction for both the whole group and individual learners or small groups within the inclusive classroom.

In addition, remember the following key points regarding co-teaching:

- Co-teaching is a collaborative strategy for *special education service delivery* within the general education classroom.
- One teach/one assist is not an optimal co-teaching model for utilizing the specific expertise of both teachers in the classroom. This model should be used *sparingly*.
- Dedicated co-planning time is essential to effective co-teaching practice.
- Ideally, co-planning should extend beyond what content will be covered on what day to a detailed discussion of *how* it will be taught, how instruction will be scaffolded or differentiated, and how student learning will be assessed.
- Co-teachers should strategically apply co-teaching models depending on the lesson content and instructional goals.
- Co-teaching fits within a framework of universally designed instruction by devoting the expertise of two teachers (a general educator and a special educator) to the needs of all learners in the classroom.

Table 16.2   Co-planning Worksheet

Action	Role: General Educator	Role: Special Educator
Differentiated Learning Goals		
Co-teaching Model(s) (types of co-teaching you will use and role of each instructor)		
Specific Instructional Methods, Strategies, and Materials		
Academic Skills (Content and Language Skills):		
Behavioral/Social Skills:		

Reflections on Co-teaching

- In what ways do you co-plan to utilize both of your strengths?
- How can we strategically apply co-teaching models other than one teach/one assist?
- How well executed was your co-instruction to effectively utilize both teachers in the classroom?
- How collaborative was the co-assessment of the lesson/unit?

Web Resources

Watch a video vignette of co-teaching:

- Part 1: https://www.youtube.com/watch?v=uLvvLc_kZys
- Part 2: https://www.youtube.com/watch?v=qUolkA4U4Ko

WORKING WITH PARAPROFESSIONALS

The Idea in Brief

Many inclusive classrooms also utilize paraprofessionals. As a teacher, you will need to plan meaningful roles and responsibilities for paraprofessionals and communicate with them in ways that support student learning and successful achievement. In this section, we describe an important aspect of classroom collaboration—working with paraprofessionals.

The Idea in Action

Ebony Bradford is a brand new teacher in a fourth grade inclusive classroom. The position at Joyce Kilmer Elementary School is her dream job in a diverse school district with a commitment to inclusive teaching and social justice. Although she can't wait to meet her students and start getting to know them as learners, an unexpected source of anxiety has arisen. Her principal informed her that she will have a paraprofessional working in her classroom, who is assigned to a student with a disability. None of her teacher education coursework prepared her for this type of collaboration. Mrs. Parker seems like a very nice woman, but she is old enough to be Miss Bradford's mother. She has worked at Joyce Kilmer Elementary for five years so she knows everyone and already has a working knowledge of the school. As a mom of a student in fifth grade, Mrs. Parker is also connected to the community in ways that Miss Bradford is not. If she makes mistakes during her first year of teaching, will Mrs. Parker air them over the backyard fence?

All of the teachers and their paraprofessionals were supposed to meet for the first time at a special breakfast on the first day of school. With her anxiety building, Miss Bradford decided to invite Mrs. Parker to meet with her before the first day of school to discuss roles and responsibilities for the school year. Miss Bradford wrote out a list of points she wanted to cover in their meeting so she wouldn't leave anything out:

1. *I will meet with you weekly (Mondays during my prep period) to let you know what my expectations are for the week. I find it best to write it out; that way you can always refer to it. I will use a plan called a Paraprofessional Planning Worksheet (see Table 16.3). I will always have a plan for you so you understand my expectations clearly.*
2. *Keep the lines of communication open. As my assistant in the classroom, you are my lifeline at school. If I have to be out, you will be the reason the classroom runs smoothly. This year I am planning to have a communication center where I can post notes for the day and an "Ask Ebony" notebook so you can write things down that I need to address at one of our meetings. I also want to include a calendar in this area so we are always on the same page regarding important upcoming dates, deadlines, testing days, etc.*
3. *I will ask you for ideas and suggestions. As the person working closely with Jayden, you are a wealth of information and sometimes will have an idea that I never thought of. This can be for anything from a lesson idea, behavior modification, or a suggestion on how to word a parent email. As a new teacher, I will need a lot of support, and I'm grateful to share my class with another adult.*

    Miss Bradford felt much more comfortable beginning the school year knowing she and Mrs. Parker had communicated clearly and established shared expectations for the classroom. At the end of each marking period, she plans to have a "check in" meeting with Mrs. Parker to make sure things continue to run smoothly for Jayden and the rest of the class.

Working with Paraprofessionals

Another key aspect of collaboration across the K–12 continuum is working with paraprofessionals. In contrast to a co-teacher who is another certified educator, a *paraprofessional* (sometimes referred to as an aide, paraeducator, or monitor) is a special education assistant who is not licensed to teach, but conducts other responsibilities with individual students as well as organizationally within the classroom. A student may be assigned a one-on-one paraprofessional as part of his or her Individualized Education Plan (IEP) or students may interact with a paraprofessional assigned to the classroom. In recent decades, the number of special education paraprofessionals has increased dramatically as more students with disabilities gain access to general education classrooms.

    Paraprofessionals are important members of the instructional team for students with disabilities. Within a co-taught classroom, the special educator and

Table 16.3 Paraprofessional Planning Worksheet

Time/ Activity	Teacher 1	Paraprofessional 1	Teacher 2	Comments/Notes
8:40– 9:00	Lead Morning Meeting	Set up computer stations for group write.	Teach/practice social skills strategy.	Student 1 in social skills group.
9:00– 9:40	Write mini lesson and group write	Get Student 1 started with writing task; circulate and check back periodically.	Teach small-group writing strategy to students struggling with descriptive vocabulary.	
9:40– 10:20	Read independent reading books and post-it	Assist Student 1 with listening center/audio book.		Speech therapist will push in to facilitate KD in comprehension.
10:20– 10:30	Snack	Take Student 2 and Student 3 to bathroom before snack.	Facilitate social skills/ communication at snack.	
10:30– 11:10	Lead Connected Math lesson 3.8	Assist with group work/ table tasks.	Teach a communication strategy during group work.	Student 3 in Speech.
11:10– 11:50	Science Lab	Assist student 2 and student 3 in their assigned groups.	Lead lab summary discussion; model graphic organizer notes.	Student 1 in OT
11:50– 12:30	Lunch/Prep Work	Lunch/Prep Work	Lunch/Prep Work	

the paraprofessional are usually viewed as the "experts" regarding the needs of students with disabilities and assume much of the responsibility for planning, adapting, and implementing instruction for identified students. Ideally, having a trained, committed paraprofessional can make an enormous difference in the implementation of a student's IEP and in the overall functioning of an inclusive classroom. Issues can arise, however, when paraprofessionals are asked to do things they are not trained to do, have been co-opted into administrative work for the school outside of their role in the classroom, or are not directed effectively by the classroom teacher.

As an inclusive educator, it is essential to clearly understand the roles and responsibilities of paraprofessionals. For example, paraprofessionals are not trained, certified *teachers*; as a result, students will not do as well or better academically or socially when they are taught by paraprofessionals (Gerber, Finn, Achilles & Boyd-Zaharias, 2001). For a busy teacher trying to meet the broad spectrum of learning and behavior needs in an inclusive classroom, relying on a paraprofessional often feels like a big relief because it can shift or redistribute responsibility for meeting the needs of a student with a disability.

However, paraprofessional support can sometimes have unintended negative effects. Classroom teachers may become less engaged and fail to communicate directly with students as the paraprofessional becomes a "barrier" to direct communication. When a student is consistently on the sidelines with paraprofessional close by, it can separate students with disabilities, isolate them from their peers, and encourage overly dependent, insular relationships between these students and the paraprofessionals assigned to them. Overdependence can adversely affect the social and academic growth of students with disabilities. These unintentional effects negate the very point of inclusive education, which is to include students with disabilities in the general education classroom to the fullest extent possible.

At times, it can be difficult to know when the level of paraprofessional support is appropriate and when it might be detrimental. When such dilemmas arise, a good question to ask yourself is, "Would this be acceptable if the student did *not* have a disability?" For example, would you allow a paraprofessional to provide primary reading instruction for a student without a disability? Would you allow a student without a disability to spend the bulk of his/her social time (e.g., lunch recess) with a paraprofessional rather than with his or her peers?

Although these examples may sound extreme, such situations occur all the time for students with disabilities. It is critical to utilize paraprofessionals in ways that minimize unintended, undesirable effects. Involving students with disabilities in determining the level and type of paraprofessional support can be helpful. Paraprofessionals can be used for whole-class support or directed in ways that free up the classroom teachers to spend time instructing students with disabilities. It is also important to keep students with disabilities actively involved with teachers and peers, seated in the midst of the entire class, and engaged in supportive, peer-assisted or cooperative learning and instruction.

The Idea in Summary

There is no substitute for the engagement of highly qualified teacher(s) in the instructional process for a student with a disability. This means that the classroom teacher(s) assume full responsibility for educating all students in their classroom regardless of whether they are identified with a disability, are well versed in the present levels of performance and expected learning outcomes for all students, and *direct the work* of paraprofessionals. Such direction includes providing training and mentoring to paraprofessionals, maintaining open dialogue and accountability, giving frequent feedback, and adjusting paraprofessional support according to student needs.

Table 16.3 provides an example of a Paraprofessional Planning Worksheet that can be used by classroom teachers to organize and direct the work of paraprofessionals. This type of tool is essential for ensuring that the work of paraprofessionals is meaningful and appropriate, especially in a co-taught classroom where the work of multiple adults must be managed effectively.

Teachers must be vigilant not to inadvertently give up their engagement with students with disabilities by allowing paraprofessionals to become a barrier. This can be achieved through some simple steps, such as:

- showing appreciation and respect for paraprofessionals' work;
- clarifying their roles and responsibilities;
- aligning tasks and responsibilities with their skills;
- orienting them to the school, classroom, and students;
- providing ongoing training, support, and feedback;
- directing their work through ongoing, supportive supervision; and
- seeking their input and providing opportunities for them to be meaningful contributors to the instructional team for their assigned student.

Reflections on Working with Paraprofessionals

- How am I co-planning with the paraprofessionals working in the classroom?
- How am I utilizing paraprofessionals to support in meaningful ways during co-instructing?
- How do I include paraprofessional input and suggestions to help our co-teaching?
- How are paraprofessionals included in my co-assessing?

Web Resources

- The National Association of Special Education Teachers (NASET) provides extensive web-based resources for working with paraprofessionals: http://www.naset.org/2877.0.html.
- Complete this online IRIS module on working with students with visual impairments, which includes important information about working with paraprofessionals: http://iris.peabody.vanderbilt.edu/module/v03-focusplay/#content.

CHECKLIST FOR IMPLEMENTATION

1. Did you find time to co-plan the lesson?
   Yes _____ No _____
   Evidence_____
2. Was the co-planning time effectively and efficiently used?
   Yes _____ No _____
   Evidence_____
3. Did the co-instruction go as planned throughout the lesson?
   Yes _____ No _____
   Evidence_____
4. Did you have time for co-assessing the lesson?
   Yes _____ No _____
   Evidence_____
5. Was the co-assessing effective and efficient for the lesson?
   Yes _____ No _____
   Evidence_____
6. Was the co-teaching model used effective and efficient?
   Yes _____ No _____
   Evidence_____
7. Did you clearly communicate expectations with your
   paraprofessionals?
   Yes _____ No _____
   Evidence_____
8. Did you implement paraprofessional feedback while co-teaching?
   Yes _____ No _____
   Evidence_____
9. Do you work closely with paraprofessionals to help aid all
   co-instructing activities?
   Yes _____ No _____
   Evidence_____

CONCLUSION

In this chapter, we presented two approaches to collaboration in inclusive classrooms to support the achievement of students with disabilities: co-teaching and working with paraprofessionals. For novice teachers, the distinction between co-planning, co-instructing, and co-assessing is crucial. Learning how to implement each of these forms of collaboration effectively will be an ongoing task in their professional development (please see the checklist below).

Most new teachers—even the most natural of collaborators—need lots of practice to teach well with another professional. Learning how you can best utilize a paraprofessional for both whole class and individual student support takes time, trial, and error. Because collaboration involves relationships, it can be messy; different people will approach any given classroom situation through the lens of their own background knowledge, schooling, life experiences, skills, and feelings.

The risks of ineffective collaboration are great: the classroom will not function as well as a whole and the learning of students most at risk for failure will be jeopardized. As a classroom teacher, it is important to be diligent to keep open lines of communication and treat each collaboration as a work in progress. Like a marriage, collaboration needs attention and effort to work well for the benefit of all learners.

GLOSSARY OF TERMS

Alternative teaching—a co-teaching model in which one teacher instructs a large group while the other works with a smaller group on different content/tasks.

Co-assessing—the aspect of co-teaching practice that involves gathering and discussing information from multiple sources in order to develop a deep understanding of what students know, understand, and can do; the co-assessment process culminates when assessment results are used to improve instruction and outcomes for learners.

Co-instructing—the aspect of co-teaching practice in which two teachers provide meaningful instruction using a model other than one teach/one assist.

Co-planning—the aspect of co-teaching practice in which two teachers work collaboratively to create a detailed plan for co-instruction and co-assessment.

Co-teaching—a model of instruction that utilizes two educators (one special educator and one general educator) in an inclusive classroom.

Paraprofessional—a school employee who works under the supervision of teachers or other professional practitioners. Their jobs are instructional and/or organizational, and they may provide other direct services to children and youth and their families.

Parity—means that both teachers in a co-taught classroom feel respected and valued for their contributions, and students perceive each teacher as equally invested and involved in their learning.

Progress monitoring—used to assess students' academic performance, quantify a student's rate of improvement or responsiveness to instruction, and evaluate the effectiveness of instruction.

Progress monitoring—can be implemented with individual students or an entire class.

Related services—the term for those services that a student with a disability needs in order to benefit from special education. Related services include speech therapy, occupational therapy, physical therapy, and rehabilitation counseling. Transportation to school is also a related service.

Social constructivism—a variety of cognitive *constructivism* that emphasizes the collaborative nature of much learning.

REFERENCES

Bauwens, J., Hourcade, J. J., & Friend, M. (1989). Cooperative teaching: A model for general and special education integration. *Remedial and Special Education, 10*(2), 17–22.

Bloom, B. S. (Ed.) (1956). *Taxonomy of educational objectives. Handbook 1: Cognitive domain*. White Plains, NY: Longman.

Bruner, J. (1985). Vygotsky: An historical and conceptual perspective. In J. V. Wetsch (Ed.), *Culture, communication, and cognition: Vygotskian perspectives* (pp. 21–34). London: Cambridge University Press.

Conderman, G., Hedin, L., & Bresnahan, V. (2014). Strategy Instruction for Middle and Secondary Students with Mild Disabilities: Creating Independent Learners. Thousand Oaks, CA: Corwin.

Cook, L., & Friend, M. (1995). Co-teaching: Guidelines for creating effective practice. *Focus on Exceptional Children, 28*(3), 1–16.

Dewey, J. (2009). *Democracy and education: An introduction to the philosophy of education*. New York: Cosimo Classics.

Dieker, L. A., & Murawski, W. W. (2003). Co-teaching at the secondary level: Unique issues, current trends, and suggestions for success. *The High School Journal, 86*, 1–13.

Friend, M., Cook, L., Hurley-Chamberlain, D., & Shamberger, C. (2010). Co-teaching: An illustration of the complexity of collaboration in special education. *Journal of Educational and Psychological Consultation, 20*(1), 9–27.

Friend, M. (Co-producer with L. Burrello & J. Burrello). (2005). The power of two: Including students through co-teaching (2nd ed.).Bloomington, IN: Elephant Rock Productions.

Gerber, S. B., Finn, J. D., Achilles, C. M., & Boyd-Zaharias, J. (2001). Teacher aides and students' academic achievement. *Educational Evaluation and Policy Analysis, 23*(2), 123–143.

Murawski, W. W., & Dieker, L. A. (2004). Tips and strategies for co-teaching at the secondary level. *Teaching Exceptional Children, 36*(5), 52–58.

Scruggs, T. A., Mastropieri, M. A., & McDuffie, K. A. (2007). Co-teaching in inclusive classrooms: A metasynthesis of qualitative research. *Exceptional Children, 73*(4), 392–416.

Slavin, R. E. (1989). Research on cooperative learning: An international perspective. *Scandinavian Journal of Educational Research, 33*(4), 231–232.

Vygotsky, L. (1980). *Mind in society: The development of higher psychological processes.* Cambridge, MA: Harvard University Press.

Section IV

PUTTING IT ALL TOGETHER

Chapter 17

"Where Do I Start?"

Guiding Novice Teachers to Improve Their Practice through Self-Reflection and Action Research

Mary Petrón and Baburhan Uzum

The purpose of this chapter is to provide novice teachers with the tools necessary to engage in continuous learning and development as an educator. Novice teachers often feel overwhelmed by the number of areas of their practice that they need to improve upon, such as issues in lesson delivery and classroom management, or differentiating instruction for diverse learners. Understanding and engaging in *self-reflection* and *action research* will help you in your role as a novice teacher identify, prioritize, and address teaching and learning problems in your classroom. In this chapter, we will first define "self-reflection" and "action research." Then, we will help you design and implement an action plan. Finally, we will illustrate how you can evaluate whether your actions have been successful or need further modification.

WHAT IS SELF-REFLECTION?

The concept of self-reflection has been widely used in educational settings. You may already be familiar with the process since you probably spent many hours reflecting on your teaching and learning experiences throughout your teacher preparation course work. Although the term can be used to mean thinking critically about past or present experiences, it has a history of systematicity and could prove to be a great learning tool if its potential is fully utilized. The notion of self-reflection dates back to John Dewey's (1933) conceptualization: thinking carefully about one's beliefs and knowledge about an issue, as well as the associated causes and effects.

There are three characteristics of reflective teaching: open-mindedness (being open to different points of view), responsibility (feeling responsible for the consequences of one's actions), and wholeheartedness (investing in educational improvement with an open mind and a sense of responsibility) (Dewey, 1933; Schön, 1983; Valli, 1997). A few decades later, it was refined by Schön (1993) to include spontaneous decisions to address unexpected events. In its simplest definition, self-reflection is thinking about what you are doing and why you are doing it.

Within the field of education, many terms have been used to refer to the process such as reflection, self-reflection, contemplation, reflective practice, and self-inquiry. What these key terms have in common is that they refer to processes with the goal of encouraging you to notice, identify, and study how your past experiences, beliefs about good teaching, and pedagogical knowledge base (or lack thereof) affect your instructional decisions (Farrell, 2015). Reflection helps you notice important processes in the classroom and study the factors that are contributing to these processes.

Most scholars agree on three basic levels of reflection: (1) *descriptive reflection*: describing a situation or problem addressing what, where, when, and who questions (e.g., What happened in the classroom? How did it affect the students' learning?); (2) *comparative reflection*: thinking about the situation from different perspectives (e.g., How do students see the same problem?); and 3) *critical reflection*: considering the problem in light of your goals, values, and beliefs (e.g., What role do my beliefs have in solving or perpetuating the problem?) (Farrell, 2015; Jay & Johnson, 2002).

Critical reflection represents the highest level of reflective engagement and is an important goal. However, the lower levels (e.g., descriptive and comparative) are also very useful, especially for novice teachers who are still learning about their new workplace and making sense of their experiences (Farrell, 2007).

In addition to the levels of engagement, there are three types of reflection: (1) *reflection in action*: making critical instructional decisions on your feet as problems occur; (2) *reflection on action*; recalling your experiences after the class is over; and (3) *reflection for action*: thinking about what to do differently building on past and present experiences. For example, in your fifth grade math class you notice that your students have difficulty with story problems. You decide to help students by mapping out the problem with diagrams and visuals (reflection in action). After your class, while planning your next lesson, you opt to change the way in which you initially present the problems to try and head off student confusion (reflection on action).

After trying out several strategies to scaffold students' understanding of word problems, you decide you need additional professional development and sign up for a regional conference organized by your state's association of mathematics teachers (reflection for action). Systematic reflection on your classroom practice, as illustrated above, can serve as the basis of action research, also known as teacher research, which involves research by teachers for teachers.

WHAT IS ACTION RESEARCH?

The history of action research dates back to the 1930s, and the method is often credited to Kurt Lewin who lived between 1890 and 1947. The original use of the term was about addressing daily problems by ordinary individuals or groups of people, using self-reflections, discussions, decisions, and actions. Action research in educational settings can be defined as a systematic study of teaching and learning problems to gather information about how well the students learn, how classrooms and schools operate, and what kind of improvements can be done to enhance the teaching and learning process (Mills, 2013).

Unlike traditional research, action research is conducted by teachers or other stakeholders in an educational context. Action research typically follows these steps: (1) identify a teaching and learning problem; (2) collect information about this problem; (3) analyze and interpret the information; (4) develop an action plan; (5) implement the plan; (6) evaluate its effectiveness in addressing the problem. In step 7, on the basis of your results, you may have to make modifications and/or go back to step 1. Action research is cyclical and self-reflection is an integral part of the whole action research cycle.

Let's consider the experiences of two novice teachers; both teach Spanish as a world language and have had similar preparation as teachers. Yet, they take very different paths during their initial year of teaching.

Deidre is a first-year Spanish teacher at a small high school where the student body is diverse. About half of the students in her classes are heritage language learners who speak Spanish in their homes in varying degrees. Most days she feels overwhelmed. She often thinks she is a failure because she believes that she is deficient in so many areas of teaching. She struggles to keep track of all the administrative tasks required of her by the school. She frequently gets behind in her grading. She has classroom management issues in several classes because the heritage language learners already know what she is teaching and are bored. She doesn't think she focuses enough on pronunciation with her beginners. Her list of defects seems endless. No one told her when she was studying to be a teacher that she would be faced with all this. She is the only Spanish teacher at the school and feels isolated. Since she finds it impossible to tackle all that she needs to work on, she just begins to follow the textbook lock-step and focuses on getting through the day.

Clearly, Deidre is overwhelmed by the complex nature of teaching. Rather than accepting the fact that she is novice and working toward continuous development, she is paralyzed by her desire for perfection. Since she cannot do it all, she opts to do nothing.

Cassidy, the second teacher, is also a Spanish teacher at a diverse high school. In fact, both Deidre and Cassidy are in very similar teaching positions and have gone through comparable teacher preparation programs. However, Cassidy chooses to take a very different route.

> *Cassidy often feels overwhelmed by the many responsibilities and tasks of teaching. However, rather than being paralyzed by her perceived deficiencies, she decides to call her former mentor teacher for advice. Her mentor reminds her that all beginning teachers have a lot to work on and cannot possibly have the same knowledge and skills as a seasoned veteran teacher may have. The mentor suggests that Cassidy prioritize her areas of improvement and set a goal or two for herself every nine weeks. This way at the end of the year she will have improved in at least four areas. The mentor also tells Cassidy to remember why she wanted to be a teacher in the first place when she sets her priorities. Cassidy recalls that one of the reasons she wanted to be a Spanish teacher was to empower students to speak the language and not just to conjugate verbs. With this in mind, she chooses to focus on improving the quantity and quality of speaking activities in her Spanish II class. She looks for resources online, both practice and research oriented.*

Like Deidre, Cassidy would also love to be a perfect teacher. However, she recognizes that this is an impossible feat and opts to work toward improvement and not toward perfection.

Our intent is to help you systematize your efforts to develop as a teacher through a cycle of self-reflection and action research. Like Cassidy, you need to target and prioritize what you would like to work on. In the section that follows, we lay out a basic path to continuous improvement using these tools.

OUTLINE FOR SELF-REFLECTION AND ACTION

Identify and Categorize Your Most Pressing Needs

- Begin by keeping a list electronically or on paper of the areas you would like to improve. The format doesn't matter; the only recommendation is that you keep it within easy reach so you can add items as you go about your day. For example, I need to find a more effective way to teach science vocabulary.
- Reflecting on your day will also help. This could involve *descriptive reflection* where you add details to some issue on your list in order to get a clear

picture of the matter. It could also be comparative reflection in the sense that you could consider the same problem you have identified from different perspectives, for example, comparing how you view the problem with how students view it. *Critical reflection* is also important, for example, taking into account how relationships of power in the broader context affect the situation.

- You may want to consider dividing your list into categories, like administrative, classroom management, lesson planning, and so on. It may help you prioritize.
- Limit the amount of time that you will use to compile this list. A week or two should be more than sufficient. If you stretch it out, you run the risk of having so many items on your list that you will be overwhelmed and choose to do nothing.

Write four of your most pressing needs below:

1.

2.

3.

4.

Setting Priorities

- Now, you should use your list to prioritize and set your goals. It is important for you to reflect on why you wanted to be a teacher and your values and beliefs about good teaching when you decide on your priorities. Very few of us would answer that we wanted to fail students or get children to stand in a straight line. Using critical reflection in this manner, you are better able to weed out relatively minor issues from ones that involve your values and professional goals. Furthermore, it provides you with the opportunity to consider your goals in light of working toward a more just society. For example, working to ensure that the special education students are successful in your class is a just goal; trying to keep them out of your classes altogether is not.
- Choose at least four goals on the list before narrowing it down. It is always better to have options. Then, select one or two and forge ahead without going back and thinking that you should have chosen something else.

- Make sure that you make the goals manageable. You want to experience a sense of accomplishment. You do the same as a teacher; you don't give a second grader a copy of *War and Peace* and tell him or her to read it. You work within a child's Zone of Proximal Development and should do the same with yourself.
- Once you have chosen your goal/s, gather information.

Select two goals that you would like focus on in this nine-week period:

1.

2.

Explore Personal Connections

- Ask veteran teachers what they would do. However, remember to seek out good teachers. They aren't hard to find and don't necessarily have to be in your content area. Secondary school teachers can learn a lot from elementary teachers and vice versa.
- If there is no one on your campus that you can talk to or you want advice particular to your content area, ask a former professor or mentor teacher. Most feel honored that you have asked them and are willing to help.

List four people who will be able to provide help and advice:

1.

2.

3.

4.

Search for Materials and Resources

- Look at teacher websites to see what resources are available. There are many out there who have great suggestions for activities, games, and so on. However, keep your goal in mind; if the material does not contribute to your goal, it is not appropriate. Again, critically reflecting on why you wanted to be a teacher as you delve into the resources is crucial. You may find some fun ideas for kill and drill, but is that who you are as a teacher?

- Consult the websites of professional organizations in your field, for example, the National Council for Social Studies or the National Council of Teachers of Mathematics.
- Consider academic resources. If you are a member of an alumni association, you often still have access to the library of your alma mater.
- Remember that you have a college degree and are more than capable of reading research. If you need to skip over some of the statistical procedures or methods of data collection, go ahead. There is not a quiz over the material at the end.

Find four websites/places to search for materials and resources:

1.

2.

3

4.

Interpret and Map Out a Plan of Action

- You may have collected quite a few resources above. Jot down a few notes that summarize your research.
- Again, reflection is important in the process, particularly that of comparative and critical, because it will afford you the opportunity to reframe the issue in light of your research.
- On the basis of what you have discovered through your perusal of the resources, determine what your course of action will be. For example, I want to make the history content more accessible for my ELLs. According to my research, I should preview the material first before having them read. Several of the sources I consulted suggested that graphic organizers, picture walks, and additional visuals are effective.
- Gather the necessary materials needed to implement the course of action. Lay out how you will use them and when.
- Set a time table for your experiment. For example, if you are trying out a new way of teaching vocabulary, try it for a couple of weeks. Don't just do it once. Generally, nothing works the first time you try it.
- Determine what your criteria of success will be. For example, if you want to increase the quality of student's writing, determine what you are looking

for with respect to quality and develop a rubric or use one that you have found in your research.

What is the goal of your action plan? What would you like to accomplish?

_____

_____

_____

What is your measure of success? How will you know if your plan addressed your goals or not?

_____

_____

_____

Apply and Evaluate Your Action Plan

- Implement your plan following the steps you outlined above.
- Be willing to modify your plan if you feel something is not working.
- Evaluate whether you have met your goals according to the criteria you established.
- Reflect on what happened; were other issues/problems solved as a result. How did students react? Analyze what you learned as a result of the process.
- If you improved one aspect of your practice, celebrate. If your action plan did not appear to be effective, consult your resources again and develop a new plan to address the issue.

Were you able to accomplish your goals?

_____

_____

_____

What did you learn as a result of going through this process?

_____

_____

_____

The diagram below illustrates the steps of action research. It is a cyclical process, beginning with identifying and categorizing needs and ending with action and evaluation of the outcomes. Please note that reflection is embedded throughout the entire process in the form of descriptions, comparisons, examples, successes, and failures.

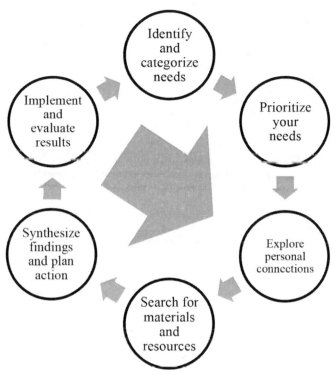

Figure 17.1

CONCLUSION

In this chapter, we set out to help novice teachers discover the path of continuous development through self-reflection and action research. In contrast to doctors who practice for years as residents under the direct guidance and supervision of highly experienced mentors, novice teachers are often in charge and on their own after they graduate from a four-year degree program. The demands of teaching are high, even for a veteran teacher. Consequently, it is easy for a beginning teacher to become discouraged and feel like a failure.

The key to surviving *and* thriving is to work toward improvement rather than perfection. By selecting a few specific goals a year and following through on them, you will experience success and continue to develop as an educator. Much like the children you teach, as a novice teacher, you have a Zone of Proximal Development. We don't teach addition, subtraction, multiplication, and division all in one day. Instead, we tackle one at time and work up from there. The processes of self-reflection and action research outlined in this chapter will guide you to becoming a better teacher.

CHECKLIST FOR ENGAGING IN REFLECTION AND ACTION RESEARCH

Check your level of engagement in reflection and action research. Read each statement below and circle the option that best represents you. Give yourself points for each answer:

5 = Always, 4 = Usually, 3 = Regularly, 2 = Sometimes, 1 = Never.

- I notice problems with teaching and learning in my classroom.
  5 = Always   4 = Usually   3 = Regularly   2 = Sometimes   1 = Never

- In order to understand and address a problem, I describe the materials, places, students, and events involving the problem.
  5 = Always   4 = Usually   3 = Regularly   2 = Sometimes   1 = Never

- I think about how students, administrators, and parents might see the same problem.
  5 = Always   4 = Usually   3 = Regularly   2 = Sometimes   1 = Never

- I take stock of my personal resources (e.g., mentors, professors, colleagues) where I can get advice about the problem.
  5 = Always   4 = Usually   3 = Regularly   2 = Sometimes   1 = Never

- I explore websites and educational organizations to find help about the problem.
  5 = Always   4 = Usually   3 = Regularly   2 = Sometimes   1 = Never

- I synthesize the information from multiple sources, like colleagues and professional organizations.
  5 = Always   4 = Usually   3 = Regularly   2 = Sometimes   1 = Never

- I develop a hypothesis and a plan of action to address the problem.
  5 = Always   4 = Usually   3 = Regularly   2 = Sometimes   1 = Never

- I allocate time in my classroom to implement my action plan.
  5 = Always   4 = Usually   3 = Regularly   2 = Sometimes   1 = Never

- I evaluate the success or failure of my action plan.
  5 = Always   4 = Usually   3 = Regularly   2 = Sometimes   1 = Never

- I explore other possibilities if my plan did not address the problem.
  5 = Always   4 = Usually   3 = Regularly   2 = Sometimes   1 = Never

- I see myself as invested in improving my practice through self-reflection and action research.
  5 = Always   4 = Usually   3 = Regularly   2 = Sometimes   1 = Never

Scoring: Add up the numbers you circled, Total: _____

Your level of engagement in reflection and action research is: (a) Strongly dedicated = 45–55; (b) On the right track: 35–44; (c) Lacking commitment: 25–34; (d) Needs work: 10–24.

APPENDIX 1: EXTENSION MATERIALS

1. *How to Formulate a Research Question?*
   The following video will help you formulate the research question which will be explored through action research: https://www.youtube.com/watch?v=SXhOZmFID4c.
2. *Examples of Teacher Action Research*
   The article here provides an overview of teacher action research and has great examples of teacher action research in the early childhood setting: https://www.naeyc.org/files/naeyc/file/vop/Nature%20of%20Teacher%20Research.pdf.
3. *Keeping a Reflective Journal*
   The following website provides information on keeping a reflective journal. It will help you decide what will work best for your needs as an educator: http://infed.org/mobi/writing-and-keeping-journals-a-guide-for-educators-and-social-practitioners/.
4. *New Teacher's Survival Guide*
   The following webpage is designed by U.S. Department of Education and has valuable information and suggestions for first-year teachers: http://www2.ed.gov/teachers/become/about/survivalguide/index.html.
5. *Online Teacher Support*
   ProTeacher is an online venue for teachers. There are forums for first-year teachers as well as grade-level/content-specific forums: http://www.proteacher.net/.

GLOSSARY OF TERMS

Self-reflection—thinking carefully about objects, places, people, events, and key incidents in your personal or professional context. In educational settings, self-reflection is thinking about your own background, beliefs, values, goals, knowledge base, strengths, and weaknesses, and how these might impact your instructional decisions in the classroom. There are three levels of self-reflection: descriptive reflection, comparative reflection, and critical reflection.

Descriptive reflection—this is the first step of self-reflection and involves asking the questions: who, what, when, where, and why? You may be analyzing a classroom procedure or problem. Describe the place, people, materials, time, and a play-by-play of what happened.

Comparative reflection—this is the second step of self-reflection and is about making connections and comparisons across the elements you described. For example, your description of a classroom event might be different from how your students see it. In order to engage in comparative reflection, you step out of your own perspective and start thinking about how the other people involved see this problem or if anyone else had similar problems and how they solved it. Exploring personal connections can be a part of the process of comparative reflection.

Critical reflection—this is the third and final step of self-reflection. In this stage, you connect your descriptions and comparisons with your goals, values, and beliefs. What is the meaning of this event in the classroom? Why does this teaching problem matter to you? Why do you think it matters to students or anyone else? Why do you see yourself as responsible for addressing this problem? How will your actions impact your students, your school, and the general community? How does this reflection transform your perspective?

Action research—this is a type of research conducted by teachers themselves. It is also known as teacher research. In traditional research (not action research), professors and scholars study an educational issue and write a scientific paper about the problem in academic journals. The researchers typically end their long reports with pedagogical implications for teachers. However, these implications have little impact on how teachers actually teach. To bridge the gap, teachers are engaged in their own research because they have the best understanding of what is happening in their classroom. In this manner, teachers are empowered to address the problems in their classroom using self-reflection and action research.

REFERENCES

Dewey, J. (1933). *How we think: A restatement of the relation of reflective thinking to the educative process.* Boston, MA: DC Heath and Company.

Farrell, T. S. C. (2007). *Reflective language teaching: From research to practice.* London: Continuum Press.

Farrell, T. S. C. (2015). *Promoting teacher reflection in second language education: A framework for TESOL professionals.* New York: Routledge.

Jay, J. K., & Johnson, K. L. (2002). Capturing complexity: A typology of reflective practice for teacher education. *Teaching and Teacher Education, 18,* 73–85.

Mills, G. E. (2013). *Action research: A guide for the teacher researcher.* Boston, MA: Pearson.

Schön, D. A. (1983). *The reflective practitioner: How professionals think in action.* New York: Basic Books, Inc.

Valli, L. (1997). Listening to other voices: A description of teacher reflection in the United States. *Peabody Journal of Education, 72*(1), 67–88.

Afterword

Using the Master Checklist in a Masterful Way

David Schwarzer

Effective teaching is a very complex set of skills to master. But, of course, you already know that by reading this book and by participating in a teacher preparation program. Like other complex skills (flying airplanes, surgery, etc.) I believe that having checklists to help the novice practitioner creates better situational awareness is crucial. Therefore, in this chapter I created a master checklist on the basis of all the checklists developed by all the expert authors throughout the book.

I crafted three master checklists, one for each one of the stages of teaching (before, during, and after—planning, documenting, and reflecting). These master checklists should be used as scaffolding tools (and not recipes to be followed) to help you plan, document, and reflect on your own teaching experiences as a novice teacher. Moreover, it could also be used as a tool for mentor teachers helping you during the first years in your teaching position, to focus your conversations about teaching.

Following is a section explaining why checklists are useful in mastering complex skills in general and how their design is important. It will explain why the use of effective checklists can enhance users' situational awareness during the task.

WHY CHECKLISTS?

As with other complex skills, for example, flying an airplane, checklists are essential. According to Degani and Weiner (1991),

> The major function of the flight deck checklist is to ensure that the crew will properly configure the airplane for any given segment of flight. It forms the basis of procedural standardization in the cockpit. (p. 3)

313

Although standardization of teaching is not the goal of any checklist we have designed here, the master checklist will allow the novice teacher and the mentor teacher center their conversations on some basic procedures that could be very useful to address as part of the observation/mentoring session.

Several positive outcomes can follow from using a checklist. According to Degani and Weiner (1991), the following objectives can be achieved when checklists are used properly:

1. Provide a foundation for verifying the configuration of the task at hand.
2. Provide a sequential framework to meet operational requirements.
3. Allow mutual supervision among colleagues.
4. Dictate the duties of each one of the teaching colleagues in order to facilitate optimum coordination as well as logical distribution of workload.
5. Enhance a team concept by keeping all teachers "in the loop."
6. Serve as a quality control tool by mentors observing novice teachers.

Moreover, according to Nagano's work (as cited in Degani & Weiner, 1991),

> another objective of an effective checklist, often overlooked, is the promotion of a positive "attitude" toward the use of this procedure. (p. 4)

Furthermore, it is crucial to reiterate what others have said about the way in which checklists should be used. Degani and Weiner (1991) state:

> The various ways of conducting a checklist are influenced not only by the checklist device and the method of using it, but also by its "philosophy of use.... The fundamental decision regarding which items should be presented on the checklist is a cardinal question in checklist philosophy." (pp. 4–5)

Therefore, the checklist created here is ONLY a tool for you to follow and change as desired. Hopefully, after experimenting with the tool provided here, you and your colleagues may design your own checklists on the basis of the needs of your local school communities.

Finally, the design of the checklist is important. According to Sanders and McCormick (1987),

> The designer can apply these principles for checklist design by:
> * Grouping the items corresponding to a system such as pressurization, hydraulic, electrical, etc., into chunks of checklist items.
> * Physically (graphically) separating these chunks while designing the layout of the checklist card." (pp. 11–12)

In order to facilitate a logical flow while initially creating the checklist, the "flow pattern" of the particular task is crucial in the development of an effective checklist (Sanders & McCormick, 1987).

This information is particularly important for teaching since, like flying, it involves a complex set of skills to master. Moreover, understanding the flow pattern of teaching to include planning, documenting, and reflecting is crucial for all reflective practitioners in the classroom.

This is why checklists used during flight are subdivided to ensure a manageable tool to be used daily.

> The complete flight checklist is sub-divided into specific task-checklists for almost all segments of the flight, i.e., PREFLIGHT, TAXI, BEFORE LANDING, etc.; and in particular before the critical segments: TAKEOFF, APPROACH, and LANDING. (Degani & Weiner, 1991, p. 4)

Like the flight checklists, the master checklists presented here are also subdivided into three sections (knowing your students, curriculum development, and pedagogical decisions) and also in the different critical segments of teaching (planning, teaching, and reflecting).

When checklists are effectively used, they may help novice teachers being present and remember all the subskills that are part of the design, implementation, and evaluation of effective classroom practices without relying solely on their memory.

WHAT IS SITUATIONAL AWARENESS?

According to (Hazlehurst, McMullen et al., 2007),

> It is commonly understood that "situation awareness" (SA) is a critical feature of effective human performance in complex tasks. In the human factors literature, four epistemic properties are taken by researchers to underlie SA: (1) the perception of relevant facts, (2) comprehension of those facts for the current situation, (3) projection forward to possible future situations, and (4) prediction of future situations given expected external influences. (p. 549)

Endsley's (1995) theory of situation awareness was developed to tackle problems faced by human factor practitioners that must deal with physical and perceptual tasks in dynamic systems. Dynamic systems are those that evolve with time and are characterized by constant change.

> True SA, involves far more than merely being aware of numerous pieces of data. It also requires a much more advanced level of situation understanding

and a projection of future system sates in light of the operator's pertinent goals. As such, SA presents a level of focus that goes beyond traditional information-processing approaches in attempting to explain human behavior in operating complex systems.... They must ascertain the critical features in widely varying situations to determine the best course of action. (pp. 32, 33)

Like surgeons and flying pilots, teachers need to be present while teaching—having a checklist to center their craft may free them to be much more responsive to the complex system of the classroom that is part of their daily work. By being "in the moment" with their students, novice teachers will be able to respond much more effectively when challenges or opportunities happen.

It is my claim that the effective use of the following master checklist used before, during, and after teaching will help you to be fully "present" in the various acts of teaching. Remember, like pilots and medical doctors, our craft is complex and ever changing on the basis of the competing realities present in our classrooms. Like pilots and surgeons again, by using the checklists as scaffolding tools, you will enhance your situational awareness and be able to promote better teaching and classroom practices in your practice.

PUTTING IT ALL TOGETHER

Many times, while observing and debriefing novice teachers' performance, I use a metaphor that many of them appreciate. I tell my students that their cooperating teacher is like a chef who has invited them to use her or his kitchen to become an apprentice in it. The student-teacher/novice teacher behaves in the class like a cook. Therefore, as a novice teacher you may have different needs than an "experienced chef."

The chef may not follow a recipe very closely. He or she may know the recipe by heart and would have had ample experiences cooking the same meal several times before. Moreover, statements like "add salt to taste" or "add water as needed" are clear to a chef but might be daunting to a cook. Therefore, taking the time to create and follow a well-designed recipe might be crucial for a beginning cook. Student teachers should spend ample amount of times planning well-written and explicit lesson plans ("recipes") for their classroom.

Furthermore, take the time to reflect on what went well and not so well by debriefing with the experienced chef before starting the new cooking experience.

Following are three master checklists that I created on the basis of all the checklists developed by different authors throughout the book. Each master checklist will consist of four sections based on the sections of the book. Moreover, I created three master checklists—one used for planning, one used while teaching/observing, and one used for debriefing/reflection. Each checklist will start with an introductory section explaining how the checklist was designed and how it is the most efficient way to use them.

MASTER CHECKLIST FOR PLANNING (BEFORE)

This checklist was designed in order to help novice teachers plan their unit/ lesson plans. Although I use both terms in the checklist, I believe that the complete checklist will be best used when planning a unit plan. However, a more concise checklist might be useful for each one of the lesson plans that are part of the unit planning. Remember, lesson planning and unit planning might be much more extensive to you as a novice teacher than to your cooperating teacher.

This checklist was written in future tense since at the planning stage you have not completed any of the activities listed in the checklist. It is important to remember that the first section of the checklist (getting to know your students) will require quite a lot of previous work and planning (visits to the community, surveying students, working with parents, etc.). Make it a priority before the beginning of your teaching assignment to complete as much of these activities as possible.

The second section of the checklist (curriculum development) has all the required elements that should appear in all the unit/lesson plans that school districts use on a regular basis. The third section (pedagogical decisions) has many options that not all of them are needed in every lesson/unit plan. Choose only the ones that apply. The fourth and final section requires you to plan for action research and reflection even at the unit planning stage (Checklist 1).

CHECKLIST 1

Master Checklist for Planning Instruction
(BEFORE Teaching)

Getting to know your students, families, and communities	Yes	No	Comments
Culture/gender			
Will you connect students' cultural/ gender expressions to your lesson/unit?			
Will you acknowledge students' gender/ culture expressions to your lesson/unit?			
Will you plan a linguistically/culturally responsive lesson/unit?			
Families/Communities			
Will your lesson/unit include information gathered from your visits to the neighborhood where your students live?			
Will your lesson include local resources from the community that the families have access to?			
Will your lesson include the various cultures that exist in your student population?			
Locus of Control			
Will you plan backwards – will you explain the final assessment of the lesson/unit clearly and explicitly to the students at the beginning of the lesson/ unit?			
Will students drive their own learning – will student activity be the focus of the lesson/unit?			

Will you check for understanding – will you plan to alter your teaching based on the level of student understanding?			
Will you allocate time for peer assessment – will this lesson/unit provide students with opportunities to evaluate each other?			
Will you encourage student choice – will the lesson/unit provide space for students to share their experiences or expertise?			
Accessible Instruction for Students with Disabilities			
Will you plan your instruction explicitly for your unit/lesson?			
Will you plan your unit/lesson to include strategy instruction?			
Will you plan your unit/lesson to include instructional scaffolds?			
Adapting Instruction for English Language Learners			
Will you have multimodal instructional methods in your unit/lesson?			
Will you provide instructional scaffolds for both the concepts and the language the students need to understand your unit/lesson?			
Will you provide a space for students' communities to meaningfully contribute to your unit/lesson?			
Will you teach one or two strategies for ELL's in your unit/lesson?			
Will you include opportunities to develop and use academic language (words, sentence patterns, and different types of texts) in your unit/lesson?			

Curriculum Development	Yes	No	Comment
Interdisciplinary Lessons and Units			
Will you assess the needs and interests of your students before the unit?			
Will you make meaningful connections between the content of your lesson/unit and your students' lives?			
Will you actively collaborate with teachers outside of your own content area for the development of this lesson/unit?			
Will your assessments encourage students' to connect to other disciplines?			
Student Engagement			
Will the unit/lesson contain a variety of learning experiences?			
Will the lesson/unit provide multiple pathways to learning?			
Will your lesson/unit have choices for students as to how they learn content?			
Will you considered the best seating arrangement that will enhance student learning and engagement?			
Will you introduce and practice essential classroom routines related to your unit/lesson?			
Academic Literacy			
Will you include activities in your lesson/unit to scaffold understanding of basic and complex concepts of the different content areas?			
Will you include activities in your lesson/unit that foster collaboration and interaction between teacher and students, and students and students?			
Will you encourage students to use their first language when needed as a resource for learning in you lesson/unit?			

Will you encourage students to have multiple opportunities to represent their understanding through different media (print, visual, interactional, & electronic)?			
Traditional Assessments			
Will you use a table of specifications to design the assessment for the unit so that the information results in valid inferences about student learning?			
Will you use selected-response items that assess lower level thinking skills?			
Will you use selected-response items that assess higher level thinking skills?			
Will you gather information from my assessments to inform my teaching (i.e., content, pace)?			
Authentic Assessments			
Will you use a rubric (hypergeneral, task specific rubric, skill focused rubric)?			
Will the learning goals or objectives match the skill and knowledge the students should obtain by the end of the unit/lesson?			
Will these authentic assessment tasks be appropriate for your grade level?			

	Yes	No	Comment
Pedagogical Decisions (Use only the ones that apply)	Yes	No	Comment
Technology Integration			
Will you use technology in the lesson/ unit that is integral to gaining new knowledge?			
Will you use a logical and intentional match between the technology and instructional activities in your unit/ lesson?			

Does the technology connect with learning outcomes?			
Grouping Students			
Will your group learning activities aligned with the learning goals of the unit/lesson?			
Will your group learning activities in the lesson/unit planned with students' cognitive, behavioral, and socioemotional needs in mind?			
Will you assess and amend the efficacy of the group learning activities during the implementation of the unit/lesson?			
Problem Based Learning			
Will the problem for the unit include opportunities for students to demonstrate what they have learned to persons beyond the classroom?			
Will the problem for the unit the problem assess grade appropriate standards?			
Will you plan for sufficient time and materials to undertake the problem in your unit?			
Dialogical Learning Community			
Will you plan your lesson/unit based on the culture(s) of your school?			
Will you plan your lesson/unit to create a democratic Dialogical Learning Community?			
Will you plan your lesson/unit to effectively navigate conflict?			
Will you plan to create a symmetrical classroom environment in which everyone is a member?			
Deductive and Inductive Approaches			
Will you probe students by asking questions about the concept to activate prior knowledge in your lesson/unit?			

Will you engage students in discussions in your lesson/unit about prior experiences related to the current concept?			
Will you incorporate specific examples and non-examples of the concept in the lesson/unit?			
Will you start the lesson/unit with an advanced organizer? (Inductive)			
Will you start your lesson/unit by posing a problem at the beginning of the lesson/unit? (Deductive)			
Collaboration in the Inclusive Classroom			
Will you use different ways to co-plan to utilize the combines strengths of both teachers?			
Will you have a clear plan for co-instruction?			
Will you have a clear plan for co-assessing the unit?			
Will you clearly communicate unit specific expectations with your paraprofessionals?			
Self-reflection and action research			
Will you collect data as part of your lesson/unit planning and delivery?			

MASTER CHECKLIST FOR DOCUMENTING—(DURING)

This checklist was designed in order to help novice teachers document their unit/lesson delivery. Although I use both terms in the checklist, I believe that the complete checklist will be best used when documenting the whole unit plan delivery. Remember, documenting what you do in class is a crucial skill to master in order to reflect on your teaching practices. Do not try to fill the whole checklist after one lesson. See this checklist as a weekly endeavor. Do not leave the class until you write down at least two comments in the appropriate sections of the checklist. Your documentation might be much more extensive to you as a novice teacher than to your cooperating teacher.

This checklist was written with empty spaces so you can write as much (or as little) as is needed to help you in your reflections. This form is intended to help you collect data on your own teaching. As before, the first and second sections of the checklist (getting to know your students and curriculum development) have all the required elements that should be part of data collected during teaching. The third section (pedagogical decisions) has many options, and not all of them are needed in every lesson/unit plan. Choose only the ones that apply. The fourth and final section requires you to document what data for action research and reflection seem to be emerging as you teach (Checklist 2).

CHECKLIST 2
Master Checklist for Documenting
(DURING Teaching)
Getting to know your students, families, and communities
Culture/gender
Families/communities
Locus of control
Accessible Instruction for Students with Disabilities
Adapting Instruction for English Language Learners

Section 2: Curriculum Development
Interdisciplinary Lessons and Units
Student Engagement
Academic Literacy
Traditional Assessments
Authentic Assessments

Section 3: Pedagogical Decisions (use only the ones that apply)
Technology Integration
Grouping Students
Problem Based Learning
Dialogical Learning Community
Deductive and Inductive Approaches
Collaboration in the Inclusive Classroom

Section 4
Self-reflection and action research

MASTER CHECKLIST FOR REFLECTION (AFTER TEACHING)

This checklist was designed in order to help novice teachers reflect on their unit/ lesson teaching. Although I use both terms in the checklist, I believe that the complete checklist will be best used when reflecting on the whole unit. However, a reflection session at the middle of the unit or after one particular lesson might be useful. You can create a more concise checklist to help you better manage your reflection. One more addition is the use of the words "meaningful, effective, and useful." Remember, reflecting on lesson/unit taught might be much more extensive to you as a novice teacher than to your cooperating teacher.

This checklist was written in the past tense since at the reflection stage you have completed all or most of the items listed on the checklist. It is important to remember that the first two sections of the checklist (getting to know your students and curriculum development) have all the required elements that should appear in a reflection session about your teaching. The third section (pedagogical decisions) has many options, and not all of them are needed in every lesson/unit plan. Choose only the ones that apply. The fourth and final section requires you to think about your next steps when planning the next unit/lesson (Checklist 3).

CHECKLIST 3 **Master Checklist for Reflecting** **(AFTER Teaching)**			
Getting to know your students, families, and communities	Yes	No	Comments
Culture/gender			
Did you connect students' cultural/gender expressions to your lesson/unit?			
Did you acknowledge students' gender/ culture expressions to your lesson/unit?			
Did you plan a linguistically/culturally responsive lesson/unit?			
Families/Communities			
Did your lesson/unit include meaningful information gathered from your visits to the neighborhood where your students live?			

Did your lesson include effective local resources from the community that the families have access to?			
Did your lesson include the meaningful cultural knowledge that exist in your student population?			
Locus of Control			
Did you plan backwards effectively by explaining the final assessment to the students at the beginning of the unit/lesson?			
Did students drive their own learning effectively by having student activity be the focus of the lesson/unit?			
Did you check for understanding effectively by altering your teaching based on the level of student understanding?			
Did you allocate enough time for peer assessment?			
Did students make effective choices to share their experiences or expertize?			
Accessible Instruction for Students with Disabilities			
Did you plan your instruction explicitly and effectively for your unit/lesson?			
Did you plan your unit/lesson to include effective strategy instruction?			
Did you plan your unit/lesson to include effective instructional scaffolds?			
Adapting Instruction for English Language Learners			
Did you have meaningful multimodal instructional methods in your unit/lesson?			
Did you provide effective instructional scaffolds for both the concepts and the language the students need to understand your unit/lesson?			

Did you provide effective spaces for students' communities to meaningfully contribute to your unit/lesson?			
Did ELL students learn one or two strategies in your unit/lesson?			

Curriculum Development	Yes	No	Comments
Interdisciplinary Lessons and Units			
Did you assess the needs and interests of your students effectively before the unit?			
Did you make meaningful connections between the content of your lesson/unit and your students' lives?			

Did you actively collaborate with teachers outside of your own content area for the development of this lesson/unit?			
Did your assessments encourage students to connect effectively to other disciplines?			
Student Engagement			
Did the unit/lesson contain a variety of meaningful learning experiences?			
Did the lesson/unit provide multiple effective pathways to learning?			
Did the lesson/unit have effective choices for students as to how they learn content?			
Did the change in seating arrangement enhance student learning and engagement?			
Did you effectively introduce and practice essential classroom routines related to your unit/lesson?			

Academic Literacy			
Did you include meaningful activities in your lesson/unit to scaffold understanding of basic and complex concepts of the different content areas?			
Did you include effective activities in your lesson/unit that foster collaboration and interaction between teacher and students, and students and students?			
Did you include useful opportunities to develop and use academic language (words, sentence patterns, and different types of texts) in your unit/lesson?			
Did you encourage students to have multiple meaningful opportunities to represent their understanding through different media (print, visual, interactional, & electronic)?			
Did you encourage students to use their first language effectively as a resource for learning in you lesson/unit?			
Traditional Assessments			
Did you effectively use a table of specifications to design the assessment for the unit so that the information results in valid inferences about student learning?			
Did you effectively use selected-response items that assess lower level thinking skills?			
Did you use successfully selected-response items that assess higher level thinking skills?			
Did you gather important information from your assessments to inform your teaching (i.e., content, pace)?			

Authentic Assessments			
Was the rubric (hypergeneral, skill focused, task specific) you used effective?			
Did students obtain the skills and knowledge necessary for the unit?			
Were the authentic assessment tasks meaningful for your grade level?			

Pedagogical Decisions (Use only the ones that apply)	Yes	No	Comment
Technology Integration			
Did you use technology effectively in the lesson/unit that is integral to gaining new knowledge?			
Did you use a logical and intentional match between the technology and instructional activities in your unit/lesson?			
Did the technology connect with learning outcomes?			
Grouping Students			
Did your group learning activities effectively aligned with the learning goals of the unit/lesson?			
Did your group learning activities in the lesson/unit effectively addressed students' cognitive, behavioral, and socio-emotional needs in mind?			
Did you assess and amend of the efficacy of the group learning activities during the implementation of the unit/lesson successfully?			
Problem Based Learning			
Did the problem for the unit include meaningful opportunities for students to demonstrate what they have learned to persons beyond the classroom?			

Did the problem for the unit properly assess grade appropriate standards?			
Did you plan for sufficient time and materials to undertake the problem in your unit?			
Dialogical Learning Community			
Did you plan your lesson/unit effectively based on the culture(s) of your school?			
Did you plan your lesson/unit to create a meaningful democratic Dialogical Learning Community?			
Did you plan your lesson/unit to effectively navigate conflict?			
Did you plan to create a symmetrical classroom environment in which everyone is a member?			
Deductive and Inductive Approaches			
Did you effectively probe students by asking questions about the concept to activate prior knowledge in your lesson/unit?			
Did you engage students in meaningful discussions in your lesson/unit about prior experiences related to the current concept?			
Did you incorporate effective specific examples and non-examples of the concept in the lesson/unit?			
Did you start the lesson/unit with a useful advanced organizer? (Inductive)			
Did you start your lesson/unit by posing a meaningful problem at the beginning of the lesson/unit? (Deductive)			
Collaboration in the Inclusive Classroom			
Was your co-planning effective?			
Was your co-instruction meaningful?			
Was your co-assessing efficient?			

Did you clearly communicate unit specific expectations with your paraprofessionals?			
Self-reflection and action research			
In order to understand and address a problem, did you describe the materials, places, students, and events involving the problem?			
Did you think about how students, administrators, and parents might see the same problem?			
Did you effectively take stock of my personal resources (e.g., mentors, professors, colleagues) where you can get advice about the problem?			
Did you effectively evaluate the success or failure of your action plan?			
Did you explore other possibilities if your plan did not address the problem?			

FINAL THOUGHTS

You have embarked on a lifelong professional journey as a teacher and educator. Teaching is a very complex and ever-evolving area of expertise that requires effort and constant refinement and adaptation to new and many a times competing ideals.

The purpose of this chapter was to provide three master checklists that summarize all the important issues raised throughout the book in a manageable and efficient way. The master checklists presented here are not recipes to be followed blindly, nor are they sealed and completed documents. It is intended as a working document for you and your colleagues to experiment with and add to as needed. However, it is my claim that by using some scaffolding tools to facilitate the sometimes perplexing first years of your professional life, it will ensure that you will be fully present while developing your craft.

A journey starts with a first step, in this case, with a first checklist—use them, change them, and improve them as you develop into an experienced and successful teacher. Moreover, we have created a website (http://

successfulteachingbook.weebly.com/) that provides live links to extension materials listed from all the chapters and an online version of the final master checklists. Please explore this website as a second step in your journey. Good luck on your professional journey!

REFERENCES

Endsley, M. R. (1995). Toward a theory of situation awareness. *Human Factors, 37,* 32–64.

Degani, A., and Wiener, E. L. (1991). Philosophy, policies, and procedures: The three P's of flight-deck operations. Proceedings of the Sixth International Symposium on Aviation Psychology (pp. 184–191). Columbus: The Ohio State University.

Hazlehurst, B., McMullen, C.K., & Gorman, P. N. (2007). Distributed cognition in the heart room: How situation awareness arises from coordinated communications during cardiac surgery. *Journal of Biomedical Informatics, 40*(5), 539–551.

Sanders, M. S., & McCormick, E. J. (1987). *Human factors in engineering and design* (6th Ed.). New York: McGraw-Hill.

About the Editors

David Schwarzer is a full professor in the Department of Secondary and Special Education at Montclair State University, New Jersey. He is intrigued by the possibility of dissolving artificial boundaries between related fields (such as early childhood, emergent literacy development, ESL, bilingual and foreign language education) in the learning, teaching, and researching of emergent literacy development in bilingual and multilingual settings. Using a holistic and sociocultural philosophical perspective that emphasizes the importance of the learning and teaching contexts as well as the creation of a community of learners is crucial to his scholarship.

Jaime Grinberg is full professor and chairperson of the Department of Educational Foundations at Montclair State University, New Jersey. His research and writings, under the larger umbrella of studying power and social "agency" in formal and informal education, cover topics such as progressivism; teacher preparation; hermeneutics; historical, political, and cultural studies in education including bilingual and ESL education; and criticality in educational research and social theories. He has studied progressive teaching practices such as those implemented by Bank Street College of Education, by the Institute for the Advancement of Philosophy for Children, and others.

About the Contributors

Maheen Ahmad is an English language arts teacher at the West Orange Public Schools in New Jersey. She enjoys finding creative ways to empower students in the classroom.

Nicole Barnes is an associate professor in the Department of Educational Foundations at Montclair State University, New Jersey. Her research interests are educational assessment, classroom assessment, teachers' data use, self- and co-regulated learning during assessment tasks, and teaching and learning in urban schools.

Melanie Bloom is an associate professor and chairperson of the Department of Foreign Languages and Literature at the University of Nebraska at Omaha. Her recent research interests include the relationship between study abroad and intercultural sensitivity, experiential second-language learning and innovations in second-language instruction.

Pohun Chen is a seventh grade science teacher in Bloomfield Middle School in Bloomfield Public Schools District in New Jersey. He is an expert in inclusive science, technology, engineering, and mathematics (iSTEM).

Stephanie Curtis is a recent graduate of the dual master of art in teaching program in the Department of Secondary and Special Education at Montclair State University, New Jersey. She is an expert in Problem-Based Learning (PBL).

Charity Dacey is the director of Teacher Education Admissions and Retention in the Center of Pedagogy at Montclair State University, New Jersey, and a PhD student in the Teacher Education Teacher Development program in the same institution. She is an expert in assessment and its implications to classroom practices.

Mayra C. Daniel is a professor in the Department of Literacy and Elementary Education at Northern Illinois University. Her research interests center on the educational needs of English language learners and on the preparation of the teachers who work with these learners in the United States and other multilingual nations.

Danné E. Davis is associate professor of elementary education at Montclair State University in New Jersey. She has published and presented papers about diversity in teacher education. Dr. Davis is currently examining LGBT children's picture storybooks as teacher education tools. She is the recipient of several awards. To unwind, Danné enjoys tennis, thrifting, and crafting.

Joseph DiGiacomo is a student and a graduate assistant in the master of art in teaching program in the Department of Secondary and Special Education at Montclair State University, New Jersey. He is an expert in Problem-Based Learning (PBL).

Helenrose Fives is a professor in the Department of Educational Foundations Department at Montclair State University, New Jersey. Her research agenda focuses on teachers' beliefs (specifically epistemic cognition and the functions of beliefs) and teachers' classroom assessment practices.

Jennifer L. Goeke is an associate professor in the Department of Secondary and Special Education at Montclair State University, New Jersey. Her research interests include teacher education pedagogy, development of special educators, reasoning and instructional thought, and conceptions of students with disabilities.

Katia Goldfarb is full professor and founding department chairperson of the Department of Family and Child Studies at Montclair State University, New Jersey. Her current research interests center on transnational Latino families in the United States. She has studied immigrant families and schools, community-based education, and family sustainability, as well as the relationship of full service schools, family engagement, and culturally diverse students and learning.

David Lee Keiser is an associate professor in the Department of Secondary and Special Education at Montclair State University, New Jersey. He is interested in the ways in which the purposes of public education intersect with notions of democracy and social justice, how school/university partnerships work to provide ethical and effective teachers to public schools, and how the nexus of mindfulness and teacher education can help navigate the unchartered waters of the current high-stakes testing climate.

Anne Lockwood is a student and a graduate assistant in the master of art in teaching program in the Department of Secondary and Special Education at Montclair State University, New Jersey. She is an expert in how effective grouping strategies affect students' learning.

Christopher Luke is an associate professor and interim chairperson of the Department of Modern Languages and Classics at Ball State University, Indiana. His research interests center on the intersection of technology and educational practices in general and foreign languages in particular.

Sandra Mercuri is an associate professor in the Department of Language, Literacy and Intercultural Studies at the University of Texas Rio Grande Valley. She is an expert in the development of academic literacy of emergent bilingual- and dual-language curricula as well as long-term professional development and coaching of teachers of emergent bilinguals.

Michael Molino is a student and a graduate assistant in the master of art in teaching program in the Department of Secondary and Special Education at Montclair State University, New Jersey. He is an expert in French as a foreign language.

Sandra I. Musanti is an assistant professor in the Department of Bilingual and Literacy Studies at the University of Texas Rio Grande Valley. Her area of expertise is teacher preparation and professional development for teachers of linguistically and culturally diverse students. Her research interests include exploring classroom-based professional development and teacher collaboration that support the learning of emergent bilinguals in content areas such as mathematics, as well as issues of equity, language, culture, and identity in teacher education.

Mary Petrón is an associate professor of bilingual/ESL education in the Department of Language Literacy and Special Populations at Sam Houston State University, Texas. Her research interests include ESL teacher education, U.S.-Mexico transnationalism, and context-specific language education.

Sejal Rana is a student and a graduate assistant in the master of art in teaching program in the Department of Secondary and Special Education at Montclair State University, New Jersey. She is an expert in engaging families and communities in the students' learning.

Sandra Rodríguez-Arroyo is an assistant professor in the Teacher Education Department at the University of Nebraska Omaha. Her teaching and research highlights the importance of providing quality education opportunities for English language learners (ELLs) in the state of Nebraska; preparing teachers to work with the growing rate of ELLs in the state; and implementation of service learning experiences with diverse learners.

Melissa Susnosky is a doctoral student in the Teaching and Teacher Education Program at Montclair State University, New Jersey. She is an expert in deductive teaching.

Niobel Torres is a ninth grade special education biology teacher in Livingston Public Schools in New Jersey. She is an expert in inclusive science, technology, engineering, and mathematics (iSTEM).

Baburhan Uzum is an assistant professor of bilingual/ESL education in the Department of Language Literacy and Special Populations at Sam Houston State University, Texas. His research interests include ESL teacher education, reflective practice, and intercultural competence.

Vincent Walencik is a professor in the Department of Secondary and Special Education at Montclair State University, New Jersey. He is an expert on Problem-Based Learning (PBL).

Susan Wray is an associate professor in the Department of Early Childhood, Elementary and Literacy Education at Montclair State University, New Jersey. She is an expert in teaching portfolios; communities of practice; teacher professional development; and school partnerships.

Mayida Zaal is an associate professor in the Department of Secondary and Special Education at Montclair State University, New Jersey. Dr. Zaal has conducted research with Muslim youth of immigrant origin to understand their everyday realities in the context of Islamophobia in the United States and in the Netherlands. On this subject she has authored several articles, including "In the Shadow of Tolerance: The Discursive Context of Dutch-Born Muslim Youth" (2014), which will appear in a forthcoming issue of *Policy Futures in Education*, and "Islamophobia in Classrooms, Media and Politics" (2012), in the *Journal of Adolescent and Adult Literacy*. She coauthored "The Weight of the Hyphen: Freedom, Fusion, and Responsibility Embodied by Young Muslim American Women During a Time of Surveillance" (2007) with Tahani Salah and Michelle Fine, which appeared in *Applied Developmental Science*.